MAKING IT IN
THE MARKET

The Insider's Guide

William C. Crawford

PEACHTREE PUBLISHERS, LTD.
Atlanta

Published by
PEACHTREE PUBLISHERS, LTD.
494 Armour Circle, NE
Atlanta, Georgia 30324

Manufactured in the United States of America

10 9 8 7 6 5 4 3 2 1

Cover design by Phil Scopp
Book design by Candace J. Magee
Typography and charts by Kathryn D. Mothershed

Library of Congress Cataloging-in-Publication Data

Crawford, William C. 1919-
        Making it in the market : the insider's guide   /
William C. Crawford.
            p.   cm.
        Includes index
        ISBN 0-56145-006-5 (hardcover)
        1. Investments. 2. Stocks. 3. Bonds.   I. Title.
    HG4521.C867   1990
        332.63'2—dc20
90-41754

TABLE OF CONTENTS

PART ONE
The Players

1. BROKERS AND THEIR CLIENTS 3
Your broker is not paid for making money for you.
He's paid for making money for his firm.

I don't ask my broker, "What do you think?" That's not
his job. He's not an analyst.

If it's prophets you're looking for, go to the Old Testament.
You won't find them on Wall Street.

2. . . . CLIENTS AND THEIR BROKERS 13
Only through your broker can you get his firm's securities
research, which you must have to invest with any hope
of success.

To get the best from a good broker, you've got to be, as he
sees you, a good client.

3. HOW WOULD YOU INVEST FOR YOUR MOTHER? 17
At 51, although I'd been in the brokerage business for 24
years, I really had never thought about the investor's needs.
My only concern was selling the stock or the bond—whatever
we had to offer.

4. SUFFERING NUMBERS 23
Numbers describe the realities of the market at different
times. The market changes; the numbers change. The
principles of investing, however, don't change.

PART THREE
The Bond Market

PART FOUR
Avoidables and Unavoidables

PROLOGUE

Six years ago, I began writing this book as fatherly investment advice for my daughters. But soon I realized that my rules of what they should do and not do, could have little value to them unless they understood investments. And although it would be easy enough to explain what they needed to know, why write just another book about investments? Why not tell them what they could get from, probably, no one else?—the risks you must take to make money, the risks you must avoid to protect your money, who can help you, who's out to get you, how to stay alive in a marketplace that gives you no second chance.

And what about the hundreds of investors I've known? Wouldn't they find that useful? Couldn't I tell almost any investor what he could get from, probably, no one else? But did I want to do that? Wouldn't I betray confidences? damage reputations?

And so for a year or more, I worked on just another book about investments, until my conscience began to trouble me. I was withholding what investors are entitled to know—about the rascals out there waiting to prey on them.

Then for another year or so, I wrote mostly about bad guys, until again some sense of fairness overtook me. Yes, some brokers are bad guys, just as some doctors and even preachers, I suppose, are bad guys. But many, many more are good guys. Why should we let the few bad guys scare us away from investing? or from getting an annual physical? or from going to church on Sunday?

What I have written here turns out to be a rather private story of what goes on in the brokerage business. It's neither a confession of misdeeds nor a one-man crusade against wickedness of Wall Street. Instead, it's a forthright account of what I learned during the 38 years of my working life.

Throughout those many years, I lived in a small, isolated world of investors and brokers and investments, a world that's always emotional and often irrational. In that chaotic world, I had to learn to survive.

For you as an investor, this is a manual for survival.

Looking back upon a career as a broker and an office manager with a major firm, I see the investor, out there in the middle of a swollen river, a man out of his depth, going under, reappearing. I see, running along the bank, shouting instructions to him, his broker, who isn't much of a swimmer himself.

In my earlier attempts at writing this book, I was blaming that broker for his client's poor investment results. I had been retired only a year or two and still viewed brokers as boys who required my supervision and direction. Now, having been away from it for six years, I see things differently. In that scene on the river, the missing element is a rope—a rope from the broker on the shore to the drowning investor who's out there taking the risks. To you as an investor, I hope this book is something of a lifeline.

I can offer you no formulas, no sure ways of making money. There are none. There is no magic. And the secret is, there are no secrets.

What I hope to give you is some understanding of why you should invest your money and how you should invest your money. I have for you no theories. Sometimes, I have no good explanations. But I can tell you what I've seen that's worked and what I've seen that has not worked. And the one thing both of us have going for us is our own, good common sense. Anything that makes no sense to you and makes no sense to me, makes no sense.

This is a book of practicalities.

The stock and bond business was good to me. I ended up with more money than I deserved. Writing this book is my way of paying back some of what I owe to investors and some of what I owe to the brokers with whom I worked.

INTRODUCTION

In 1946, along with 22 other boys just home from the war, I went to work with Merrill Lynch, Pierce, Fenner & Beane as a member of Training Class No. 4. Most of us lived at the Henry Hudson hotel up near Columbus Circle and each morning rode the subway down to the Wall Street station. Lower Manhattan then couldn't have been much different than it was in the 1920s. On a pretty day, we could walk down to the East River and out onto an open wooden pier that extended from Wall Street. The Fulton Fish Market was only a few blocks away, and the American Stock Exchange was still called the Curb. On Saturdays, we worked only half a day, because the N.Y. Stock Exchange closed at noon. Those must have been the last of the great years to have lived in the city, and none of us could have found a more exciting civilian job.

The quality of our six months' training was excellent. But we got a big surprise after we'd been there for a couple of months when a classmate had the temerity to ask, "What will we be doing after we complete all this training?" Then, for the first time, we were told that in four more months, we'd all become salesmen.

Salesman? I'd never been anything but a soldier. I couldn't imagine myself selling anything. One of our classmates was from Argentina. He spoke almost no English. But we did understand him to say, "I thought this was an accounting firm." I couldn't spell his name any better then than now. It was something like Urey-burey. He was no dumber, however, than I.

So I became a securities salesman, and as a salesman I made my living for 38 years.

Because you are reading this book, I shall assume that you're an investor or a would-be investor. You probably feel that you don't know enough about investing, that you can't trust the experts, that you want to know about the real world practicalities of the market. You want to make money, but you're scared stiff that you'll lose the money you've got. I share both your wish and your anxiety. I, too, am an investor.

Out of the selling business now for six years, I've learned to see things as you see things, as an investor. But I have an advantage. I know the investment business; I know investments. I've seen it all, and I know how to dodge the bullets. That's why I wrote this book. If I can teach you what I had to learn to survive, it will be my most gratifying accomplishment. And that's what I'm setting out to do, to help you, and maybe some other folks, avoid the booby traps and land mines—to help you become a confident, self-reliant investor.

For your part, you've got to concentrate on learning the few things you must do and must not do to make money and keep from losing money. You've worked hard for what you've got—and remember, it is your money.

You may not like this book. I'm going to tell you some harsh, disagreeable facts.

> Most corporate CEOs are out for themselves, not the stockholders.

> Some investment professionals you trust may not be trustworthy.

> Wall Street firms sell investment "products" to make money for themelves, not you.

You may not like me. I'm going to tell you some things you don't want to hear.

> You cannot forecast the market. Nor can I. No one can.

> You're not capable of selecting stocks to buy. Nor am I. It's a job for full-time securities analysts.

> Much of what you think you know about investments, just isn't so.

I couldn't justify the years I've slaved away on this book unless I told you the truth about investors and brokers and investments. And the truth sometimes is hard to take. Throughout my years in the business, I saw no more than a dozen investors who had even the foggiest idea of what they were doing. Hoping not to offend you, I shall guess that what you know about investing is, at best, foggy.

But who will admit that he doesn't understand half of what he hears and reads about investments? And who wants to show how dumb he is by asking dumb questions? Well, if it makes you feel any better, neither do I understand a lot of what is said and written about investing and securities. There's a reason for that. Much of what we hear and read makes no sense. How could we understand?

Investing is a simple business. To be a successful investor, you need no more than a good high-school education. Anything about an investment that you can't understand has been introduced, deliberately, to obscure the high risk you're being asked to take or the high price you're being asked to pay. Possibly the best investment advice you'll ever get is this: If you're unable to readily grasp the reasoning, the logic that would make an investment attractive to you, don't make the investment.

You can have two reason for investing your money, only two reasons. You invest to get income, or you invest to make a profit— buy low, sell high. Of course, you could invest for both income and profit. But that's it; nothing more. You invest either for income or for profit.

"Is that so," you say. "What about taxes?" My answer would be, pay your taxes. But don't confuse investing with taxes. Later in this book, you'll find out why so-called tax investments just haven't worked.

Or, "What about trading the market?" Trading is not investing. I'll try to convince you that you can make no money trading.

And, "How about commodities? options?" The same. "And gold?" Gold is not an investment, although a few coins might be nice to have for bribes. Further on, we'll get into all of that.

And we could go on and on, but again the only two reasons to invest are either to get a flow of income or to make a profit. Investing is just that simple.

Investments, too, are simple. Either you lend your money out at interest to get income or you buy property, equity, hoping to sell at a profit.

Unless you want to become a loan shark, the only way to lend your money at interest is to buy either mortgages or bonds. Mortgages would be hard to buy and hard to sell. Where would you go to find a market? The only practical way that we can lend our money is to buy a bond. When you buy a Treasury bond, you're lending your money to the U.S. Government. Buy a corporate bond and you're lending money to a corporation. Buy a municipal bond and you're lending to a state, county or city. So to invest for income, you lend out your money at interest—you buy bonds.

How about investing for profit? What kind of investment property is available? For you and me, it's either real estate or stocks.

"What about an oil well?" you ask. Yes, oil is a great investment—if you're in the oil business, know something about underground reserves and know where to sell your oil. But we're not in the oil business.

"Buy an interest in a shrimp boat," did you say? I guess you could, but you'd soon find that you have to operate that boat yourself, spending all night in a rolling tub somewhere out from

Brunswick. I don't know about you, but I have no interest in an investment that might become an occupation. I'll stick with securities. And I believe that you, too, will be happier investing in either stocks or real estate.

But if it's real estate that interests you, I can't help you. You'll have to talk with someone who's spent his life selling real estate.

So you and I can agree that we want either income or profit. And to get income, we buy bonds; to make a profit, we buy stocks. That's it. Nothing more.

How you go about investing is just as straightforward. Telling about it, learning about it, however, takes a bit more time.

In writing this book, my purpose is to help you invest your money, not to attack Wall Street. Yet I must tell you that you and your broker may have conflicts of interest. Even an honest broker is in business to do business. And a dishonest broker, to do business, is willing to damage his clients. But among brokers, the ratio of crooks to good guys is about the same as in the general population. Of course, we do get our share.

The securities business is a narrow channel through which enormous sums of money slosh back and forth. In a typical retail office of a major brokerage firm in any one of the 15 or 20 major U.S. cities, annual revenues at the beginning of the 1990s were roughly $20 million. Assuming that those revenues, consisting of commissions and mark-ups, averaged one percent of the principal amounts of all transactions, that typical office, each year, bought and sold securities worth about $2 billion. That's enough to attract several unprincipled people whose main purpose is to divert a bit of that money into their own pockets. They're out there. And unless you know what you're doing, one of them surely will nail you.

The brokerage business, however, is just another selling business—no more wicked than your favorite department store or auto dealership. With a brokerage firm, I must admit, you could lose a lot more money than you would if you bought a lemon from your friendly auto dealer. So when you talk to a broker, you'd better have your wits about you.

Yet your broker is not your enemy. It's you, yourself, you've got to beware of—your own emotional reactions to ups and downs of the markets. Your enemies are your own greed and your own fear. Market action taken in response to those emotional signals almost always is wrong. Swept along with the crowd, you find yourself doing what almost everyone else is doing. You're buying only now when the whole world has decided to buy, and no money is left to push prices any higher; selling only now when the whole world has decided to sell, and stocks are being given away.

I hope that I can show you how to make money by going against your own, strong emotional reactions.

Investing is accepting risks. Risks, however, can be controlled. Without foregoing opportunity, you can avoid some risks altogether. The skill or art of investing, I believe, is containing risks within reasonable limits, accepting the least exposure to risk while waiting, patiently, for the market to recognize the value of the investment you've made and bid up the price.

Yes, investing is risky business. But not investing is risky business—the value of your dollar always is eroding. It buys less and less as prices go higher and higher. What $1 bought in 1967 cost $3 by 1985. To protect yourself against inflation, you must own property, either real estate or common stocks. Once you step into our marketplace, however, you find yourself exposed to get-rich-quick schemes, something for nothing. Anyone who believes fervently that there is something for nothing, who has a bit of larceny in his heart, is just waiting to be discovered by some unscrupulous broker.

If you own property, if you invest for price appreciation, you have a chance, at least, to stay ahead of inflation and increase your net worth.

Most rich folks that you know made their money from investments. They started out modestly. Hard working, they broke out of hand-to-mouth subsistence and saved some money. But no matter how hard they worked, how thrifty they were, those people never could have saved enough to have become wealthy. Their savings had to be used as seed corn to buy property—real estate or stocks. They invested, and their investments made them rich.

PART ONE

THE PLAYERS

Chapter 1

Brokers and Their Clients . . .

As young brokers in the 1940s and 50s, we used to see them, coming into our office, obvious strangers to the market, trying to look like pros.

Back then, most folks down South had apprehensions about discussing investments over the phone and, therefore, transacted business in person.

Here in Atlanta, our office on Pryor Street was fairly typical. We had ground floor, storefront space with glass windows painted green about halfway up. Above that, wooden Venetian blinds kept passers-by from seeing in. Entering from the street, you could go directly in to the manager's office at the right, or to the cashier's cage at the left, without entering the boardroom.

More genteel clients, and certainly any lady, preferred not to be seen in a boardroom. Along the longest wall, floor to ceiling, was a green chalkboard on which boardmarkers recorded stock prices that moved across the Translux projection of the New York Stock Exchange ticker tape. Facing the board, brokers worked at desks in small, low cubicles. Behind them, for the comfort of clients, whom we called sitters or tape watchers, were two rows of enormous, leather-covered, wing chairs. On the floor at every other interval between chairs, polished brass spittoons sat on black rubber mats. Chewers sometimes missed. Everybody smoked cigarettes or cigars.

Wearing a long, white apron, Nick, a Greek immigrant who operated a lunch counter at the corner, occasionally appeared to book bets on the horses. Our office was not as nice as a gentlemen's club but not as bad as a saloon.

Now and then, the stranger would come in with a slight swagger that betrayed his discomfort—here, money was made and lost in ways he didn't understand. Ego, however, would require that he fake sophistication and easy familiarity: "How're the dogs running today?"

Commenting upon such a visitor, a fellow broker said he could think only of a first timer in a sporting house, trying to look like one of the regulars. Although I lack experience that would allow me to confirm that comparison, I'm sure that in either place a rube could get rolled.

As an investor, you've got to do business with a broker, a retail broker whose clients are individual investors, people like you and me. Institutional brokers, on the other hand, do business with banks, large corporations and pension funds. The New York Stock Exchange calls them all registered representatives. Some firms use titles such as account executive and financial consultant. It's less confusing, however, to call them simply brokers.

Even into the 1950s, most retail brokers waited passively for prospective clients to find them, to walk in or call in. Young brokers who came into the business after World War II were trained to go out to call in person upon businessmen who might have an interest in investing. As that proved time consuming and inefficient, we began to identify prospects by canvassing on the phone. Also we held public seminars and used direct mail. But prospecting by phone produced the best results.

By the 1980s, almost every business executive in the U.S.A. was getting one or two calls a week from new brokers "dialing for dollars." Yet brokerage offices still get call-ins and even a rare walk-in.

Hard working, aggressive brokers with all firms, continue to prospect actively on the phone to identify the larger investor. That investor finds himself buying from several brokers and, therefore, having accounts with several firms. But the most successful brokers get their big prospects by referral. They ask their clients for names of wealthy friends and business associates. All of that is to tell you that the broker more often finds the client than the client finds the broker. The brokerage business, you must remember, is a selling business.

Most brokers, however, are poor salesmen, because so few of them understand the investment needs of their clients. Most brokers are young men and women; most investors, older men. Young people don't understand the needs and concerns of investors 10, 20, 30 years older. They've never been 40, 50, 60 years old. Also, it's because few brokers, young or old, ever have money to invest. Most of them speculate, but not many become investors in the same sense that their clients are. They just don't have the money. That's true, however, of people in any business or profession. Few are successful.

Most investors are concerned with the long-term, with their financial security. In retirement, they want to be able to maintain their standards of living. They don't need a CPA to tell them that a pension and Social Security won't be enough; they know they must have supplemental incomes from their investments. But they don't have enough capital to produce the investment incomes they'll need. Before retirement, they've got to invest for growth of capital. Although they sense urgency, they're afraid—afraid of losing the money they've got.

Even though the investor understands his dilemma, he probably doesn't know enough about securities to travel in the right direction. His broker, not understanding his client's needs, too often is tugging him in the wrong direction.

Until they've been burned a few times, investors can be too trusting, willing, even eager to turn over their money to persons they scarcely know. We're all a bit lazy. It's an easy out to tell yourself, "This is too much for me. I'd better turn things over to an investment expert."

Although the investor frequently can't see the logic of what he's being told, he doesn't question expert opinion. He'll accept even the absurd, nodding affirmatively in response to complete nonsense, trying to appear knowledgeable and experienced. Along with his ego, throw in a dash of greed—visions of something for nothing. What an easy mark for even a second-rate confidence man.

Still, investors must depend upon brokers for many services. Most investors, in fact, depend entirely upon their brokers as investment advisors. Although that relationship doesn't always prove satisfactory, most investors view their brokers—at the outset, anyway—as experts and counselors they can trust. Some are.

Yet brokers are not paid for making money for their clients. They're paid for making money for their firms. So, you must expect conflicts of interest.

Brokers are salesmen. Having something to sell, few brokers give much thought to their clients' investment needs. Most simply leaf through their books of clients and begin calling those who are least sophisticated and most trusting. So when your broker calls with some some great investment idea, he may have given less thought to your investment need than to his own need of doing business. Nothing wrong with that, just so long as you remember: You're on your own. You must rely on your own good judgment, your own common sense.

To work with your broker, to get the use and benefit of his firm's services, you must know how your broker can help you. To protect yourself, you must know how your broker can damage you. But first, you must identify your own investment needs and understand how securities can meet those needs. You must retain for yourself the *yes* and *no* decisions over everything recommended to you. And to make good decisions, to become a successful investor, you must gain a practical knowledge of stocks and bonds. You cannot allow yourself to be dependent upon someone who may prove to be less of an expert than he led you to believe.

If already you don't have a good broker, you should phone the local office of a large, national firm with the best reputation and ask for the manager. Then and there, he'll want to assign you to one of his brokers. But that manager might be thinking, *This could be a nice client to help one of my new boys along,* or *George has been talking with the competition. If I feed him some prospects, maybe he'll stick around. I'd hate to lose a broker just now.* You'd rather that the manager be concentrating on your problems, not his. So, instead of having a broker assigned to you over the phone, make an appointment to see the manager. Go to his office, tell him what investments and capital you have, describe your need of investment income or capital appreciation, and ask him to recommend a broker. Ask him about that broker's qualifications.

Not all brokers, I'm sorry to tell you, care about the interests of their clients. Some skim accounts by excessive trading. That's called *churning.* Some push, indiscriminately, only those securities that make the most money for themselves, regardless of the investment needs of their clients. That's called *unsuitability.* So long as such brokers are producing satisfactory volumes of business, most firms wink at what they're doing.

A conversation I had some years ago with one of my young brokers gives you an idea of what to watch out for. New to the business, he told me, in all innocence, "I spent two hours yesterday with a prospect who's got a lot of money in the market. We really hit it off. Great rapport. He's had some bad experiences with brokers and doesn't trust anybody, but I think he liked me, because he may transfer his account from this other firm to me. I want to ask you how you think I should cement the relationship."

Without a pause, he went on, "Now what I plan to do, as soon as I can move the account over, is to lay back and not do anything for a while, tell him I'm gonna wait until the market's right and my stocks are ready to move. I want him to see that I'm different from those other brokers, that I'm not interested just in commissions. By the way, what's our policy about taking prospects and their wives to dinner?"

First, my "policy" was, no dinners. But would you like to know what that young man was saying? Proudly, he was telling me that he planned to gain the man's trust and confidence (thus, confidence game), then wear him out trading. Somewhere, probably in our New York training school, he'd been told about clever salesmanship. With his prospect, he was pretending, moreover, an ability to forecast the market and pick stocks. Although I'm sure that the young broker wanted his clients to make money, he was more interested in doing business the quick and easy way.

Another way of baiting the hook is the familiar pitch: "Why don't you deposit fifty thousand with me and let me show you what I can do?" That, too, suggests a special talent of market forecasting and stock picking. The prospect, dumb enough to bite, simply invites the broker to play double or nothing with his money.

Less competent, less conscientious brokers believe that picking hot stocks is the secret of success. Starting out as brokers, all of us in our fantasies imagined ourselves becoming oracles. Eager investors would flock to hear us name the stock about to explode in the market. With many brokers, that delusion continues throughout their careers. They fancy themselves to be great stock pickers.

You won't make much money trading with a stock picker. More reputable firms allow their brokers to recommend only those stocks that the firm's securities analysts recommend. That's another reason why I'd do business only with one of the most reputable firms.

Most brokers pretend to have an ability to forecast the market. In fairness, however, we should appreciate that many honest brokers are responding to the demands of their clients. How often have you asked a broker, "What do you think of the market?" And if that broker were to have answered you, honestly, "I don't know what the market's going to do," you'd have said to yourself, "What's wrong with this guy?" So the poor broker has to say something about the direction of the market. Even when I'm introduced as a retired broker, I'm asked, "What do you think of the market?" Now I can say, "Nobody can forecast the market."

You'll have a far better understanding of investments and get far better investment results than most professionals if you can accept that obvious fact: No broker, indeed, no one, can forecast markets. Not the stock market, which goes up and down with change of present expectations for future earnings. Not the bond market, which goes up and down with change of present expectations for future rates of interest. Not any free and open market. Nor does anyone know what's going to happen to the price of gold, of wheat, of lumber or, indeed, the price of any commodity.

At any given moment, the stock market reflects all that is then known about every company with securities that trade publicly; all that is then known about every industry; all that is known that instant about the national economy. The bond market reflects all that is then known about borrowing demand, the supply of money, inflation or anything else that can impact future interest rates. At any given instant, prices represent a point of balance at which buyers and sellers agree as to the worth of securities.

What will happen next year, next week or the next minute to disturb that balance, no one knows. But millions of things will happen. And countless decisions, therefore, will be made to buy and sell. The aggregate of all those transactions, together with the pervasive sense of either optimism or pessimism, become "the market." Every investor is trying to peer into the future, to anticipate events and to forecast the market. But if it's prophets you're looking for, go to the Old Testament; none are to be found on Wall Street.

When you hear some investment professional telling you what the market is going to do, you can know that you're listening to either a fool or a fraud, or maybe both.

Some brokers I've known pride themselves on fast answers. To them, it's important to speak confidently on any subject. As a client, I'd never ask a broker, "What of you think of XYZ?" Apart from the fact that he's not thinking of XYZ and probably never has thought of XYZ, your broker is threatened by that question. You are just about to force him to read his firm's research opinion and the latest news items on the company. You are about to put him to work.

It's easier for him to give you one of two quick answers. Lowering his voice to suggest confidentiality, he may say, simply, "Buy it." That's an easy way to get an order on a slow day. Or he may be working on an offering of some security that carries a big sales credit. In that case, he says, "I don't like it. But let me tell you something you ought to buy."

I don't ask my Broker for his opinion of a stock. I ask his assistant to read to me from the CRT screen of her quote machine recent news items about the company and to send me a printout of the firm's research opinion and a copy of the Standard & Poor sheet. Too, I may ask her to wire for a technical interpretation of recent market action.

I don't ask my broker, "What do you think?" That's not his job, He's not an analyst. But I do ask my broker about changes of his firm's investment strategy, their outlook for various industries and stock groups, and I might ask him to watch out for a high quality Georgia municipal bond maturing in 10 years.

In 1949, the senior broker in our Atlanta office was sometimes called Pierpont. Robust at 75, he was distinguished in appearance, strong face, luxuriant white hair combed straight back—and just as dumb as could be. A client once became upset with his response to the question, "What do you think of XYZ?" Pierpont had said, "First, I'd have to know whether you want to buy or sell."

Training a man or woman to become a retail broker is expensive. Supporting a trainee during the time necessary for him to develop a clientele is even more expensive. And as most new brokers fall by the wayside within two years, all of the money wasted on them becomes part of the cost of bringing on the survivors.

Once a retail broker becomes known as a big producer, managers of competing firms that don't train their brokers try to recruit him. They'll offer a bounty that can be twice the broker's annual income. In 1987, a broker I knew, whose '86 pay-out had been about $400,000 on production (commissions and credits) of $1 million, got a $1 million sign-on bonus for walking across the street.

Changing firms, a broker tries to take along his clients. That's what his new firm is buying, the clients. To the firm that trained that broker, that paid the cost of his success, losing him is a whopping loss.

If you're the client of a broker who changes firms, perhaps you ought to question that broker's loyalties—to his employer, to his client, namely, you. And as for his new firm, why don't they train their own brokers?

Maybe one out of ten brokers would make a real effort to learn what he's got to know about you, your financial circumstances and your investment needs. Maybe one out of a hundred might be able then to show you how to invest to meet your needs. Unless you're lucky enough to do business with one of those rare, hard-working brokers, you'll have to analyze your own circumstances, identify your own needs, and make your own investment decisions—all without much help from anybody.

If you're dissatisfied with your broker, for whatever reason, I can suggest several ways to get the service you want. If the relationship is salvageable, start with that broker. If already he doesn't have a list of your investments, give him a copy. Identify your investment objectives. How much income do you need? Taxable or nontaxable? What about capital gains? Acceptable degree of risk? Make notes of the services you want and don't want. Then, invite your broker to lunch so you can talk to to him away from his office where he feels secure and confident. After telling him of your objectives and needs, ask him what you can expect. Make notes of what he's telling you so that in the months ahead you can review your understanding.

If the results of that exercise prove unproductive, phone the office manager. As most firms allow only one broker to service a client, explain your needs and ask that he reassign your account to another broker. With that new broker, start all over again, having lunch just as you did with the first broker.

Often an investor who finds himself assigned to an incompetent or even an offensive broker is reluctant to ask for a transfer— he's afraid he'll hurt the broker's feelings. Whatever feelings that broker has, do not extend to his clients. Typically, an unhappy investor will say nothing but just go across the street to another firm and take his chances with a broker randomly asssigned over there. As for me, I do business with the firm that I believe to be the best in Wall Street. I wouldn't switch to what might be a second-rate firm because of my concern for the feelings of a sorry broker. I'd see the manager.

Surely, by now, you think I'm down on brokers as crafty, greedy rascals. Well, in fact, some are, but the percentage is no greater than among salesmen in other businesses.

In any occupation, the more successful people tend to be entrepreneurial, ego-driven loners. Although executive positions offer prestige and authority, most successful persons are after the money. Apart from what it can buy, money is a convincing measure of success. Successful brokers are no different from other successful businessmen. They want to be seen as successful.

As in any business, however, nothing happens until the salesman makes the sale. Brokers, both good and not-so-good, are essential to the flow of money into investments that fuel our economy. And without brokers out there selling stocks and bonds, few people ever would become investors. Our money would be buried in tin cans. Obviously, some brokers are working only for themselves and some investments turn sour and some folks lose their money. But most investors have profited, long term, from the investments they've been sold. We need the brokers and, of course, they need us investors.

Almost every broker, surely every broker with a conscience, wrestles every day with the devil. Always, the temptations are there. And often he himself doesn't know whether the advice he gave to that old lady was in her interest or in his. That's the way the business is. Maybe a surgeon who takes out appendixes doesn't know either. A good broker will put his client's interests first. That's not just honesty. In a repeat business, that's good business. If he loses his best clients, he may not be able to replace them. But the devil sometimes out-wrestles the broker and his clients pay the price.

You and your broker have conflicts of interests. Without becoming paranoid, you've got to be aware of that. You've got to accept, as fact, that no one is as concerned about your money as you are; that you're on your own.

Still we hear, so often, "Well, okay; you're the doctor." What does that statement mean to a doctor? It means that you don't want to know, that you don't want to be bothered trying to understand what he's talking about. You're saying you are willing to trust implicitly whatever he chooses to do. Yes, medical science is complex and our knowledge limited to our own, few, unpleasant ailments. But even when you're dealing with your doctor, blind trust can be dangerous. Why do hospitals examine tissue to see if the surgeon had good reason to remove it? Why do they have peer review boards?

Investing, however, is part of what we see, every day, all around us. Every store, factory, means of communications, transportation, all are businesses that you see operating. For yourself, you can see that some prosper, others fail. Often you can see why. If you apply your own, good common sense, develop confidence in your own, good business judgment, you stand an excellent chance of profiting from your investments. Based on the same set of facts, your judgment and that of the expert probably have equal value. If you don't know all the facts, well, that's something quite different. But your modestly deferring to opinions of an expert is a mistake. Further, if that expert can give no satisfactory, easily understood explanation in response to your question, "Why?" he has just disqualified himself as an expert. As investors, we must have confidence in our own judgments. Don't sell yourself short.

By the way, if I were you, I'd avoid the discomfort of going into a brokerage office, even though the spittoons are gone and there's not as much smoking. I'd prefer that my broker meet me on my own ground.

➤   ➤   ➤

You hear someone ask a broker, "What firm are you with, Frank?" Then the next question, "Are you retail or institutional?" And although institutional sounds a bit more impressive, Frank admits that he's only a retail broker. Unless you're in the securities business, the difference may not mean a whole lot.

The distinction between institutional and retail is size. Retail business, buying and selling securities for individuals, is little business. Institutional business—transactions with trust departments of large banks and investment counseling firms that manage pension and profit sharing funds, and with state and other public funds—is big business. If there's such a thing as an averge size of a single order, I'd guess that institutional orders, in dollar amounts, are 50 times larger than retail orders. Retail orders might average $20,000; institutional orders, $1 million and more. Institutions, along with major corporations, have become the dominant players in both stocks and bonds.

Institutional business and retail business are so different that brokerage firms have had to separate their sales forces in order to develop both.

Intense competition for the enormous volume of institutional business has driven down institutional commissions far below rates charged retail clients. On the larger orders, institutions are charged about six cents a share. On an order to buy or sell, say, 500 shares at 50, a retail client is charged about 75 cents per share. Even so, institutional business can be quite profitable.

Institutional brokers deal with limited numbers of readily

identifiable, large institutions with big pools of money to invest. Because large institutions have organized their personnel in sections that specialize in types of security (common stocks, corporate bonds, Government bonds, short term stuff like commerical paper, etc.) institutional brokers also have had to become specialists. That's been done, in part, to accede to the ego requirements of the institution's buyer-specialist who wants it known that he can deal only with a broker-salesman whose "level of knowledge" is comparable, at least, to his own. The full-time buyer-specialist will talk only with a full-time salesman-specialist of the brokerage firm.

Institutional brokers, whose accounts are assigned to them, don't have to hustle for new business. Their jobs, therefore, have become more servicing and less selling, which means that a firm can replace an institutional broker more easily than a retail broker. As you would suppose, institutional brokers, even though they handle large volumes of business, are paid a much smaller part of their commission dollars than are retail brokers. Compared to the 40% or more of his production that a retail broker gets, the institutional broker might be paid 10% or less. In fact, many firms pay their institutional brokers a salary plus a year end bonus that's not directly related to production.

To keep their retail brokers from jumping ship, firms must pay them handsomely. If you include various employee benefits, retail brokers get up to 50 cents of every commission dollar. It's a lot like professional athletics—only the players make money. As long as Wall Street firms continue outbidding one another for retail brokers, they'll have a tough time making any money for their stockholders.

Chapter 2

...Clients and Their Brokers

As an office manager, I heard from no happy clients. I got all the complaints. A client with a complaint is not pleasant. He has thought about, talked about his complaint for several days. His wife has called him a fool for not standing up for himself, for them. "They've got our money. How did you get us into this? Why don't you get it straightened out? Why don't you get our money back?"

He didn't sleep much last night. He tossed and turned, thinking about what he's going to say. But now he's got his speech all ready. He dials the number.

My secretary answers the phone.

"Mr. Crawford's office . . . . I'm sorry, he's not in his office. He may be out in the boardroom. I can page him for you. Shall I tell him who's calling? . . . Do you have an account with us, Mr. Smith? . . ."

She puts the client on hold and calls the broker. "Your client Mr. Smith's on the other line, asking to speak with the manager. Do you know what he might want? Any problems?"

Then back to the client, "I'm sorry, Mr. Smith, Mr. Crawford doesn't answer the page. If you'll give me your number, I'll have him return your call."

Now the secretary tells me that an upset client was on the phone, that he's lost some money, that I'd better speak with the broker before returning the call.

The broker tells me what he knows about the loss, whether it's a big client we want to keep, what sort of person he is. I decide whether the complaint is serious, whether we were right or wrong and, if wrong, what our dollar loss might be. If I have complete confidence in my broker, I know right then how to respond. If I don't have complete confidence in the broker, I'll give the client benefit of any doubt, and the broker . . . well, he won't be with me too long anyway.

I don't return the call right away. I wait for the client to cool off, to be distracted by something else and forget the ugly speech that he was about to unload on me. Thirty minutes later, I call the client. Now, maybe we can talk rationally.

If a complaint turned out to be serious, I'd ask the client to meet with the broker and me in my office, because there's always a disagreement over who said what. It was better to have both client and broker present, looking at one another. If I concluded that we were wrong and the client was right, I paid off. If the client was wrong and we were right, a beautiful relationship probably had come to an end. But most of the time, fault could be found on both sides and we negotiated a settlement.

At an office in which any broker found to be a bad guy is promptly fired, most complaints arise from honest misunderstandings or a client's pigheadedness.

You don't go around making people mad. Neither do I. But some folks seem to go out of their way to be unpleasant. The ratio may be no more than one out of 100, but even one impossible client was one too many for me.

From your broker, you want the best information, the best service that you can hope to get. Even then, making money is tough. You want your broker working for you, not against you. To get the best from a good broker, you've got to be, as he sees you, a good client. It's important, therefore, that you know how a good broker sees his overbearing or ill-tempered client.

The unreasonable, demanding client must believe that he can bully his broker into giving him better service, better information and better executions. It just doesn't work that way. You'd think they'd learn. Although a broker, as any other salesman, wants to please his client, who's going to put up with abuse?

I used to tell my brokers that we couldn't afford an abusive client. No matter how much business he gave us, our cost was too great. He inflicts emotional trauma that wipes out his broker for the rest of the day and costs him a full day's business. I'd instruct my broker to tell that client to go elsewhere with his business. And to assuage the injured feelings of that harassed broker, I'd explain that the s.o.b. serves an important social need: he causes us to appreciate the other, 99-out-of-100 nice people. But even nice people, unwittingly, can cut themselves off from the help that they must have to get good investment results.

Even a nice guy can expect too much of his investments. He's probably heard some big swinger scoff at reasonable yields on high quality bonds and reasonable profits on good quality stocks. He believes that brokers hold back on the good stuff. So he, too, sneers at reasonable returns.

If it's for income that he's investing, he presses his broker for the highest yield that can be found: "I can do much better than that. Doesn't your firm get in on any of the sweet deals?"

What would you expect of the broker? He's a salesman. Why pass up a good ticket? The broker asks, "What sort of yield do you have in mind?" And however ridiculous the reply, the broker can find a bond offered at a price low enough to produce that yield—although the bond may go into default at the next interest payment date. Any firm can fill an order for a junk bond. And when the client asks the broker, "You think this is a pretty safe bond, don't you?" the broker replies, as would any salesman: "Sure," and says to himself, "If he doesn't buy it through me, he'll buy it somewhere else."

If it's a stock bought for a profit, the client wants a steal, something for nothing, the undiscovered high flier of tomorrow, or certainly next week: "I'm not interested in those high-priced blue chips. A five dollar stock can double a lot easier than a fifty dollar stock can go to a hundred." (Really?) So how does the broker respond? He can think of several five dollar numbers, and one or two that trade over-the-counter, that can be offered at a net price. On a $5 OTC stock, a mark-up of three-eighths of a point that the client never will know about, is $375 on 1000 shares. For the broker, that beats the commission on a N.Y. Stock Exchange trade. So the client buys a stock only because it's below $5 and trades OTC. And the broker makes twice as much on the order.

An otherwise nice guy also can be a complete know-it-all. Believing himself to be an expert, he wants the broker to know how smart he is. Anything the broker says, he challenges. If the broker is aggressive, the two develop an unproductive, adversarial relationship. More likely, the broker will just say to himself, "Well, mister, since you know so damned much, I have no problem of conscience in selling to you whatever will make the most money for me. Protect yourself. Good luck."

A nice but naive investor will be discovered, in time, by some bandit of a broker who will take advantage of his trusting nature and cause him to lose a lot of money. Once burned, he becomes suspicious of everyone in the investment business.

Dealing with a suspicious person is impossible, because he tends to accuse everyone of being a crook. A broker reacts just as you would. He provides only what the client specifically asks for, volunteers nothing, and silently watches as the man rushes over the precipice.

I can understand why some people would be secretive about their investments and their income. If I hadn't been paying my income taxes, I'd probably be closemouthed myself. And people can be secretive for many other reasons. You'd be surprised to know (or maybe you wouldn't) how many men don't want their wives to know what they've got. And I found that some people won't disclose financial information because they're ashamed of how little money they've accumulated.

For whatever the reason, withholding from your broker any information about your investments, available capital, your income, liabilities or, indeed, anything else that he needs to know, is not too smart. Most brokers want to do a good job for their clients. They want to keep their clients and, through referrals from them, get new clients. Unless your broker has the information and fully understands your needs, he can't do a good job for you. A broker working in the dark can only go through the entire menu of investment products, offering one security after another, hoping to hit on something that appeals to your appetite. As a result, you may find yourself buying bonds when you don't need investment income or buying stocks when you can't afford the market risks. My broker knows what I've got and what I need from my investments.

I'm not telling you to trust every broker, to believe everything a broker says or accept everything a broker recommends to you. Professionals who are both honest and intelligent are rare in all businesses. But you must find a broker whom you can trust and with whom you can work. Only through your broker can you get the product of his firm's securities research, which you must have to invest with any hope of success.

An intelligent, hard-working broker can do a lot for you. He can guide you to good value and low risk, get you out of securities that turn sour, keep you from going overboard on the upside and selling out at the bottom. He can protect you from yourself. I like my broker.

Your broker is a salesman. He wants your business. He wants to keep you as a client. He tries to be pleasant and accommodating. It's in your selfish interest to have a good relationship with him.

➢   ➢   ➢

Each morning, as an office manager, I would review the executions, buys and sells, for my office on the previous day—a couple of hundred trades. All of those orders were taken over the phone, clients talking with brokers, no one else listening, no witnesses. Yet I experienced scarcely one repudiation a year. That says a lot for the honesty of most folks, both clients and brokers.

CHAPTER 3

HOW WOULD YOU INVEST FOR YOUR MOTHER?

At 51, although I had been in the business for 24 years, I had never been, really, an investor. Yes, I'd owned stocks but mostly as haphazard speculations bought with the hope of a fast run up and for the fun of being right on the market. Anyhow, most of my money was in the stock of the firm with which I worked. The firm then was owned almost entirely by its officers—no public market for the stock. We could buy or sell only through the firm and at book value (which you'll read about in another chapter). That was my all-time greatest buy, but I don't want to imply that I had made some astute investment decision. I just bought the stock whenever the firm offered it to me. I owned no bonds, because my earnings were adequate, and I had no need of investment income. So I suppose you might say that I was a passive investor and a small speculator.

I never had thought much about investment needs, about buying securities to meet needs. Along with everyone else in the brokerage business, I always had thought first of the stock or bond that we were selling and then of the clients for whom that security might have been suitable. We never began by identifying the client's investment needs and then, working backward, selecting the securities that would meet his needs.

As to my own investment needs, I had only the vague purpose of making a lot of money so that I could feel successful and, in retirement, could afford to live as I might wish without money worries. So my own experiences had not been instructive.

It wasn't until 1970 that I began to learn something about investing, and then only because it was up to me to solve an investment problem that arose.

In the spring, my father died leaving an estate consisting of common stocks and money in savings accounts. The aggregate value was $133,000. Federal estate tax and the bank's executor fees reduced that the $111,000.

My widowed mother had stocks worth $97,000 and, in her

name, a house that we later sold for $47,000. (Ten years after the sale, that house was worth probably $200,000—just to give you an idea of what happened to real estate prices during the inflation of 1972-80.) So Mother's capital was $97,000 plus $47,000 for the house, a total of $144,000.

According to my father's will, his $111,000 went into a trust. The bank and I were co-trustees. For my mother's lifetime, she was the income beneficiary of that trust. At her death, assets of the trust were to be divided between my brother Jack and me. That arrangement, under estate tax laws of the time, reduced the taxes on my parents' estates.

Immediately after my father's death, Mother told me that she wanted to sell the house and move into an apartment. But I'd seen too many bad decisions made too hastily by distraught persons. After a death, divorce or other disruptive event, one should let a year pass before making any major change that can be postponed.

We found a nice apartment for Mother. But we didn't sell her house until many months afterward when she decided for herself, unemotionally, that she could not be happy alone in a large house. I wanted to be satisfied that she wouldn't regret the decision.

Before making any investments for her, I had to know what her needs would be and what I had to work with. What did she require from her own money and the trust at the bank? How much investment income did she need? What about investing for appreciation, to protect her against inflation?

First, I had to know how much money, how many dollars would be available to me for reinvestment. To get an accurate figure, I assumed that everything had been sold at the close on the previous day.

Now, with that information, I would be ready to start working, working backward, to invest her money to meet her needs.

I knew what assets were available. From my father's estate, was the $111,000 that went into a trust for the benefit of my mother during her lifetime; and belonging to my mother, $144,000 that included the proceeds from sale of the house. The total was $255,000. That's what I had to work with.

Next, I had to know how much income my mother required. I asked her to go back through her checkbook, for she had always paid the household bills, to get an idea of what her living expense was apt to be.

Mother's estimate was $700 a month. (That, mind you, was in 1970. From 1970 to June, 1984, the purchasing power of a dollar dropped from 100 cents to 37 1/2 cents. That $700 in 1970, therefore, was the equivalent of $1,866 in June, 1984.) Mother was frugal.

During the Great Depression, she had raised two boys on about $200 a month. Suspecting that her $700 estimate was cutting it a bit close, I upped it to $800. From there, I continued working backward.

Her Social Security of about $200 a month reduced her need of investment income to $600 a month, $7,200 a year. Before even thinking about anything else, I had to provide that income. The continued flow of $7,200 had to be a certainty. I could buy only high quality, fixed-income securities, triple-A bonds.

The prices of high grade bonds at that time resulted in yields of about 6 1/2%. To determine the quantity of bonds, at 6 1/2%, necessary to bring in $7,200 a year, I simply divided $7,200 by 6 1/2% or 0.065. That gave me a figure of $110,769, the amount I had to invest at 6 1/2% to produce the necessary income. As that figure, by chance, was almost exactly the available $111,000 in the trust created under my father's will, I instructed the trustee bank to invest all of that money in corporate bonds. They bought three different issues, $40,000 par value of each, all AAA-rated. The bonds were selling at discounts of about 10%, so the cost was close to $900 a bond for a total of 108,000. Altogether, the three issues paid interest of $7,400 a year or $616 a month. Of the $111,000 in trust, the remaining $3,000 went into the bank's cash management fund.

Each month, the trust department of the bank transferred $600 of investment income to Mother's checking account. Her $200 monthly check from Social Security then brought her income to $800 a month. The income need was met, and I still had Mother's $97,000 and, later, $47,000 from the sale of her house. That total of $144,000 could be invested in high quality common stocks for profit. And if needed, I could count on dividend income of about 5%, at that time, on the stocks bought with the $144,000. That was another $7,200 of investment income which, if not needed, could be reinvested in stocks.

Stocks for an 81-year-old widow? Yes. Had she lived to be 100 in 1989 (and lots of folks do live to be 100), I would have been thankful to have had the $144,000 in stocks. The profits would have been more than enough to have paid the ballooning costs of medical and nursing care for her. More realistically, however, I was buying stocks, not so much for Mother as for Jack and me, because we wanted to see some growth of that capital during her lifetime. Was I risking Mother's money? Of course. But do you know what the big risk turned out to be? You guessed it, the $108,000 in corporate bonds.

When Mother died in September, 1976, 20-year corporate bond prices were down at levels to yield about 8%, so I had small losses in the three issues bought to produce income for her. Inflation, even then, was picking up steam, and interest rates were rising. If we had continued to own those bonds for five more years, we would have had big losses. By 1981, bond prices had gone down so far that high grade corporates were yielding 14% and more. The three corporates that we'd bought for $108,000 carried coupons of 6% and 6 1/2%. Yielding 14% in 1981, those bonds were way down in price. The three issues then were worth less than $65,000.

Stocks during the decade of the 1970s were no great shakes either. In 1970, the mean level of the Dow Jones Industrial Average was 753; in 1976, 974; and in 1980, 891. Few people got rich in stocks. Mother's stocks, however, were up enough to offset the small losses we took, shortly after her death, when we sold the bonds. For ourselves, Jack and I put that money, too, into stocks. Having adequate earned income, neither of us needed investment income. So why own bonds?

Surely, you are wondering, what's so remarkable about investing a widow's money to meet her needs? Who wouldn't find out, first, how much money the lady had available for investment? Who wouldn't determine how much income she required? how much she could afford to invest in common stocks to protect against inflation? And you're right. Who wouldn't?

Just about nobody would. In the brokerage business, nobody that I'd ever heard about would. All of us started with the security, the product. We concocted a sales presentation that made whatever we had to sell sound appealing to the widest number of investors, and with that as our script we all got busy cranking the phone. Thus we began, never with the investor and his investment needs; we began always with the security, the product.

As that, probably, doesn't make a lot of sense to you, the question is, why? I'd have to blame both brokers and investors.

Brokers are salesmen. They're in business to do business, to make the sale. As most salesmen, they can be so intent upon the sale that they forget about the needs of their clients. Only in more recent years have I begun to see brokers meeting, in person, with their new clients to learn everything possible about the clients' financial circumstances and investment needs and only then recommending investments that meet the needs.

Some investors, I believe, can be as much to blame as brokers. Among investors, the ratio of suspicious, secretive people may be small, but they're out there in the gray area between unreasoned fear and paranoia. Those folks can be so offensively indignant when asked a harmless question about what they've got, what they earn, that some brokers are afraid, ever again, to ask those questions that set off the explosion.

I offer that only as an explanation as to why some brokers don't find out what capital, what investments their clients have and what needs must be met with that capital. Although you may not believe it, brokers can be just as timid as people in other businesses. Some are afraid that asking questions will cost them the client. Want of courage, however, is not an excuse.

In my later years, whenever one of my brokers talked to me about a client, I'd ask, "May I see a list of his holdings?" So often, the broker had no list. And why not? "Uh, well, that's getting rather personal, and I didn't want to offend him by asking." And, "How much investment income does the client need?" "Can he take market risks to buy stocks?" The broker wasn't too sure.

Whether the fault is that of the broker or the client, the broker is left guessing, probing, offering a stock or a bond to see how the client responds, trying to find out what the client wants—and that may not turn out to be what the client needs.

You're right. It doesn't make a lot of sense.

The logic of investing is in determining, first, the capital you have to work with and, next, your investment needs, income or growth of capital or both. From that, you work backward to get the answers. If you don't try to get too clever, your answers will be good, useful answers.

Emotional considerations, however, are important. Stock and bond prices can go down. Will market losses so upset you that you'd be better off in nothing more venturesome than Treasury bonds or notes maturing within five years? It's no fun to see your stocks selling at 15 or 20% below the prices you paid. But if you're out to make money, you must be prepared emotionally for just that.

Mother's investment needs, even if clear and simple, were my introduction to the use of capital to accomplish the purposes for which everyone toils and struggles. And there I was, 51 years old, 24 years in the business, figuring out, for the first time, how to put money to good use. Better late, I suppose, than never.

CHAPTER 4

SUFFERING NUMBERS

This book is in two parts. The first and longest part is about investing for profit, investing in common stocks. The second part is investing for income, investing in bonds and other fixed-income securities.

You can't talk about baseball without mentioning batting averages, runs batted in, league standings. It would be just as tough to talk about investing without quoting prices, price/earnings ratios, interest rates. At any present time, those numbers seem real, because for that moment those are the real prices, the real rates, what we must pay if we buy, what we will get if we sell. Reading something that was written a year, a month or sometimes even a week earlier, you find the numbers unreal. Prices and rates of 10, 25, 50 years ago can be not only unreal but quaintly amusing. Prices and rates out there waiting for you in the years ahead, I can promise you, will be just as unreal—but maybe not so funny.

Numbers describe realities of the market at different times. Because realities change, numbers change. The principles of investing, however, don't change. To give you examples that illustrate those principles, I must use stock prices, corporate earnings, interest rates that are forever changing. Don't be distracted by changing numbers. What you're looking for are principles that can see you through all kinds of markets.

Also, we'll have to use some simple arithmetic, not much, just multiplication and division that I do for you. Nothing is requried of you, no problems to solve, no final examination.

So don't let the numbers throw you.

PART TWO

THE STOCK MARKET

CHAPTER 5

INVEST FOR PROFIT

"Okay," you say. "So what's in all this for me?"

The answer is money. You're investing your money today to get back a lot more money in the years ahead. Anyway, that's your hope. Money, however, is the only benefit you'll ever get from an investment. You're buying future dollars. Whether interest on bonds and mortgages, rent from real estate, profits from your business, or earnings and dividends on stock, the only benefit to you will be a flow of money, a flow of future dollars.

Buying a bond, which is lending your money, you'll receive a flow of interest payments in fixed amounts. You're investing for future income.

Buying real estate or stock, you're convinced that you'll get an ever increasing flow of rents or earnings that will make your property worth more, so that you can sell at a higher price. You're investing for future profit.

And so what's wrong with future dollars? Well, nothing, unless the rate of inflation accelerates and your future dollars won't buy as much as today's dollars. Further along, we'll get into the damage that inflation does to future dollars and to the worth of investments that produce those future dollars.

Investing for profit is buying property at a reasonable price and owning that property over time during which some favorable change occurs to make your property worth more money. And that's what you'll be reading about, buying property and waiting patiently for your property to enhance in value.

If you want to invest for profit, if you want your money to make money, you must buy either real estate or common stocks. Rich folks that I've known made it either in real estate or stocks. Yes, many have become wealthy from the sales of their businesses. But owning one's business is much the same as owning stock.

None of that is to suggest that ownership of either real estate or common stocks guarantees riches. For every person who's gotten rich from real estate or stocks, many, many more have gone broke.

What does that tell you? Investing for profit is risky business—unless you know what you're doing.

Apart from real estate and common stocks, there's not much in which you and I can invest for profit. If you buy property that has no prospects ever of producing a flow of future dollars, you're not investing. You are speculating on the hope that the scarcity of what you own will cause other speculators to bid up the price and let you out at a profit. Although French impressionists' paintings, porcelains of the Ming Dynasty and baseball cards all have skyrocketed in price, none of that, for you and me, is investment property.

What about gold? Just like paintings, porcelains and baseball cards, gold pays no interest, no dividends, no rent. So to own gold, you must forego the interest or dividend or rent that you'd get on the same amount of money invested in bonds, common stock or real estate. What you *don't* receive as investment income is the cost to you of owning gold—*opportunity loss*. For a specific, dollar amount of the minimum cost of owning gold, look at the rate of interest on U.S. Treasury bills (about which, more later). Multiply the cost of gold by the rate those T bills are paying. That's what you'll have to give up each year for the pleasure of looking at your gold. Owning gold is expensive. Gold is not an investment.

As a speculation, gold can be bought with the hope that the price will rise. From $35 an ounce in 1972 when again after many years U.S. citizens, legally, could own gold, the price soared to more than $800 in early 1980. For anyone who owned gold, it was a great way of making money. But in 1982, gold was back to $300, a great way of losing money.

Nuts, who think they hear voices through the walls of ancient European castles, pretend to be privy to the machinations of some cabal of mysterious men who control the world by manipulating the price of gold. Don't rely too much on the goldbugs. Gold is a commodity that trades like other commodities, wheat, cotton, soybeans, pork bellies. No one can forecast the price. Gold is not an investment.

During times of madness, gold coins would be nice to have for bribery. For European Jews in the 1930s, the ticket out of Nazi occupied areas was gold. For any of us, gold some day could be useful again but only for bribery. If money ever were to become worthless, I wouldn't plunk down a Krugerrand at the grocery store. Someone with a gun would follow me home to rob me of the rest of my Krugerrands.

Investing for profit, you and I can buy either common stocks or real estate.

I never invested in real estate. I should have. During the 15 years from 1970, real estate was the investment to have owned. The

Baby Boom of the 1940s and '50s had become a huge, rising wave of young adults. Cities were badly deteriorated and inadequate—not enough houses, apartments, office buildings, parking, shopping malls, warehouses. Demand for space exploded. Developers could get unheard-of rents for space in new, modern, well-located buildings. And that lifted rents in older buildings. Moreover, some leases contained escalator clauses that tied rents to the Government's Consumer Price Index. As the CPI went up, those rents went up and property values, too, went up. So those rents and property values became indexed to inflation.

As a tax dodge, the highly leveraged real estate investment was a marvelous contrivance. (Leverage means investing as little as possible of one's own money and as much as possible of borrowed money.) As the real estate boom expanded, the price of land and cost of construction rose. To make a profit on rents that tenants could afford, developers became increasingly dependent upon loopholes in the tax law. Big developers of real estate must have been among the most generous of contributors to campaign funds of U.S. senators and representatives who write and vote upon our tax laws.

By the 1980s, however, the real estate lobby may have gotten from Congress every possible tax concession and, therefore, may have stopped making campaign contributions, because the income tax law of 1986 eliminated many of the attractive real estate tax breaks—including the low, 20% maximum tax on all capital gains from sales of not only real estate but stocks, bonds or anything else. It was just about that time that everyone had agreed that real estate offered the surest investment opportunity. But whenever everyone agrees upon anything, something different seems to happen. Just before a boom tops out, everybody goes crazy, lemmings rushing to the sea. As always, the best time to sell is when everybody wants to buy.

An investor in real estate or, indeed, in anything, must be alert to changes of the tax law. Whether sanity and fairness ever will be a part of our method of taxing ourselves, who knows? But so long as politicians are allowed to accept money, whether as a campaign contribution, honorarium or whatever you wish to call it, tax laws will be warped to accommodate contributors.

Except for owning homes, I've had no experience in real estate. Before buying any real estate, I'd have to know a whole lot more than I do now. If you want to invest in real estate, talk with someone who sells real estate.

I've spent my life selling stocks and bonds. I can help you there. In the next chapter, I tell you what I learned buying and owning stocks for profit.

Chapter 6

Common Stocks

The structure of a corporation seems democratic enough. Ownership is divided into identical shares of common stock. Every share has the same value, receives the same dividend and is entitled to one vote at stockholder meetings.

As to organization, stockholders exercise basic authority. To represent their interests, they elect directors. Directors develop broad strategies, establish policies and, to implement their decisions, elect officers—the management. Management is responsible to the board of directors. Directors are responsible to the stockholders, the owners.

Anyhow, that's the way it's supposed to work, all in consonance with our cherished democratic ideals. But in publicly owned corporations, that is not always the way it does work. Managements of most publicly owned companies serve, not the interests of the stockholders—they serve their own interests.

The control that stockholders exercise over managements of public companies is limited to nonexistent. Once a year, before the annual meeting, stockholders receive proxies that they are asked to sign to authorize management to vote, yes or no, on four or five proposals.

Those proposals, typically, include perfunctory actions required by law: Election of directors, usually the CEO's friends who may know nothing of the company's business, and the reappointment of an outside auditing firm. Other proposals could be, for approval, a plan to award valuable stock options to management (they do take good care of themselves) and, for disapproval, maybe the adoption of corporate policies introduced by reformers who have bought a few shares of stock to gain a forum in which to advocate their irrelevant causes.

Almost never is the CEO required to explain his blunders; almost never is he held responsible for his poor performance. If the company has been losing standing in its industry, if it is reporting losses instead of profits, if the stock has dropped down into the pits, stockholders are allowed not even that one, fair question, Why?

Well, why not?

The CEO gains control by default. Individual stockholders are scattered over the country. They have no communication among themselves, no organization to represent their ownership interests. What they know about the company is only what the CEO wants them to know.

Large blocks of stock owned by pension funds are bought, held, sold, by professional investment managers who are concerned less with the long term fortunes of the company than with the price of the stock from now until end of the current quarter. As they are paid only for the portfolio profits they can rack up, investment managers have no reason to join in revolts against corporate managements. The CEO, therefore, is answerable to no one.

The CEO may own only nominal quantities of stock and hence have interests than can conflict with stockholders interests. Like what?

➤ CEO ego. He wants a bigger job for himself. He buys out another company and, in so doing, puts his own company so deep in debt that the next recession just might take it under.

➤ CEO greed. He rewards himself extravagently, pays himself a salary of $1 or $2 million plus big bonuses, stock options and an unreasonable pension, not only for himself but for his wife, even though the company just has had a disastrous year or a string of disastrous years. What some of the rascals pay themselves is a scandal.

➤ CEO job security. To thwart an unfriendly buy-out he makes the company unattractive as an acquisistion. He increases the debt to the brink of insolvency by selling an enormous bond issue, then squanders the proceeds and panders to the stockholders by buying in a large quantity of the company's stock or paying out a huge cash dividend. (I'm not implying, mind you, that corporate raiders are a bunch of swell guys.)

Investors forever are being told that competence of corporate management is a major consideration in making their investment decisions. Yet no useful, reliable evaluation of management is available to us. Yes, a few blue chip companies consistently, successfully, profitably dominate their industries. A long record of outstanding results tells us that management at all levels is effective, that management is being developed for the future.

Some major corporations are managed successfully as one-man shows. A driving, ruthless man can get good earnings results for maybe a few years. His picture appears on national business magazines. Cover stories tell us of his genius. Employees respond to bullying, however, for just so long. At lower levels of management, intelligent, innovative persons drift away. The CEO, probably psychotic, views his more capable executives as threats and runs them off. When that CEO departs the scene, he leaves no leadership, only weaklings, a void.

Business schools, I suspect, have taught managerial arrogance. Their young, aspiring MBAs are told that they're being trained as problem solvers, that knowing the nuts and bolts of a business is for dolts whom they can hire. Instead, they're taught sleight-of-hand corporate finance. That's how conglomerates came into being: scheming CEOs manipulating the finances, cooking the books, to gobble up companies in unrelated businesses. To explain what they were doing, they found a new word, synergism.

Most major brokerage firms bought life insurance companies. (Some brokerage firms were "buyees.") Management revealed to us the mystery, synergism. Once under the umbrella of the same holding company, life insurance salesmen and stock brokers would team up, "cross selling" each other's clients. It never happened.

I had a glimpse of a buy-out by one of the earliest conglomerates that I'll call Food Company, Inc. In the mid-1960s, someone in my firm's investment banking department in New York asked that I accompany Food Company's CEO, Bill H., to a meeting with the owner of a local candy manufacturer that Food Company wanted to buy. I'll say that the owner's name was Woody and for his company's name I'll use Woody's.

Seated at a large conference table at Woody's offices, Bill and I heard from the executive in charge of their franchised candy stores—stations, as they spoke of them. We heard from the plant manager who told us about making candy. From the financial V.P. who gave us the figures—revenues, expenses and profits, about $5 million after tax. Woody, a big, tall engaging man whom we'd call a good ol' boy, had little to say. He never was much of a talker.

Bill of Food Company was a good listener. He asked no questions. He took no notes. He'd come alone, no attorneys, no accountants, just himself. After he'd heard what he needed to know, Bill did about 30 seconds' worth of arithmetic on a scrap of paper and said, "Woody, I'll give you two million shares of Food Company stock for your business."

Woody excused himself to discuss the bid with one of his fellows. He wasn't gone too long. When he came back, he said, "That sounds okay, Bill."

Bill suggested that Woody call in his secretary to dictate a brief agreement that both could sign. That offended Woody. "Down here," he said to Bill, "a man's word is good enough. We don't need anything in writing." Bill said that was all right with him. Across the table, they shook on the deal.

Driving back home, I asked Bill how he had arrived so quickly at his two million share bid.

"That was easy," he told me. "The only reason I'm buying Woody's is to increase Food Company's per share earnings and the price of our stock. Woody's will add five million dollars to our profits. If I'd given Woody any more than two million shares of Food Company, it just wouldn't work. It's simple arithmetic.

"This year, Food Company will earn two dollars a share. If I'd given Woody, say, two-and-a-half million shares, the five million profit from his company would be just two dollars per share on the additional stock I'd have outstanding. That wouldn't add anything to Food Company's per share earnings. And if I'd given him more than two-and-a-half million shares, Food company's earnings would be diluted, and I'd end up reporting something less than two dollars.

"On the two million shares he's getting, the five million dollars profit from Woody's will be two-fifty a share. Spread that additional fifty cents over all of Food Company's stock and that'll add about five cents a share to our earnings this year. I'll be able to report two-oh-five instead of two dollars. Just on this one small acquisition, I'm adding a nickel a share to Food Company's earnings for this year. Not bad for spending a day out in the boonies."

That's the way conglomerates grew. I wouldn't buy stock in one, because the music always stops. Nevertheless, I liked Bill. He was straightforward.

About two weeks later, I read in the paper that Woody's had sold out to a dairy company that also had gotten in the buy-out business to become a conglomerate. I'll have to guess that the dairy company upped the bid—and got their agreement in writing.

I've heard folks from up North complain that our good ol' boys can good ol' boy you to death.

Corporate raiders learned from the conglomerates and carried forward the idea: Yes, buy out a company, a publicly owned company, but with that company's own money and credit. Strip it of whatever can be sold and then, to cash in, take it public again.

Flashy management leads to trouble. Before buying the stock of some high flying company run by some hot shot CEO, ask yourself, Do I want trust this sort of guy with my money? At least, that's one way of evaluating the competence of corporate management.

Stockholders ought to attack and drive out a CEO who proves

to be a bandit. The problem, however, is belling the cat. As it is now, a stockholder can express his dissatisfaction with management in only one way, sell his stock. Persistent selling, of course, will drive down the price of the stock, but that doesn't remove, necessarily, a CEO who is damaging the company but who continues to rule by what would seem divine right.

How might stockholders, the owners, regain authority? The answer is, they can't, unless they can communicate and organize without the interference of the CEO. And that can be accomplished, I'm afraid, only through the courts. Creative attorneys must develop arguments to overcome courts' refusals ever to question business judgments of corporate managements or to consider charges against them of misfeasance. Then stockholders might engage an auditing firm paid, at company expense, to evaluate performance of management. As directors are personally liable to stockholders, they'd begin to feel the heat and just might decide to hire a new CEO.

In this exercise, I writing and you reading, neither of us has the purpose of introducing reform into the corporate boardroom. Our concern is surviving, even thriving, in the world as it is. If management is leading the company from one disaster to another, sell your stock.

Owning one's own business is an investment in common stock, 100% of the stock, but I'd say it's a lot different from investing in stocks of publicly owned corporations. The sole owner of a business has complete, effective control. He has the confidence that he can correct things that go wrong and, therefore, has little concern that all of his eggs are in one basket. I'd suppose that the sole owner views his business more as a source of income flow and less as an asset to be sold at a profit. Selling out, in fact, might be tough. Among possible buyers, will one be willing to pay what the owner thinks his business is worth? And does he want to buy all of the company or just part?

An investor in stock of a publicly owned company enjoys the advantage of liquidity. Perhaps he's not happy with the market price, still he can get out whenever he wishes. As quick as you can say Jack Robinson, he can switch his money from a company in one industry to a company in another, or from stocks to bonds or to cash.

Common stock, just as real estate, is property that has an unknown and uncertain future. Who can foresee, ten years out, changes of corporate fortunes? Some corporations will have disappeared. Others will have prospered beyond anything we can imagine. Most, however, probably will be doing pretty much what they're doing now.

What about a bond? Its future may be somewhat more predict-

able than that of a common stock. We know, as a certainty, that the
bondholder never will receive more than the stated rate of interest.
We know that interest will be paid on the bond so long as the
corporation is even marginally profitable and that the principle will
be repaid at maturity if the company's still solvent. Yet a business
can go broke. Squabbling over the bones of a dead business, bondholders would find that their first claim on the corporation's assets
is worth, probably, not too much.

Stockholders of corporations that prosper also prosper. Bondholders don't. As earnings grow, dividends to stockholders grow.
Bondholders' interest payments don't. Flip a coin. If it comes up
heads, stockholders win; bondholders just don't lose. Tails? Stockholders lose; bondholders lose.

What gives value to a stock? Further along is a chapter on that,
but your first thoughts, probably, are that publicly traded stocks can
be sold immediately at the market price; that you can get money for
your stock. Yet that's only because the buyer recognizes a value in
owning the stock. The price that buyer is willing to pay reflects his
evaluation of benefits to him. If you were the buyer, you'd ask,
What's in this for me?

You buy a stock for two reasons: to sell at a profit; to get
dividends. Although everything seems to change in time, stocks
have been bought, at least since the mid-1950s, with the hope that
later they could be sold at higher prices. Dividend returns have been
attractive only during times when the market has been way down
and the outlook bleak. Most of the time, dividends, in relation to
current stock prices, have been around 4 1/2-to-5% of market value.
At market bottoms, dividend returns have been maybe a couple of
percentage points higher; at tops, a couple of percentage points
lower.

During the 1940s and early 1950s, yields on Government bonds
were about 3%; on corporate bonds, about 4%. Dividend returns on
stocks were 6%, 7%, 8%. Bond yields were so low it took twice as
much money invested in bonds to get the same dollar income as you
could get on stocks. Investors who needed income had to buy stocks.

For many years after WW II, bond prices slowly fell, and the 3%
and 4% yields slowly rose. Stock prices, meanwhile, advanced
erratically. (We thought that every sell-off in the stock market was
the end of the world.) As stock prices rose, dividend returns declined,
because even though dividends were being increased as earnings
grew, stock prices were rising faster.

In *Barron's Weekly* during the late 1940s, H. J. Nelson in his
column "The Trader," made a convincing argument that rising stock
prices would bump against a ceiling. He saw the risks of owning

stocks as greater than the risks of owning bonds. For accepting those greater risks, he reasoned, stock buyers would demand higher dividend returns from stocks than the yields they could get on less risky bonds. In the rising stock market, once dividend returns on stocks dropped below yields on bonds, he warned, investors would stop buying stocks and begin buying bonds. Stock prices then would decline until dividend returns again became more attractive than bond yields. Only then would investors go back to buying stocks.

Dividend returns on stocks, Mr. Nelson implied, could not remain below interest yields on bonds. That was the ceiling he saw above stock prices. Advancing stock prices would reduce dividend returns, and higher yields on bonds would begin to attract the flow of investment capital away from stocks and into bonds.

That didn't happen.

I'd guess that investors compared bond yields, not only with dividend returns of stocks, but with dividend returns plus price gains of stocks—total return. Stocks were in a bull market. Investors began to expect continued appreciation. For many years, stocks did continue up. The economy of the country was growing. During the five war years, only military weapons and equipment had been manufactured—no automobiles, no new buildings, factories, machinery, highways; of consumer goods, only bare necessities. In the 1950s, the country still was catching up, building new, modern plant facilities, carving out the routes of interstate highways. On top of that came an awareness of the tidal wave of the Baby Boom, the great, post-war population explosion that had begun in 1947. Looking back, one must wonder that the stock market did anything but go up. That, however, is hindsight.

Viewed retrospectively, everything always seems clear and logical. But just as at any present time, every tomorrow is a frightening abyss. Companies, nevertheless, were making more money. Dividend payouts were increasing. Investors began to anticipate both higher earnings and higher dividends. They were willing to buy stocks at prices that included their expectations. They bought prospects of growing corporate profits. They were right.

Moreover, that portion of earnings that corporations did not pay out as dividends but retained and reinvested, became something of a tax shelter for wealthy investors who then were paying income taxes at rates as high as 70%. After taxes, the investor in the top income tax bracket could keep only 30 cents of his dividend dollar. But that part of a corporation's earnings not distributed to stockholders as dividends was available to build new plants, to modernize for greater efficiency and to move into new markets. The top bracket stockholder, instead of getting a dividend dollar that, after taxes, left him with only 30 cents to reinvest for himself, was happy to let the corporation retain a large part of its earnings and, in his behalf, reinvest 100 cents of each dollar of earnings.

As corporate revenues and earnings grew, stocks advanced in price. If the investor sold his stock to take a profit, that profit or capital gain was accorded preferential tax treatment. With various changes of the tax law, capital gains on property held more than six months or, later, 12 months, became long-term and were 50% tax-free, a tax break eliminated by the 1986 tax law. Tax advantage was a force behind the rising stock market. And around 1950, something big happened, but only in later years did we begin to appreciate the significance.

The state of New York threw open the doors to allow trustees of employee benefit funds, for the first time, to invest in all common stocks. Pension funds, profit sharing funds could go into the stock market. Elsewhere in the country, state regulators of other public pension funds and trustees of corporate pension funds began to tell one another, If New York thinks it's okay to invest in stocks, it must be okay.

Labor unions were demanding that corporations guarantee workers more generous pensions. And to cover the costs of larger pensions, corporations had to come up with larger annual contributions to their pension funds. Corporate managements began to see that the rising stock market offered opportunity. Employee benefit funds invested in stocks produced profits that reduced those annual contributions. Savings went direct to the corporations' earnings. Over the years, almost every person employed full time, union, nonunion and white collar, became participants of a pension or profit sharing fund program.

Incidentally, the pension and profit sharing fund business became a bonanza for Wall Street. It wasn't until the early 1970s, strangely enough, that brokerage firms began to recognize that pension funds and other institutional investors required something beyond the services of the high-pressure stock salesman who had developed in the retail business. Pension and profit sharing funds became the nation's biggest investors in common stocks.

It's interesting that ownership of corporations now is held, largely, for the benefit of employees. That makes just about everybody an investor in stocks, directly or indirectly.

The stock market always has gone up—long term. People in the U.S. are aggressive, grasping and driving—maybe not always attractive, but always innovative, vigorous and productive. Most of the natural resources we need we've got right here. The U.S. economy has continued to grow. Free enterprise has worked. And I don't see any of that changing.

I can't forecast the market, but I can assure you that the market will continue to go up—maybe not tomorrow or next month or next year, but long-term. Economic growth, technological change and inflation will drive up stock prices—long-term. To make money, you must be a long-term investor in stocks. To make money, you've got to be patient and financially able to ride out the market, if need be, for five years or more—for the long haul.

CHAPTER 7

EARNINGS ESTIMATES AND ANALYSTS

You've heard him, telling you how smart he is, the local stock market expert, "All I do is, heh, heh, play my own hunches."

The dictionary tells me that hunch, as a noun, is ". . . a feeling about something not based on known facts; premonition or suspicion: from the superstition that it brings luck to touch a hunchback." I don't know about you, but that's not the way I want to risk my money.

The buyer of a stock believes that the price he's paying is cheap in relation to his expectations of future earnings. The seller believes that the price he's getting is high in relation to his expectations of future earnings.

Decisions to buy and sell are not, of course, as precise and scientific as that sounds. More realistically, the buyer believes that the company's business is good, that the stock is going up. The seller believes that the company's business isn't all that great, that the stock is going down. Or maybe he sells because he sees another stock that he believes will do better or because he just needs the money. However the buyer or the seller might describe his reasoning, his expectations of earnings underlie his investment decision.

As large numbers of investors come to believe that a corporation's earnings will rise, they buy the stock, and the price goes up. As large numbers of stockholders come to believe that a corporation's earnings will fall, they sell, and the price goes down.

Further along, I hope to convince you that earnings expectations govern the prices of stocks. For the moment, just take my word for it. Earnings expectations govern the prices of stocks.

Now, you must be saying to yourself, Great, but how in the world can I know what the earnings of a corporation might be five years from now, or even next year? If you mean, know with any precision, you can't. No one can. But we can get some pretty good guesses from top-notch securities analysts who work with the major brokerage firms.

The New York Bond Club, on the occasion of their spring outing, used to put out a once-a-year edition of the *Bawl Street Journal*, a humorous take off on the securities business. One year during the late 1950s, the paper carried a major firm's ad that read, "Don't buy stocks until you consult with our Research Department. Best in Wall Street. Our motto: We like what you like."

In fact, a firm that would be so shortsighted as to lean on their analysts to recommend stocks only to increase business, soon would have an empty research department. Most analysts are fiercely independent and pride themselves on their reputations for integrity and objectivity.

Securities analysts know that big institutional clients listen only to analysts whom they believe and trust. Yes, that's true, long-term, of anyone who makes his living selling advice and counsel. Analysts' results, however, are immediately measurable. At any moment, important persons at those institutions can be asking, "How have that guy's recommendations worked out? How much business are we giving to his firm?" When you know that your results are measurable and being measured, you know, too, that performance is all that counts.

For estimates of corporations' earnings, we depend almost entirely upon Wall Street analysts. Why is all the analytical talent concentrated in Wall Street? Because only the major brokerage firms can afford to pay the competitive, six-figure salaries that attract and keep superstar analysts. Among the many analysts that cover each industry, two or three will be viewed as the most competent. They've spent years doing research work on companies within that one industry. They know, personally, the important corporate executives, they understand the business, they can compare strengths and weaknesses of the companies of that industry.

Sometime during the 1970s, *The Institutional Investor* magazine began an annual poll to identify the outstanding analysts of various industries. So-called "money managers" at banks, mutual funds, investment counseling firms and elsewhere vote for their favorites, and the year's All American Research Team is selected. Making the team, an analyst becomes something of a celebrity and, more important, commands extraordinarily high pay.

As you would guess, analysts want those votes. That means getting to know money managers and being available to answer their questions and to discuss with them industry and company developments. Most analysts already were doing that, but national recognition was an additional incentive.

During the years that I was manager of both retail and institutional offices here in Atlanta, at least one of the firm's analysts came to town each week—as they still do. An All American analyst is always in demand. The analyst would meet with money managers and research people at investment counseling firms and trust departments of major banks. At lunches, we'd have folks from insurance companies, the state and other institutions. I tried to make most of the lunches, because I could pick up ideas for my retail brokers.

Other institutional brokerage firms were having their analyst luncheons, too, so private dining rooms at Atlanta's Commerce Club had to be reserved well in advance. Meetings like that go on every day in every major city in the country. Local investment people enjoy what they call exchange, two-way discussion with a prominent analyst. Everybody in the business wants everybody else in the business to know how much he knows about an industry and the companies of that industry. Information flows freely.

Analysts can be called fundamental analysts, securities analysts, industry specialists—all the same thing. Other research people concentrate on market psychology. They're called technical analysts, market analysts, technicians—again, all the same thing. To distinguish between fundamental and technical analysis, let's call the fundamental analysts, analysts and the technical analysts, technicians.

You and I as private investors, retail clients, don't talk with analysts and technicians. We have no need to. The firm with which you do business will give you copies of their research material, but you'll have to ask for it. Most office managers discourage mailing lists. I did. Postage costs are high and, anyhow, few people read much. Most importantly, retail brokers get their business, their buy and sell orders, from oral presentations, over the phone, on the outgoing phone call. Why clog up the postal system? Mail order just doesn't work. If it did, firms would hire no brokers.

The main purpose of securities analysis is to arrive at estimates of companies' earnings for the current year and for one, two, five years out. Analysts are concerned with the persistence of trends, both evident and developing, and changes with which companies are struggling and changes that they anticipate. As general economic conditions will affect profoundly the profitability of companies, most analysts accept the business forecasts of their firms' economists and try to project how their companies will fare in the assumed economic enviornment. Estimating earnings is an iffy business.

Investors want analysts' earnings estimates, because stock prices are a product of earnings expectations. Do analysts' earnings estimates affect stock prices? Indeed, even if those estimates prove wide of the mark when companies report actual earnings.

An earnings estimate made, say, two years in advance of an earnings report can't be nearly as accurate as an estimate made just one month before the report. So analysts continually are adjusting their longer range estimates to take into account happenings that they could not have anticipated. Sometimes an analyst will write this sort of self-congratulating comment, "Earnings reported at $2.57 were slightly better than my estimate of $2.55." Sounds impressive enough, but that $2.55 estimate was made, not a year ago, but last month. A year ago, that analyst could have been estimating $5.

To get information about a company, analysts study annual reports, quarterly reports, 10-K reports that companies must file with the Securities and Exchange Commission, management's statements made to the press—all of which is publicly available information. Analysts develop personal relationships with the CEO, the Chief Financial Officer and other company executives. That allows for free exchanges of information useful to both the analysts and the company officers. That is not to suggest exchanges of so-called inside information. Trading on inside information is a felony. Any analyst or company officer who would divulge or use inside information would expose himself to prosecution.

Even so, what about inside information? Do people buy and sell on inside information? Of course they do. How would you stop it? Almost anyone can say that he bought a stock because he saw an increase of trading volume or that he bought on a hunch. A prosecutor, to get a conviction, must show intent to do wrong. Proving what might have been in someone's mind is difficult. But if it's a company officer or director who knew and who traded? C'mon.

If ever a broker touts a stock to you on his claim of having inside information, tell him you're not interested. Then find for yourself a new broker.

Analysts' principal sources of information are corporate officers. To keep open their pipelines, analysts avoid giving offense to those officers. To publish a derogatory opinion of a company is to risk shut-down of sources of information. The analyst then is on the outside while his competition, analysts of other firms, remain on the inside, basking in the confidences of the CEO and other officers. Ego, too, is a consideration. Analysts enjoy their personal relationships with prominent figures of business and industry—nice parties, photographs with the mighty. Although neither you nor I has the purpose of changing the relationships between analysts and corporate officers, we need to know that relationships do exist.

During any future time, half of all stocks traded in the U.S. will outperform the market; half will underperform. That suggests that if analysts have buy recommendations on, say, the 10% of those stocks they expect to be top performers, they should have—wouldn't you think?—sell recommendations on the 10% of those stocks they expect to be among the poorest performers. Seldom, however, do analysts recommend sales of stocks. They don't want to damage relations with companies they cover.

Technicians, by contrast, will recommend not only sales but short sales. Technicians have no need of information from corporate executives, because they rely almost entirely upon stock price and trading phenomena.

I'm not telling you than analysts are conned by corporate managements. Their buy recommendations, you may be sure, reflect their best thinking. But because they don't want to be cut off from the companies they're paid to follow, analysts convey negative opinions by use of euphemistic phrases: "Temporarily reducing opinion from Buy to Neutral"; "Would not be an aggressive buyer"; etc. Moreover, analysts are paid to identify, not losers, but winners. So if you hang on to a stock that's a bummer, waiting for the sell recommendation, you might get, first, news of bankruptcy. But whenever an analyst lowers either his opinion or earnings estimate on a stock, watch out.

Withal, analysts do expose mismanagement in a limited way and, thereby, give CEOs reason to consider possible reactions of stockholders, the public and even government regulatory agencies.

Analysts, I believe, are excessively concerned with the preciseness of their earnings estimates. Maybe that's because of the abuse they suffer for their misses. Stock buyers at institutions are quick to tell them of some other analyst whose earnings guess was a few cents closer—as though it made any difference.

Analysts must work carefully and deliberately, for they surely live in fear of overlooking a sign of trouble buried deep in the footnotes that accompany a corporation's financial statements. Although vital to the avoidance of land mines, methodical examination of figures must be time consuming drudgery.

I go into all of that because I don't want to seem insensitive to the demands of an analyst's job. Seldom, however, have I found an analyst who could answer the most important question about his strongest buy recommendation: What's going to make the stock go up? That probably was a more glaring deficiency to me because I was a salesman. I had to explain to my clients—or in later years, to my brokers—a rationale for expecting the improved profitability that the analyst was forecasting.

For myself as a client, I cannot buy a stock simply on the

analyst's increase of his earnings estimate or a statement that he's raised his opinion from Attractive to Most Attractive. I've got to know why. What makes sense to the analyst may not make sense to me. As an investor, I want to know what the analyst's reasoning is. It's my money at risk, not his.

To invest successfully, profitably, you must have access to the team of analysts and technicians of a major brokerage firm. The big Wall Street firms are the source of almost all securities research. Almost any investment advice that comes to you from anywhere else is, at best, secondhand stuff; at worst, it's not based on research at all. Like it or not, we're all dependent upon those major firms.

Ask yourself, How can I possibly know more about a company, an industry than a professional, superstar analyst? more about market analysis than a professional, superstar technician? You can't. I can't. Forget it. Forget about hunches.

CHAPTER 8

WHAT YOU GET FROM DISCOUNT BROKERS

"I make my own investment decisions," the well-dressed executive type with jutting jaw confides from the TV screen, "so I trade with [this discount firm] instead of a high-priced, full-service broker."

I, too, make my own investment decisions, but I make those decisions based on the best research on Wall Street. To get that research, I do business with a brokerage firm that has the best research on Wall Street. Although I probably could bellyache enough to get that firm to cut its commission charges 30% to 40%, I prefer to pay commissions at that firm's standard rates. No, I'm not a simpleton. It's just that I've been around long enough to know that I won't get what I don't pay for.

When my broker sees himself getting paid on commissions that are only 60% to 70% of his firm's standard rates, the service I get from him will be 60% to 70% of his standard. It's through him that I get the firm's research.

Every now and then, I used to hear a client say proudly, "I do my own research." And I always wondered that anyone could expect to pick up from casual reading that vast reservoir of information that an analyst acquires over many years of full-time study and direct contact. How could any individual investor expect to gain the breadth of knowledge that an analyst must have to assess accurately the prospects of the many companies of an industry? And even if he could, why undertake an enormous task that already has been done for you? But that's not the worst of it.

Before even thinking about the stock to buy, you must know which industries, which groups of stocks are beginning to gain strength or to lose strength in relation to the entire market. A technician can tell you which industries, which groups of stocks to be in, and which to avoid. For that, I want direction from the best technician in the Street. Just as the best analysts are with full service firms, so are the best technicians.

With no apparent, fundamental explanations, the price of a stock, or the prices of stocks within a group or an industry, will begin to exhibit a change of strength relative to the entire market. A technician picks that up immediately. Price action alerts him to something that's happening. It could be news that's been overlooked or news that has an impact that wasn't anticipated. Sometimes the technician can identify strength or weakness that can't be explained. He may tell you to wait and see—don't sell out on this strength or don't buy on this weakness.

The technician is invaluable, too, at market extremes. During highly emotional panic selling at the bottom or reckless buying at the top, the technician can give you the courage to go against the direction of the mob. During that other 99% of the time, he can't tell you whether the market will go up or go down. And he doesn't pretend to. Advice from a leading technician is worth many times the cost of commissions.

For someone so foolish as to believe that he can make money trading actively in the market, a discounter offers all that he needs: execution of his buy and sell orders. An in-and-out trader, as you'll see further along, is untroubled with facts. He's playing blindman's buff.

Just plain old service, too, is important. On the television news right after the crash of October, 1987, we saw some of the discounters' irate clients. They complained bitterly of having been unable to get their brokers on the phone, unable to enter their orders.

And even in more normal markets, poor execution—the price at which your order is executed—can wipeout any savings of commissions. That's especially true of orders for multiples of a thousand shares. An eighth of a point on 1,000 shares is $125. You'll never be aware of the eighths and quarters you lose, but it's costing you. Over the years, traders at the large institutions have told me that among brokerage firms, they see a night-and-day difference in execution— even of their small orders.

The best way to control your commission expense is to reduce your frequency of trading—which, incidentally, will improve your investment results. Before making a transaction, I prefer to wait at least until the following day. That keeps me from making knee-jerk switches from one stock to another.

Commission cost, however, is a minor consideration. Your major consideration is the amount of money you might make or might lose on an investment. Either way, that figure can be a hundred times the commission charge. And a discounter can't help you there.

CHAPTER 9

YOU'VE GOT TO UNDERSTAND T BILLS

Until you understand U.S. Treasury bills, T bills, you can't have a good understanding of any investment—stocks, bonds, real estate or anything else you ever put your money in. T bills are safe. You are lending your money to the U.S. Government. T bills are simple. You know when you'll get your money back and exactly how much. T bills are the basic investment. So before going any further with common stocks, I must be sure that you know what you need to know about T bills.

To borrow money, the U.S. Government issues securities that are sold at public auctions. For its long-term borrowing, out as far as 30 years, the Government sells bonds. For intermediate term borrowing, for more than one year but less than seven, it sells notes. For short-term borrowing, for 90, 180 and 360 days, it sells T bills.

On its bonds and notes, the Treasury makes semiannual payments of interest. Holders get a flow of interest income and, at maturity, return of principal. On its bills, the Treasury pays no interest. The holder gets only return of principal. His interest is the difference between what he pays for his bills and the principal he gets back at maturity. That difference is called the discount—bills are bought at a discount and paid off at par.

T bills maturing in 90 and 180 days are sold at auction every Monday; bills maturing in 360 days, every fourth Thursday. Bids are accepted until 1 pm ET. For principal amounts, or par values, of more than $1 million, bidding is competitive.

Starting with the highest bid (the smallest discount) the Treasury accepts successively lower bids until it sells all of the bills that it must, to borrow all of the money it needs to stave off bankruptcy for another seven days. Remaining bidders at lower prices are sold no bills.

But how about us folks who don't happen to have a million dollars this week? How do we buy bills on the primary offering?

Through the Federal Reserve Bank, a commercial bank or

other financial institution, we can buy bills on a noncompetitive bid—we subscribe to bills. The minimum amount we can buy is $10,000. Above $10,000, bills come in multiples of $5,000. Bills are sold to us at a price that is the average of all bids that the Treasury accepted on the week's competitive auction. So we are assured of buying our bills. And the price is reasonable—not the highest, not the lowest, but the average.

Until the early 1980s, the Treasury issued engraved certificates for T bills. When I worked in downtown Atlanta, I occasionally subscribed to bills at the Federal Reserve Bank, just up the street from our office. Walking two blocks, I could save the $25 service fee that our firm charged. About a week later, through the mail, the certificate came in bearer form—no registration, no name, just the same as having $10,000, or whatever amount, in currency.

Three or six months later, taking that certificate back to the FRB for redemption, or earlier to a bank for sale, and elbowing my way through the crowds around the bus stops at Five Points, I always was amused by the thought that several of those law abiding citizens, had they known what was in my pocket, cheerfully would have done me in. But walking along and looking dumb, I was safer than I'd have been riding in an armored car.

Since then, certificates have been eliminated for all Government securities. For individuals, the FRB will carry a Treasury Direct account in which you can subscribe to new issues of bills, notes or bonds. But the FRB won't execute any purchases or sales in the secondary market. So if you subscribe and afterward find that you need your money before maturity, you must have your bills transferred, by book entry, to a bank or a brokerage firm for sale. The transfer can take about a week, which may be an inconvenience.

Subscribing through a bank or broker, you'll be charged a fee, now about $50. And they'll ask that you deposit a check for the full face amount on the Friday before the auction. Your personal check is okay. If you sell your bills before maturity, you may get hit for another fee. Except as an accommodation for a good client, brokerage firms don't want to fool with T bill subscriptions. They lose money on the transactions.

Investing in T bills or in anything else, you spend today's dollars to buy a larger number of dollars that will come to you in the future. I don't want to sound like a preacher, but let's run that by again: Investing, you spend today's dollars to buy a larger number of dollars that will come to you in the future. You're buying those future dollars at a discount. What you pay now, is the present, discounted value of future dollars. Whenever you invest, in whatever you invest, you are buying tomorrow's dollars. You expect to make money on the deal.

Likely, you're asking yourself, How much of that future money are we talking about? How long before I get it? What's it going to cost me now?

Right. Those are the three questions you should ask before making any investment, whether you're investing for income or for profit.

How much, today, would you pay for $10,000 that you won't get until one year from today? Well, to begin with, you certainly wouldn't pay $10,000. Why would put your money beyond your reach for a year simply to get back nothing more than what you started with? You wouldn't leave $10,000 in a noninterest-paying checking account for a year or $10,000 in currency in a safe deposit box for a year. You'd say, Surely, I can do something better than that with my $10,000. And so you could.

Buying a T bill, you know exactly what you're going to get back. On a $10,000, 360-day bill, you'll get $10,000—360 days from now. But what would you be willing to pay for that bill today? Because all calculations of prices and yields of bonds, notes and bills are based on 12, 30-day months and a 360-day year, let's call the 360-day bill a one-year bill. To figure what you'd pay, you've got to begin with the $10,000 that you won't see for a full year and work backward.

Before doing that, however, let's see what $10,000, invested today, would be worth in 12 months. We'll start with today and work forward. We'll say that today you lend $10,000, risk-free, for 12 months. And that the current rate of interest on a risk-free, 12-month loan is 7 1/2%. At the end of the 12-month term of that loan, you'd get back your investment, 100% of the $10,000. As interest, you'd be paid 7 1/2% on your $10,000. So to figure what you'd get back after 12 months, you'd multiply $10,000 by 107 1/2% or 1.075. That comes to $10,750—$10,000 invested at 7 1/2% for 12 months.

Now, to see how much you'd pay for a $10,000, one-year T bill, let's work backward. To end up with $10,000 after 12 months, how much money would you have to invest at the risk-free rate of 7 1/2%? What we do is *divide* $10,000 by 107 1/2% or 1.075. That comes to $9,302. So the value of $10,000 discounted at 7 1/2% for 12 months is $9,302—which isn't the exact price. My bond calculator tells me that it's $9,292. So let's work with $9,292 and a discount of $708.

Put another way, when you subscribed to those T bills, you gave up today's $9,292 to get back $10,000 next year. Although you can sell those bills at any time at some discounted price in the secondary market, you've told yourself that for the $708 difference, you're willing to give up your $9,292 for 12 months. That's what you do when you buy a T bill.

Buying T bills, you are paying now for money that you won't receive for 90, 180, 360 days. You can buy those future dollars at a discount, because today's dollar is worth more than a future dollar. With today's dollar, there's the opportunity to invest, to get a return on your money during the time that must pass before that future dollar becomes available to you. And owing to continuous inflation, today's dollar will buy more than you will be able to buy with a future dollar. The current rate of interest takes that into account. If the expected inflation rate is high, interest rates rise.

Investing your money in stocks, bonds, real estate or anything else, you're buying promises of the future; you're buying future dollars. You must have some idea of how many of those future dollars you expect to get, how long you'll have to wait and how many of today's dollars you'll have to pay to get those future dollars. Buying stocks, as we shall see, your answers to the first two of those questions are nothing better than estimates—estimates that may prove to be nothing better than bad guesses. Looking ahead several years, you don't know what dividends you'll receive, you don't know the price at which you'll be able to sell your stock, and you don't know how long it will take for your expectations to be realized.

Buying a stock, you've got to be convinced that the price you're paying discounts fully the value of future earnings and dividends and the price that you hope to get for your stock if you sell. That's a complicated way of saying that you want to buy a bargain.

The current return on T bills is something of a baseline. It tells you what you're passing up if you don't invest—your opportunity loss. The interest rate at which a T bill is discounted is the free-market cost of money, the risk-free, near-term cost of money. Before investing in something else that promises a higher return, ask yourself, Is the risk I'm about to take worth the difference in return?

In whatever you invest, you're giving up today's dollars to get back, at some time in the future, a greater number of dollars. And you must remember that stocks, bonds, real estate or any other investment rewards you only with dollars.

Investing, you are buying future dollars at a discount. What you pay now is the present, discounted value of those future dollars. Understanding T bills, you understand *discounting*. And if you don't invest your money, what opportunity are you passing up? You could buy T bills and, risk-free, be paid the current rate of short-term interest. That's one measure of *opportunity loss*.

That's why I had to be sure that you know what you need to know about T bills.

CHAPTER 10

WHAT YOU'RE PAYING FOR WHEN YOU BUY A STOCK

Who'd go into a business unless he was convinced that he could make a profit? Nobody. The purpose of business is profit. The owner takes the risk of losing his money; he's entitled to the profits. As a share of ownership, a share of common stock is an entitlement to its proportionate share of profits. That's the only reason for buying a stock. With today's dollars, you're buying a flow of what you expect to be a lot more dollars coming to you over future years. You're buying a flow of future profits—a flow of per share earnings.

The price of a stock is the product of two, marketplace guesses. The first is a guess as to future earnings. That, of course, is in terms of dollars, dollars per share. Let's call guesses as to future per share earnings, simply, earnings expectations. When you buy a stock, that's what you're paying for—earnings expectations, a flow of future earnings.

The second guess is the percentage rate at which those earnings should be discounted. Future dollars aren't worth as much as present dollars. Just as the present value of a T bill is the discounted value of that future $10,000, the present value of a stock is the discounted value of that flow of future earnings. You'd discount future earnings at the current, long-term interest rate, which is the sum of "rent" on your money at about 3 1/2% plus the rate of inflation that's being anticipated in the market.

Thus the present price of a stock, theoretically, would be the present earnings expectations discounted by the present, long-term interest rate, which includes the marketplace forecast of the future rate of inflation. The higher that inflation forecast, the less those future earnings are worth and the less the stock is worth.

Actually, you and I never would attempt such a reckoning. Some analysts may do some such hypothetical stuff on their computers, but the arithmetic couldn't tell them much. By the time someone completed that discounting exercise, both earnings expectations and anticipated rate of inflation would have changed. The theory, nevertheless, describes a rational thinking process. Buying a stock, you're buying a flow of future earnings. Estimating present value of future earnings, you must discount that flow of future dollars by some percentage figure that takes into account loss to inflation.

The decision to buy a stock can't be made on a computer. Trying to prepare a nice, neat table of calculations would be like raking leaves in a tornado. Buying a stock is a subjective, seat-of-the-pants judgment. From something you've seen or heard or read, you're convinced that a company enjoys a unique advantage: a new product, a special marketing skill, some service that's in big demand. As a result, you expect revenues to increase. You hope that management can get wider profit margins and that earnings and dividends will go up. You believe that price of the stock will outrun inflation. At the price you're paying, you believe that you're getting a bargain, that you're buying a bright future.

Most investors are pragmatic. They evaluate the prospects of a stock in a simple, practical way. For many years, investors have watched and, indeed, studied the relationship of stock prices to earnings—the present price of a stock in relation to current per share earnings and to earnings expectations. Price divided by earnings results in a ratio, the number of times price is greater than per share earnings. It's spoken of variously as times-earnings figure, earnings multiple, price-earnings or P/E ratio. I'll stick with P/E ratio or just P/E—price divided by earnings. Rather than undertaking a confusing explanation of P/E, I'll use two, simple examples.

Suppose that in the current year, ABC Company has profits, after taxes, of $1 million, and suppose it has outstanding 1 million shares of common stock. ABC then earned $1 per share. If you decided to buy ABC stock, what price would you be willing to pay?

I'm sure that, first, you'd want to know what ABC might earn next year. If you were convinced that ABC would make $1.50 per share next year and if beyond you saw growth of earnings, you might be willing to pay $15 a share. That would be 10 times next year's earnings of $1.50 but 15 times current earnings of $1.

Now, let's suppose that XYZ Company's profits, this year, will be the same $1 million. Shares outstanding, again, 1 million. So earnings this year, also $1 per share. But you've decided that XYZ's earnings may drop; that earnings of $1 in the current year could be only 50 cents next year. Based on that earnings estimate, you might be willing to pay no more than $5 for the stock of XYZ. That, too, would be 10 times next year's earnings of 50 cents but only five times current earnings of $1.

Current earnings of both companies are $1 a share, yet you'd be paying three times as much for ABC as you'd pay for XYZ. At 15,

ABC is selling at 15 times current earnings. At 5, XYZ is selling at five times current earnings. Based, however, on estimates of next year's earnings—$1.50 for ABC and 50 cents for XYZ—both stocks are trading at 10 times earnings: ABC at 15, earnings of $1.50; XYZ at 5, earnings of 50 cents.

Stocks trade on earnings expectations, on expectations of future earnings.

On the financial page of the newspaper, P/Es appear along with stock prices. Those are called current P/Es. Yesterday's closing prices have been divided by current earnings. "Current" means earnings of the four most recently reported quarters, which may be the company's first quarter of this year plus the fourth, third and second quarters of last year—not necessarily the calendar year or the company's fiscal year.

Run down the column of those P/Es in the newspaper. The range is wild, possibly from two to 100. Are stock prices, you ask, all that crazy? Not really. Those P/Es, remember, are current prices divided by what we call current earnings, but current earnings actually are of the most recent past, the most recently reported four quarters.

Investors don't buy and sell stocks on multiples of last year's earnings. Stocks trade on multiples of earnings expectations, future earnings. If all the current prices in the newspaper were divided by the best earnings estimates for the coming 12 months, those P/Es would fall in a much more narrow range than the 2-to-100 that you saw. What value then are the newspaper's current P/Es?

Although the overall market is pushed up and down by recessions and recoveries, by inflation and disinflation, by fears and hopes, a sort of neutral P/E for the stock of a sound but slow growing company is something around 10—or maybe above 12 toward the top of a rising market or maybe below eight around the bottom of a falling market. Assuming that no big change of future earnings is expected, the current price of that stock would be around 10 times estimates of the next year's earnings. So for the moment, we'll think of a P/E of 10 as some sort of median number.

In the newspaper, P/Es significantly above 10 signal investor expectation that future earnings will be well above recent earnings. The higher the P/E, the more optimistic the expectation. It may be the stock of a company that's growing rapidly, each year's earnings expected to show handsome gains over earnings of the year before. Or possibly it's the stock of a company that took a big nonrecurring hit against earnings of the most recently reported 12 months but now is running well ahead of past operating earnings. A high current P/E tells you that earnings expectations are high. That's why ABC was selling at a P/E of 15. Earnings were expected to increase from $1 to $1.50.

How about a P/E well below 10? The price of that stock reflects investors' fears that the company's earnings are about to drop—just as XYZ was selling at a P/E of only five, because current earnings of $1 were expected to fall to 50 cents.

Earnings don't always go up just because the current P/E is high, and earnings don't always go down just because the current P/E is low. The market's not always right. But prices that buyers are paying for those stocks are a measure of their anticipations, expectations of earnings for the next 12 months, the next two, three, five years. They may be wrong. Their earnings guesses may be overly optimistic or overly pessimistic. But of the little that can be known of the future, that's what buyers and sellers risk their money on.

Every moment of the trading day, they're out there on the floor of the Exchange, the most optimistic buyer eager to take the best offer, the most pessimistic seller willing to hit the best bid. When they come together, the stock trades. The price of that trade reflects all that is then known of the fortunes of the company, of the market, of everything else that can affect that price. And it happens thousands of times every day.

The P/E figure you see in the newspaper represents well informed consensus. Unforeseen happenings probably will intervene. You get a good idea, nevertheless, of the market's present evaluation of every company's earnings prospects.

Still you hear someone say that a P/E is too high or too low; that the stock is too high or too low. That, of course, is but one man's opinion. If earnings of the next year or two don't improve, maybe the P/E was too high. But if earnings double, maybe that high P/E wasn't really high after all. Perhaps that stock will prove to be a great buy—which takes us back to earnings expectations. If those expectations pan out, the P/E, high or low, represented what was an accurate consensus.

From your broker, you can get his analyst's estimate of a company's earnings for the next year and a projection of the rate at which earnings might grow for the next five years. Other sources are the large statistical services. In most brokerage offices, you can find either Standard & Poor's or Moody's. As a reference for home use, I subscribe to Value Line. Those services will give you good estimates and projections.

Another way of looking at what you're paying for a stock is to use the analyst's projection of the annual rate of growth of earnings. It's a percentage. Say the analyst projects a five-year growth rate of 15% annually. That means earnings should double in

4.8 years.* If you were buying such a stock with a current P/E of 20, it would take almost five years for the earnings to double and catch up with the with the price you paid. Although earnings growth of 15% is excellent, five years is a rather long time. The longer the time, the further out the earnings projection, the more likely that unexpected things can happen.

A fairly good rule of thumb for determining a reasonable price at which to buy a stock is to compare that projection of annual rate of growth of earnings, a percentage figure, with the P/E, a multiple. If earnings are expected to grow at 15% annually, don't pay much more than 15 times current earnings, a current P/E of 15. I know of nothing scientific about that relationship. Still, it can keep you from getting carried away with excessive enthusiasm.

Just as earnings expectations affect the prices of individual stocks, expectations as to rate of inflation affect the prices of all stocks, the entire market. Inflation means a depreciation of the dollar, a dollar that won't buy as much. Even though the future per share earnings may increase in terms of dollars, if investors believe that the dollar is losing value, they won't pay as much to get those future earnings dollars. Future flows of dollars will be discounted at higher percentage rates, rates that include anticipation of rising inflation. Stock prices will fall. Bond prices will fall. Interest rates will rise. In terms of today's dollars, future earnings are not worth as much. That affects the prices of all stocks, the entire market.

The most widely used indexes of the market are the Dow Jones Industrial Average (DJIA) and Standard & Poor's 500 Stock Price Index (S&P 500).

The DJIA comprises stocks of 30 major corporations, mostly high quality, blue chip issues. When the average first was begun in the 1890s, only 10 stocks were used. Per share prices of the 10 were added up and divided by, I suppose, 10. After all, that's the way you get an average. With time came changes. Stocks were added, stocks were taken out and others substituted. Also, when one of those stocks is split 2-for-1, the price drops 50%, overnight. To obviate a wide gap in the average between one day's close and the next day's opening, to provide continuity, the divisor has been adjusted many times to produce, on the day after a change, the same average as the day before. That divisor has gotten down to around one half—0.50. If 29 of the 30 DJIA stocks remain unchanged and one stock rises a full point or $1 per share, the DJIA is up about two full points.

---

*You probably recall the Rule of 72. To find out how long it will take, at some annual percentage rate of increase, for your money to double, divide that percentage rate—here, 15%—into 72. Thus 72 divided by 15 = 4.8. That's 4.8 years. In 4.8 years, earnings growing at an annual rate of 15% will double.

The DJIA is what you read about when news of a big stock market hits the front page. The DJIA, up or down, is what the TV newscasters tell us about in the evenings. The DJIA is what your broker talks about with great enthusiasm—if the market's up.

The S&P 500 gives a broader picture. Also, its component companies are weighed in by size. For each of the 500 companies, the total number of outstanding shares is multiplied by the per share price to arrive at the total value of the ownership of that corporation.

Institutions follow the S&P 500. In analyses of investment performance, the stock portions of institutional portfolios are measured against the S&P 500. It's the S&P 500 that money managers try to beat. Few, however, do with any consistency.

Both indexes tell the same story: What the market did. For a single day, a move of more than one percent in either index, either way, up or down, is big.

In each Monday's *Wall Street Journal,* you can find the current P/E of the DJIA. Most recently reported per share earnings of all 30 stocks are added up and divided by that divisor of about one half. Average earnings then are divided into the average price to give the current P/E ratio of the DJIA.

Historically, what's a low P/E for the DJIA? Probably from 10 down to six. And what's a high P/E? Probably above 17. A P/E of something around 13 would be neutral.

Looking at a single, isolated stock, you simply can't say that its P/E ratio, in an absolute sense, is high or low. Only in a relative sense is a P/E high or low. It's high or low only in relation to the overall market and high or low only in hindsight, only in relation to what happens to earnings in future years.

While present expectations of earnings largely govern the P/E and, of course, the price of an individual stock, rate of inflation— high, low, rising or falling—has a most profound impact upon interest rates and P/E ratios of all stocks, of the overall market.

A chart of the DJIA for the past 40 or more years is a picture of continuous changes: changes of earnings expectations and changes of investors' evaluations of those earnings. As stock prices are the product two variables, earnings expectations and P/Es, the picture or chart doesn't tell you much more than when the market was up and when it was down. You will be able to make out waves, however, that correspond to the business cycles, because fears of business recessions are fears of lower corporate earnings, and stock prices drop. The market, in fact, has been probably the most reliable lead-indicator of turns in the business cycle. Otherwise, a chart of the DJIA, to me, is not especially illuminating.

Looking at a DJIA chart, you say to me, Okay, so prices went up and down, but what I want to know is, why?

Well, we know that earnings expectations largely govern stock prices, but how can $1 of earnings at some times be worth as much as $20 (a P/E of 20) and at other times be worth as little as $7 (a P/E of seven)? Explanations of market phenomena are never hard to come by. You can get a lot of answers. Looking back, starting in 1946 when I began in the business, I must say the the rate of inflation seems to have had a lot to do with the P/E of the DJIA. Let me explain two charts that follow.

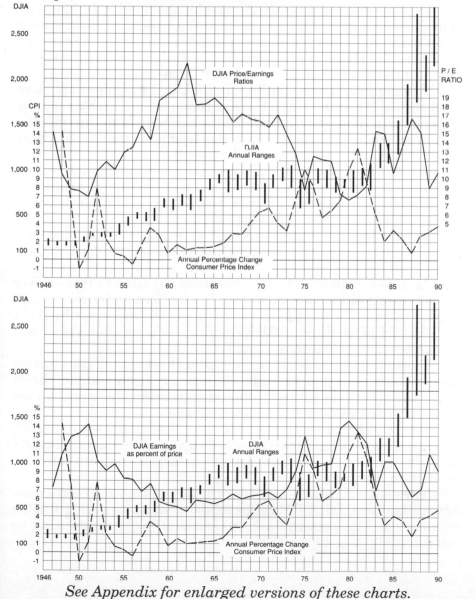

See Appendix for enlarged versions of these charts.

To get the median P/E of the DJIA for any past year, that year's median price of the DJIA is divided by that year's earnings of the 30 stocks. During that year, the prices of the 30 stocks were governed, of course, by earnings expectations—earnings that would not be reported until two or three months after year-end.

P/Es based on earnings expectations, even of only a couple of months in the future, are more realistic than comparing prices with earnings reported some months earlier. Investors were buying and selling, not on earnings already reported, but on expectations of earnings.

On that chart of the DJIA, let's plot the median P/E for each year. Now you have a picture of both the wide ups and downs of DJIA prices and the even wider ups and downs of the P/Es.

Here I'm about to show you how inflation impacts P/Es. (For rate of inflation, I'll use the Consumer Price Index, the CPI.)

When annual rates of inflation are plotted on the chart along with annual P/E ratios of the DJIA, a remarkable, inverse relationship appears. When the inflation rate has been high, the P/E has been low. When the inflation rate has been low, the P/E has been high. That's what you see charted on page 59.

When a rising rate of inflation has been anticipated, future dollars have been seen as worth not as much, and interest rates, we know, have risen. Future earnings, too, have been viewed as worth not as much, and P/E ratios have fallen.

The median P/E of the DJIA, just as any other P/E, is a ratio—price divided by earnings. That's what we see on the chart on page 59.

To give you an even more convincing picture, I've flipped over those P/E ratios. Instead of dividing DJIA prices by DJIA earnings to get P/E ratios or multiples, I've divided DJIA earnings by DJIA prices to get percentages—DJIA earnings as percentages of prices. A high percentage figure is a low P/E.

Plotting those percentages, we get a chart of multiples turned upside down. And now on page 59, you see a remarkable, direct relationship between rates of inflation and earnings as a percentage of prices. The two lines are roughly parallel.

The two charts are the same, except that on the second chart, P/E ratios have been turned upside down to show more strikingly that when inflation rises, stocks sell at prices that are lower in relation to earnings.

Through business cycles and wars, Republican and Democratic administrations, DJIA P/E ratios follow or maybe anticipate rates of inflation. The patterns are too parallel, too persistent to be coincidental.

Immediately after World War II, when wage and price controls were removed, the rate of inflation rose, a sudden adjustment from artificial price restraints to a free market. Corporate earnings were surprisingly good. But investors, convinced that a post-War recession was inevitable, had little enthusiasm for stocks. The P/E ratio of the DJIA stayed below 10.

In 1950, upon outbreak of the Korean War, the rate of inflation jumped briefly to about 10%, and the P/E of the DJIA dropped to about six.

Early in 1951, inflation began to subside and continued down to zero in 1955. The P/E doubled to about 15. Until 1969, inflation remained below 5%—for many of those years, at 2% and 3%. The DJIA P/E ranged from 15 to above 20. Low rate of inflation, high P/E.

By the early 1970s, costs of the Viet Nam War and Lyndon Johnson's Great Society had begun to fuel inflation. And in 1973, the big jolt came when Arab countries embargoed shipments of oil. The price of crude, maybe $3 a barrel, started up and was to continue up until 1980, topping out around $40. By 1974, inflation hit 11%. Moving inversely, the DJIA P/E, which had begun to slide in 1972, dropped to about eight.

In '76 when inflation came back down to below 6%, the P/E rose to around 11. But as inflation again heated up to hit 13 1/2% in 1980, the DJIA P/E, by 1979, had fallen below seven. During the 1980s, as inflation cooled down to something around 3%, the P/E once more began to rise.

To look at it another way: Back in the 1960s when the U.S. was experiencing almost no inflation, earnings of $1 were worth $17 to $21 in terms of market values of stocks—P/E ratios, that is, of 17 and 21. But during inflation years of the 1970s, per share earnings of $1 were worth only $7 or so—P/E ratios of around seven.

So what's the relationship between rate of inflation and P/E ratios at which stocks trade?

I've heard it expressed as the Rule of 20. It assumes that with no inflation, per share earnings of $1 are worth $20 in market value—a P/E of 20. From 20, subtract the rate of inflation. That gives an approximate P/E to expect of the overall market. At an inflation rate of 12%, as an example, the DJIA P/E would be about eight; at 3%, a P/E of about 17.

So what's a high P/E? What's a low P/E? Those questions, remember, started all this.

Based on that long-term relationship of inflation to the P/E ratio of the DJIA, I must say that during periods of inflation at rates of 10%-to-15%, a P/E above 12 is high, indicating market risks, and a P/E below seven is low. With inflation at 2%-to-3%, a P/E above 20 is high, and a P/E below 12 is low.

I'm not suggesting that the effect of inflation on P/E ratios has any value for market forecasting. The relation of inflation rate to DJIA P/E gives you only a benchmark as to degree of market risks: Relatively high P/E warns of risks. Relatively low P/E, however, suggests opportunity.

CHAPTER 11

WHAT'S ALL THIS ABOUT BOOK VALUE?

You've heard the expert speak knowingly about a stock's book value, and because the importance of book value is supposed to be widely appreciated, everyone, reverently, falls silent. No one wants to make a display of his ignorance, so no one asks, "What does book value have to do with me and my investments? In fact, what is book value?"

The balance sheet of a corporation's financial statement shows assets and liabilities. Assets include cash on hand, inventories, securities owned and depreciated value of plant and equipment. Liabilities include unpaid bills, borrowed money, bonds outstanding. From assets, subtract liabilities, and you get net worth. Divide net worth by the number of shares of common stock outstanding, and you get net assets per share or book value.

Of course, you wouldn't try to figure a book value for yourself. The big statistical services, S&P, Moody's and Value Line have done that for you. They'll give you almost every company's book value for the past year and for 10 or more years back. But what does book value have to do with you and your investments? If you mean the book value of just one company, the answer is, not much.

If the owners of a company decide to close the doors, to go out of business, what can they get for the building? machinery? inventories? What cash is in the bank? What do they owe? The only way to find out is to go out of business. Accountants, however, have ways to figure out liquidation value without going out of business. But accountants' formulas fail to include, in their complex accounting, realities.

Yes, assets have value. But try to sell the assets of a business that's no longer in business. In the secondhand market, those assets will go at only fractions of their replacement costs. Most assets have value only in a going business.

Each year, some part of the original cost of an asset is depreciated, written-off. The idea is to create a reserve with which to replace that asset once it's worn out. But think for a moment of a plant that makes, say, shoes. For how many years will the machinery produce economically? competitively? At what annual rate ought that machinery be depreciated? And, too, what does the Internal Revenue Service say? What arbitrary assumption do they make as to the useful life of that type of equipment? At what annual rate does IRS require the company to depreciate that machinery? Actual productive life may be much longer, or much shorter, than was assumed for accounting and tax purposes. On the books of the corporation, the value of its machinery may be wildly understated or wildly overstated—and the book value just as unrealistic.

Technological change can bring an abrupt end to the economic life of machinery, a factory or even an entire method of production. That happened to companies in our steel industry when the Japanese introduced more efficient processes. A more advanced competitive product can wipe out an industry, just as electronic calculators did-in the manufacturers of adding machines.

Relating book values of stocks to market values, you'll discover wide disparities from company to company, industry to industry. In industries that require expensive heavy equipment, book values of companies, generally, are high in relation to the market values of their stocks. Some examples: auto manufacturers, electric generating utilities, airlines, railroads, oils, steels. In industries that sell services, information and technology or that manufacture highly sophisticated products, book values of companies tend to be low in relation to market values of their stocks. Examples: prescription drugs, computer related companies, and publishers of books and newspapers.

Among financial companies such as banks, brokerage firms, life insurance companies, prices of stocks seem to be tied more closely to their book values. Perhaps that's because those companies work with money and their assets are more readily converted into money.

Except for financial companies, the book value of a stock seldom seems to have much to do with the market value.

But viewing the overall market, book values appear to have more significance. The book value wildly understated by one company seems to be offset by the book value just as wildly overstated by another. Averaged out, book values have some correlation with stock indexes. Look at the chart on page 65. The vertical lines show annual ranges of the DJIA. The dotted line shows year-end book values of the DJIA—the average of the book values of the 30 component stocks. The solid line shows the annual times-book value

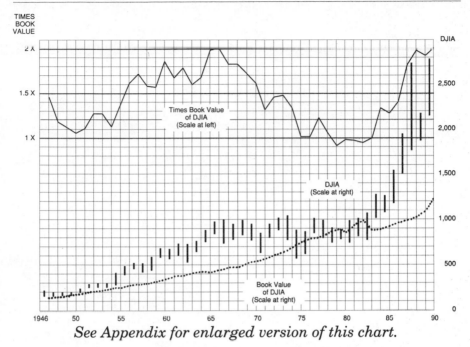

TIMES
BOOK
VALUE

See Appendix for enlarged version of this chart.

of the DJIA. (You can find current book values of the DJIA, S&P 500, and other indexes on one of the back pages of *Barron's Weekly*.)

Since 1946, the DJIA has ranged from a high of two-times book value to a low of one-time book value. During years that the DJIA has sold at or below book value, stocks have been a bargain. When the DJIA has sold at two-times book value, stocks have not been great buys. That won't help you forecast the market. Nothing will. Book value of the overall market, however, can tell you when market risks, probably, are low and when market risks, probably, are high.

That's about all I get from book values.

CHAPTER 12

CHANGE IS BOTH OPPORTUNITY AND DISASTER

All around us, all the time, change is going on. We see it. But what we see, we seldom recognize as change. And even if we do, rarely do we ask ourselves, what does this mean? Who will benefit from this change? Who will be damaged? Every change creates its own winners and losers. To one company, change is opportunity; to another, disaster.

Seeing a change, recognizing what you see as change, applying your own imagination, you can make some pretty good guesses as to companies that might be affected. Some will do more business, make more money; others will lose business and and maybe lose money. Because of that change, some stocks will go up; some will go down.

Investing is taking advantage of change. An investor buys a stock because, out there in the future, he sees—or believes that he sees—some important change. For whatever reason, he expects the company's business to improve and its profits to rise. He's buying the future; he wants to profit from change.

To us as investors, a company's past and present earnings only suggest direction, up or down, of future earnings. But we believe in trends. If earnings have been consistently good, rising every year for the past seven years, we all begin to believe that earnings surely must go up again next year and maybe for another seven years, at the same rate each year, just as we have come to expect.

We all resist change. We're adjusted to the present; we'd rather not be disturbed. If stocks are high, we can't imagine—or don't want to imagine—a drop of 25% or 50%. If interest rates are low, we can't believe—or don't want to believe—that rates could double or triple. And when times are bad, earnings down and rate of unemployment high, who is so brash as even to suggest that it's an opportunity to buy stocks?

All of us tend to believe that, good or bad, things as they have been, things as they are, will continue. It's called inertia: nothing, really, is going to change. We all seem to think that way. Yet every personal experience tells us that nothing remains the same, that everything changes. In the market, the one great value of experience is to have seen unlikely things happen and to know that, likely, the unlikely will happen again.

Trying to identify changes that I should watch for, I once undertook to identify every change, whether trivial and important, that I could remember. All seemed to fall into one of six major areas of change: economic, demographic, political, social, technological and changes of nature. As an example, business recessions and recoveries, financial panics, inflation, deflation—all were economic changes. But simply identifying changes had no practical value to me as an investor, so I've just kept on doing what I had done for many years.

Each morning after reading *The Wall Street Journal* and *The New York Times,* I go back over what I've read and ask myself, with respect to each item, What change does this suggest? What impact? Who are the winners? Who are the losers?

When still in the business, I especially enjoyed having lunch with one associate who has an active imagination and an interest in change. To me, our discussions always were useful. Having to communicate orally sharpened my thinking. Unless I put an idea into words, I find myself dreaming instead of thinking. If you have no one with whom to exchange ideas, the next best exercise, I've found, is to write down your thoughts. Your imagination, in any case, must range uninhibited, just short of fantasy, for strange things do happen. Possibly you can anticipate a few.

Some pages back, we got into one of the changes caused by rising rate of inflation. Financial assets, stocks and bonds, owned by investors as sources of continuing flows of money, are losers when inflation threatens the value of future dollars that investors expect to receive as earnings, dividends and interest. Inflation comes on gradually. The effects are pervasive. Investments lose present value.

Other changes can be sudden and unexpected. The 1973 oil crisis was a good example. Stock market reaction, at first, seemed slow and almost tentative. Yet commodity prices move up and down, anticipating changes of supply and demand, and supply of the world's most important source of energy, oil, was threatened. Energy costs were bound to rise and cut deeply into corporate profits—and stock prices.

Changes in annual numbers of births, past and present, produce population waves that advance each year as the new crop of babies is born and everyone becomes a year older. As each age group grows older, their activities and requirements change somewhat predictably. As numbers of people of any age, zero to 100, gradually increase or decrease, companies identified with the demands of that age group gain or lose business. Profits and the prices of their stocks go up or down.

Improved means of transportation and communication have internationalized industry, business, commerce, finance. As everything is bought and sold with money, one must understand the impact of change in rates at which currencies are exchanged, one for another. Depending upon the country in which a corporation is located and the locations of its customer and competitors, currency exchange rates can either damage or improve that company's profitability and the price of its stock.

Ups and downs of the national economy produce sometimes frightful change. To corporations, economic recessions mean reduced revenues, more intense competition, narrowing of profit margins and lower earnings. To us as investors, lower earnings result in dividend cuts and lower prices for our stocks.

Changes that we *anticipate* determine stock prices—even though what actually happens can be unexpected and quite different. Changes out there in the future that we can't foresee cannot affect stock prices. Those are the surprises awaiting us. As we move further into the future, some of those present unknowns will begin to appear through the mists, and prices will adjust continuously to the clearer picture of change. So it's not what ultimately does happen, it's what we think will happen that governs the price at which a stock trades.

I'm neither an economist nor a historian, but as a broker I'll try to tell you how some important changes have moved the market. I've watched the market react to changes in rate of inflation, the price of oil, numbers of births, currency fluctuations and swings of the business cycle. Each of those changes produced market reactions that are instructive. And each is a change that probably will repeat, again and again. Knowing how the market reacted at an earlier time, you'll be better prepared take advantage of those changes when they happen again.

Chapter 13

Inflation—Winners and Losers

Investing in stocks, you surrender your money in exchange for pieces of corporate ownership. With today's dollars, with money that can buy present needs and enjoyments, you elect to buy, instead, hopes of bigger and better things: growth of earnings, increased dividends and a big run-up in the price of your stock. By choice, you put your money beyond your reach. You do that, you surrender today's dollars, only because you expect that in the future you'll get back a lot more dollars. Investing, you are buying future dollars. Therefore, you must have some sort of idea, however vague, of the money you'll make on your investment.

Further, you must take into account the value or buying power of those future dollars. That is to say, you must take into account the possible rate of inflation, the rate at which the purchasing power of those future dollars will be eroded.

From what we saw a few pages back, the marketplace seems to use the current, long-term interest rate as the percentage figure to discount future dollars, to reckon their current value. You can see why. Interest rates are prices at which investors are willing to lend their money. Buying a bond in the open market, an investor is lending his money either for the remaining life of the bond or until he sells it. As a lender, the bond buyer demands a return or yield high enough to compensate him for loss of future buying power, to offset depreciation of the dollars with which that bond will be paid off at maturity. So the interest rates or yields at which bonds trade include compensation to the buyer for expected damage from inflation.

The yield of, say, a Government bond consists of risk-free rent on money, historically about 3 1/2%, plus expected inflation damage—the marketplace consensus of rate of inflation, which, no doubt, is a better guess than that of any economist. Bonds of longer maturities, of course, generally sell at higher yields (lower prices), because the longer the time before the bond is paid off, the greater the risk of higher inflation.

A rising rate of inflation, as we learned painfully in the 1970s, plays havoc with the prices of both stocks and bonds. Investors begin to wonder what inflation will do to the future value of money, to the future value of earnings and dividends. They begin to doubt that those future dollars will be worth as much as present dollars. They become convinced that the cost of everything will continue up at an annual rate of 10, 15% or more. They assume that interest rates will be 15, 20%, or more. With that in the offing, what's the present value of those future returns they expect from common stocks?

An investor buys stocks, owns stocks, for growth of earnings and dividends. But even at the rate of growth that the investor optimistically might expect, what will the earnings and dividends be worth next year? five, 10 years out?

What $10,000 is worth at an annual inflation rate of . . .					
	8%	7%	6%	5%	4%
after					
1 year	9,259	9,346	9,434	9,524	9,615
2	8,573	8,734	8,890	9,070	9,246
3	7,938	8,163	8,396	8,638	8,890
4	7,350	7,629	7,921	8,227	8,548
5	6,806	7,130	7,473	7,835	8,219
6	6,302	6,663	7,050	7,462	7,903
7	5,835	6,227	6,651	7,107	7,599
8	5,403	5,820	6,274	6,768	7,307
9	5,002	5,439	5,919	6,446	7,026
10	4,632	5,083	5,584	6,139	6,756

After five years, a 15% rate of inflation will reduce the buying power of today's dollar from 100 cents to 50 cents; after 10 years, to 25 cents. Through a period of such inflation, earnings, just to stay even, would have to grow at 15% a year. And dividends would have to be increased 15% a year just to maintain buying power of your dividend dollar. Even so, you'd just be treading water.

The higher the anticipated rate of inflation, the less the present value of a future dollar. As expectations of a rising rate of inflation force up interest rates, the present value of a future dollar falls, and the present values of future earnings and dividends fall. In comparison with what today's dollar will buy, future earnings in depreciated dollars that a corporation will retain for reinvestment won't buy as much research and development, new machines, as many talented people. Future dividends paid to stockholders won't have as much buying power as today's dollar.

Who wants to spend good dollars today to buy not-so-good dollars in the years ahead? Accordingly, prices of common stocks fall. That's the combined affect of higher inflation rates and higher interest rates.

During the inflation of the 1970s, we made another frightening discovery. Earnings reported by corporations—especially manufacturing corporations—were suspect. Profits were being overstated, because costs of goods sold were being understated. Materials from which those goods were fabricated had been bought earlier at prices way below current, replacement prices. The difference between cost and sale price resulted in paper profits, money that was not available for plant expansion or for distribution to stockholders as increased dividends. That "profit" had to be spent on new inventories of raw material now available only at higher, inflated prices.

Inflation hit corporate earnings in another way. From its taxable income, a corporation is allowed to subtract, as a business expense, annual depreciation of the value of machinery, buildings, trucks and other tangible production equipment. The tax savings allows the corporation to create a reserve fund that can be used to replace worn-out equipment and aging facilities. But the tax law allowed corporations to depreciate—write off—no more than original costs. Inflation, meanwhile, had increased replacement costs so much that reserve funds were woefully inadequate. Corporations found that they hadn't enough money in their reserves to pay the inflated prices for purchases of new production equipment. Reported earnings, in consequence, became overstatements of real profits—real money that could have been used for expansion or paid out to the stockholders.

An accountant, I'm sure, could give more examples of how inflation results in overstated earnings. But that's what someone is talking about when you hear a comment about quality of earnings. During rising inflation, reported earnings are viewed as poor quality. Investors won't pay as much for a dollar of reported earnings. P/Es fall. The market falls. During disinflation, quality of earnings improves. As the rate of inflation drops, reported earnings include fewer bookkeeping credits and more real dollars—spendable money. Reported earnings, therefore, are worth more. For a dollar of reported earnings, investors now are willing to pay more. P/Es expand. The market goes up.

During inflation of the 1970s, we were hearing that stocks of companies producing lumber, copper and other natural resources would be splendid "hedges against inflation." Most weren't. The investment that paid off was real estate.

Everyone agreed that the only investment to own during inflation was tangible property. Real estate is tangible property. That was seen as the magic of real estate. Stocks, it was argued, weren't doing well because stock is an intangible. Looking back, I don't see that as an explanation.

Real estate developments during those years met the demands for shelter for a growing work force. Rents could be raised as high as the traffic would bear. Furthermore, Congress had all but exempted real estate investors of income tax. All of that is to say, real estate was a great investment from which to get a flow of high income along with tax savings that resulted in enormous, rising, after-tax returns. I used to hear developers brag about paying no income taxes. Small wonder fortunes were made developing and owning office buildings, shopping centers, apartment houses, warehouses.

Yet some real estate values did not increase along with inflation. New York City's rent controls, first imposed in 1943 during WW II to provide cheap rents for apartment dwellers, precluded rent increases. Those property values suffered. If rents can't be raised to offset higher costs of operation, who wants to invest in rental property? Hence owners of New York City apartments reacted predictably. They continued to collect rents but spent nothing for repairs and maintenance. When tenants finally moved out of those dilapidated buildings, landlords stopped paying taxes. As buildings were abandoned, the city took them over to provide public housing. By 1988, New York City operated 4,100 apartment buildings and rented to 37,000 families—almost as many folks as live in Macon, Ga. The buildings were not condemned only because NYC doesn't require itself to comply with its own housing codes.

Nationwide, investors in rental property got a shock on February 24, 1988, when the U. S. Supreme Court reaffirmed the constitutionality of rent controls imposed by cities and states.* Any investment in apartment houses, especially in major cities, would seem vulnerable to imposition of rent controls.

So maybe the magic of real estate had nothing to do with its being a tangible property. Maybe the real estate boom was the product of the Baby Boom of 25 years earlier, a product of generous tax incentives created by Congress, a product of uncontrolled rents.

The important distinction, in my view, between what we call a tangible investment—real estate—and an intangible investment— common stock—is that, for yourself, you can see and examine the

---

*Pennell v. San Jose, No. 86-753.

real estate that you are about to buy, but for yourself, you can't see or examine a common stock. Buying stock, you must depend almost entirely upon someone's oral representation of its future value. Our laws recognize that. The real estate business is not regulated. Although laws protect us against fraud, real estate is bought and sold in an unregulated market. The stock and bond business is closely regulated. It must be. Otherwise, opportunity for misrepresentation would be limited only by the salesman's imagination.

In the 1980s, entrants into the work force leveled off. With the 1986 tax law, Congress closed up some of the loopholes and stopped some of the abuses. For real estate, that could have marked the end of a heyday. Surely, I don't know. I'd be wary, nevertheless, of an argument that real estate is attractive simply because it is a tangible.

Anyone investing money asks himself, What's in this for me?

Whether tangible or intangible, real estate or stock, the present worth of any investment is the anticipated, future flow of money to the owner. The flow can be property rents or corporate earnings. The worth of farmland is the anticipated profits from the sale of future crops. Of mining properties, the anticipated profits from future sales of extracted minerals. Of oil property, anticipated profits from future sales of oil.

However you invest, you're buying expectations, hopes. To me, hopes seem intangible. If so, then every investment is the purchase of an intangible.

That could be quite a different story, however, in an environment of hyperinflation—rates of 50, 100% and higher, when money rapidly becomes worthless. You could expect people to buy anything—gold, diamonds, stocks, real estate—any kind of property, just to get rid of money as quickly as possible, before it lost more of its value. Buying gold and diamonds, who'd care about flow of income, about opportunity loss? Concerns, I should suppose, about discounted values of corporate earnings and dividends and the poor quality of earnings would be lost to panic to do something, anything to exchange money for property. Because of immediate availability and liquidity, stocks could be especially attractive. Even in the worst of circumstances, moreover, a corporation can survive. Corporate know-how has immeasurable, intangible value.

At the end of World War II, standing at the outskirts of cities in the industrial Ruhr, one had an unobstructed view across the bombed-out ruins. A few years later, those factories were up and running, outproducing the rest of the world.

During inflation, it's easy to rationalize extravagence. That's what someone is doing when you might hear, "We really can't afford this expensive furniture, but if we wait until next year, the same furniture will cost a lot more." It's a sense of less and less constraint upon spending—even for things we don't need. As a pervasive attitude among both consumers and corporate executives, rationalized spending stimulates further inflation, which soon justifies reckless spending.

Once inflation becomes widely accepted, once everyone views money as a deteriorating asset, money becomes something to get rid of, to turn immediately into property, into things. Having no intrinsic value, money buys things only because people of a country believe that it will continue to be accepted in exchange for things. Once that confidence in money is lost, a government only can declare its money worthless and start all over again, with a new money, with a new name for it.

Rising inflation—up, at least, to the 15% that we saw during the 1970s—results in rising interest rates which kill the stock market. And of course, the bond market. In the 1980s, when the rate of inflation began to moderate, investors began to see hope of recovery from the damages caused by inflation. Although inflation continued, the rate was declining. We spoke of it as disinflation. Interest rates, too, began to decline. Flows of earnings, dividends and interest began to be discounted at lower rates. Quality of earnings was seen as improving. Prices of stocks and bonds began to rise.

In the past, an inflation rate below 5% has been the ideal environment for stocks. Only for one or two years during the Great Depression of the 1930s have we had deflation when the dollar was worth more, bought more goods. But who wants to return to those dreadful times?

As an investor in common stocks, you've got to watch the trend of inflation. To get an immediate picture of change in the rate of inflation, I look at charts of commodity futures. When you detect a trend in the price of an individual commodity, you ask yourself what it means. When you see all commodities moving in the same direction, you're getting a message you'd better heed. Rising prices in commodity futures markets tell you that the rate of inflation is rising.

Nothing is more sensitive than prices of futures. Persons who do nothing but deal in, say, soybeans, immediately relate every happening in the world to its effect upon the price of soybeans; their evaluations are accurate and reasonably predictive—until something different happens the next day.

In October, 1980, a month before the Carter-Reagan presidential election, commodity futures prices that had been, according to one index, 100 in 1972, topped out around 335. On the charts at that time, the break was visible. It marked the end of what was called double-digit inflation. By 1983, that commodity index was down to 230. Disinflation had begun in 1980.

Try to remember, however, that every trend—including the trend of inflation—is a chart of the past. This present moment, within only a minute, becomes the past. Any trend is past tense. A trend only points to the direction in which something—inflation— has been moving. A trend tells you nothing of the future. If you are a strong believer in momentum or inertia, you can draw a dotted line on your chart to extend into the future the direction of the trend. But you'd be kidding yourself. Looking into the future, no one ever can know how far up—or down—a trend will go or how long it will last before it reverses itself.

From experience of recent years, however, I shall watch the trend of inflation. If the rate should pass 10%, I'll have to assume that stock and bond markets are getting into deep trouble. I must consider switching some money from stocks to short-term Treasury bills until inflation subsides. But should the rate get above 20% or 25%, I must assume that we're getting into hyperinflation, admit that probably I've been wrong and consider investing everything in the stock market. In hyperinflation, of course, there would be no bond market, as bonds would become just as worthless as the money.

In Germany, the inflation of the early 1920s completely wiped out the value of the mark. Toward the end, the government maintained the supply of paper money by overprinting, say, 10-mark notes to make them into 1,000,000-mark notes—which even then wouldn't buy a loaf of bread. Bonds, too, became worthless. Yet ownership—stock—of the industrial giants, Krupp, I.G. Farben, Seimens, survived, and the owners prospered to welcome Hitler in 1933. That ownership still survives and prospers.

In the early 1980s, when bond yields were extraordinarily high, investment professionals were expressing their doubts that common stocks ever could outperform yields of 14% then available on Governments. For many decades, the annual return on common stocks had average about 9 1/2%—that's from both dividends received and increased market values. So why not sell stocks and lock in, for 25 years, 14% on risk-free Governments?

The attraction of that 14% surely diverted to bonds a heap of money that, otherwise, would have gone into the stock market. One major corporation announced that it had switched its entire pension fund from stocks to bonds—only to return to stocks after the market took off in 1985. But at that time, I saw little of such switching by individual investors. Their judgment was more foresighted than we could have known.

No one can forecast the onset of inflation or rate of inflation or beginning of disinflation. Yet, when the rate of inflation is rising, the only stocks to own are those of blue chip companies. Some companies, even of high quality, I'd want to avoid; others, I'd be willing to hold or buy, even though the trend of inflation might be pointing up—because I can never know when that trend can begin to level off and point down.

What companies to avoid? I can tell you only what I saw during the inflation of the 1970s. Among those I would avoid:

➤ companies that depend upon sales of big ticket consumer durables such as autos, housing, appliances—anything bought "on time." As interest rates rise along with inflation, folks find that they can't afford the monthly payments and stop buying.

➤ companies that have high labor costs, because unions negotiate contracts indexing wages to inflation.

➤ manufacturing companies vulnerable to rising costs of raw materials, because when manufacturers try to pass along those costs, they run up against customer resistance.

➤ banking, brokerage, finance companies, because big users of money can be caught in a squeeze between the higher and higher interest rates they must pay for deposits or short-term borrowing and the lower rates they're getting on their long-term loans and investments. Also, bank loans can go bad.

➤ electric utilities and natural gas distributors, because their rates are regulated, and elected public service commissioners drag their feet in granting rate increases. Also, utilities can be borrowing money for construction of new power plants.

What stocks to own at a time when the trend of inflation has been rising? From what I saw during the inflation of the 1970s, I'd want stocks of . . .

➤ blue chip companies with little or no debt, with relatively low costs of wages, raw materials.

➤ companies that provide consumer necessities such as packaged foods, beverages, drugs, medical services and supplies, because those are daily needs that cannot be deferred.

Inflation never goes away. Probably, it's one of the constants with which we always must live. Only the rate of inflation changes. When the rate is rising moderately, you hear complaints about the cost of living. At a rate something above 15%, we see extravagant spending. At higher rates that break through some sound barrier, reactions and behavior, I believe, will be different. So inflation is not the change, it's change of rate of inflation that you can expect to drive stock prices.

Looking back over 10, 20, 50 years, you'll see that the best hedge against inflation has been common stocks, the stock market. Long term, the stock market not only has kept up with inflation, stocks have paid off at a rate far exceeding rate of inflation. But you've got to monitor, manage your stock portfolio—weed out stocks of faltering companies, substitute stocks of emerging companies. If you're willing to work at it, you can count on stocks to be your best investments in the future.

CHAPTER 14

OIL PRICES—WINNERS AND LOSERS

The great surge of oil prices began with the 1973 Arab-Israeli war. As the U.S. supported Israel, Arab countries retaliated. On October 21, oil shipments to the U.S. were embargoed. On December 9, nine Arab countries announced a 28% cut of September rate of production. That hit Western Europe and Japan. On December 23, 1973, seven Arab nations, with the tacit approval of other members of the Organization of Petroleum Exporting Countries—OPEC—doubled the posted price, to $11.65 a barrel. Although the embargo against the U.S. was lifted on March 18, 1974, OPEC had made a useful discovery: it could get away with extortion—all the way to $40 a barrel.

Suddenly, Islam had slashed out, and the shock waves collided with every economy in the world. It was something more than just a change.

U.S. oil companies, both domestic and international, with important underground reserves, were accused of being delighted. If they weren't, they shouldn't have been in the oil business.

In the U.S., Congress and the Administration saw political opportunity and promised that we'd never pay exorbitant prices for gasoline, heating oil and natural gas. How to do that? Price controls and allocations, of course. At year-end, 1973, with OPEC selling oil at $11.65, our Government's Cost of Living Council capped the price of oil produced in the U.S. at $4.25. Results were predictable.

The lid on prices of domestic oil and natural gas was a guarantee that fuel supplies would dry up. Producers cut back to wait for higher prices. Gasoline shortages in some areas began to appear. In long lines, motorists waited at filling stations that often ran out of gas before those toward the back of the line got up to the pumps.

During the cold winters of 1973-74 and 1974-75, we were told that natural gas reserves were almost exhausted. The Government-controlled price of natural gas, sold interstate, was 52 cents per 1,000 cubic feet. Intrastate, within Texas and Louisiana, uncontrolled gas sold at $1-to-$2 and, not too surprisingly, was in ample supply. And once gas newly discovered below 10,000 feet was exempted of price controls, drilling promptly began. Nothing more was heard of a shortage of natural gas.

In 1977, shortly after his election, President Carter declared his energy program to be "the moral equivalent of war." He stated, "We will not let the oil companies profiteer." That, no doubt, was good politics. And there may have been some near-term benefits. Certainly it was consistent with one's sense of equity. Long-term, however, it proved to be a high-cost slogan.

A tax was applied to "gas guzzlers," new cars that got fewer miles per gallon than Federal minimum standards, and the speed limit was reduced to 55 mph—probably two good ideas that came out of the panic. The Government subsidized production of corn alcohol to blend with gasoline—an expensive way to consume some of the corn surplus. Electric utilities were required to buy electricity from factories that generated for themselves more than they used. Investors in windmill-driven generators were allowed big credits against their income taxes—and the utilites were required to buy that electricity, too. Office buildings were encouraged to keep temperatures at a chilly 65 degrees in the winter and a hot 80 degrees in the summer—patriotic landlords were happy to comply.

Government price controllers allowed the price of newly discovered oil to rise over three years to the free market level by 1981. Thus we had one price for old oil and a higher price for new oil—both of which looked a lot alike. Congress appropriated billions of dollars for the development of synthetic fuels. Firing furnaces with ten-dollar bills would have been less expensive.

Saudi Petroleum Minister Sheikh Zaki Yamani, one generation out of the Arabian desert, favored Western nations with lectures on economics.

The 1973 oil crisis was followed by aftershock in 1979 when Iran's Shiite Moslems deposed their Shah. The enormous flow of oil from Iran was threatened.

Rising prices of the world's major energy source resulted in rising prices of everything dependent in any way upon oil. Money, therefore, bought less and less of everything. That's inflation. Inflation produced higher and higher interest rates. And borrowers found that rising costs of money could lead to bankruptcy. That's recession.

Industrial countries, having become dependent upon abundant supplies of cheap, imported oil, began to scramble to cutback nonessential consumption and to encourage conservation and use of other fuels.

On the world market, oil is bought and sold with U.S. dollars. Thus Arab countries were awash with dollars. And U.S. bankers saw opportunity. To attract Arab deposits, they offered high interest rates and, to make a nice spread, or profit, they gleefully lent that money, at much higher rates, mostly to Latin American governments—which meant lending billions of dollars, in some of those countries, to two-bit military dictators.

To give respectability to that lending activity, our bankers dreamed up the catch phrase, "recycling petro-dollars." Piously, they told us that they were supplying the money to allow world trade to thrive in spite of rising energy prices. Sovereign states, our bankers explained to us, cannot repudiate external debt—although South American countries had done so in the 1920s. The dictators and their cronies deposited millions of those U.S. dollars in their own Swiss bank accounts and left their countries busted and deep in debt. Most of those loans would never be repaid. The heroes of the banking fraternity retired just before the chickens came home to roost, and their stockholders discovered that they were the losers— holding the stock, holding the bag.

The Arabs weren't so dumb. They themselves could have made those same loans, direct, at the same high interest rates. Instead, they decided to play it safe. Why worry about Latin America? The Arabs were happy to take lower rates paid by U.S. banks, let the banks carry the big risks, and be sure of getting back their deposits.

In late 1980, the price of oil peaked out at around $40 a barrel. Oil then began to drift down along with most other commodities. OPEC began to fall apart. Having reserves for the next 200 years, Saudi Arabia was said to have been fearful that too high a price for oil would promote development of competing energy sources. But other countries, such as Nigeria, wanted both high prices and all-out production to get maximum dollar revenues. Most OPEC countries ignored their cartel quotas limiting production and continued to flood the market.

For some time, Saudi Arabia took up the slack by reducing its output to support the world price, but by late 1985 they had tired of bearing the burden for their uncooperative OPEC partners and began opening the valves. Some said that their purpose was to run marginal producers out of business so that afterward the Saudis again could jack up the price. Oil then was trading on the New York Mercantile Exchange at more than $31 a barrel. Four months later, it was $10.

In the U.S., the Government's price control and allocation apparatus already had been dismantled, quietly, more in response to public exasperation than as an admission that controls don't work. Rising prices had done what no Government program could have accomplished. Users of petroleum products switched to cheaper fuels—coal, natural gas, nuclear—and found ways to conserve energy. In the spring of 1977, the U.S. was importing 8.5 million barrels a day. By 1985, imports had dropped to 4.2 million barrels. When the demand fell, the price fell.

Just as in the stock market, the bond market or any other open, freely negotiated market, price brought supply and demand into balance. The free market responds immediately to any change or anticipated change of either supply or demand. The only effective discipline is price—when rising, price encourages production and discourages consumption; when falling, price discourages production and encourages consumption. At every opportunity, politicians intervene in that supply-demand relationship to seek favor of their constitutents by identifying themselves with handouts, something for nothing. It's the cheap way to get reelected.

So what were some of the consequences of the oil crisis? Who were the winners? Who were the losers?

Across the board, the stock market was loser. Future dollars wouldn't buy as much, so corporations would be earning depreciated dollars. That's inflation. And inflation meant higher interest rates. Those future corporate earnings, when discounted at higher interest rates, weren't worth too much in terms of current dollars. The market hit the skids. And with President Nixon's Watergate scandal being exposed, it was a bad time for the country.

Government price controls and a windfall profits tax postponed benefits to oil and gas producers. When the market began to recover in late 1974, oil stocks followed along, even though Government controls precluded earnings gains until 1979.

Gasoline, diesel fuel, fuel oil and other petroleum products always had been dirt cheap in the U.S. That cheap availability had increased our dependence on oil. We've always been the world's most profligate consumer. Abruptly, the price now had gone up and kept on going up. Every industry, business, every home, every person, was hit. Oil and gas had become expensive—for many purposes, too expensive. Cost became a severe discipline.

Users of oil began frantic efforts to locate supplies of coal or natural gas, so those prices, too, went up. For transportation—autos, trucks, airlines, railroads—there is no substitute for oil. As the cost of oil went up, earnings went down and stocks fell.

Since most of a barrel of oil becomes gasoline and since automobiles consume most of that gasoline, you'd expect the auto industry to be among the hardest hit by the high price of gasoline. It was.

For years, autos in Japan had been designed for its densely populated string of small islands. And in Japan, every barrel of oil is imported. Almost overnight, small, light Japanese cars that got great gas mileage were what U.S. car buyers wanted. Too, Japanese cars were better than ours—and cheaper, owing to extraordinarily high U.S. wage settlements that had been negotiated over many years with the United Auto Workers.

Japanese cars began to penetrate the U.S. market where the large, uneconomical, domestic car long had been a status symbol. U.S. auto makers needed several years to redesign their products to reduce size, weight and consumption of gasoline, which cost about three times what it did before the embargo. It was a tough time for U.S. car makers and their parts suppliers. On top of that came economic recession. GM, Ford and Chrysler took their lumps.

And who wanted to pay the high price of gasoline to drive to the beach, the mountains or wherever people go to get away from it all? You couldn't sell a vacation home. And resorts, of course, had a rough time. Filling stations went out of business. Suburbanites began to rethink their decisions to buy homes many miles from where they worked. In-town homes became more expensive, suburban homes less so.

Many electric generating utilities that fueled boilers with oil switched to coal. The cost of electricity went up. The all-electric home with electric heating almost put families in the poor house. To save on the cost of heating oil or natural gas or electricity—to keep warm in the winter, cool in the summer—homeowners stuffed fiberglass insulation into the walls, installed storm windows. Great business for building materials companies such as Owens-Corning Fiberglas.

Chemical companies that used petroleum and natural gas as feed-stocks for synthetic fibers and plastics were caught in the cost squeeze. Airlines saw jet fuel going out of sight. Truckers saw the rising cost of diesel fuel eat up their profits.

Rising energy prices cut into consumers' discretionary spending.

Directly or indirectly, sooner or later, almost everybody was a loser, as money from the U.S., Western Europe and Japan was sucked up by the Arabs and other oil exporting countries.

How about some winners?

Most conspicuously, stocks of oil and gas producers—first recovering with the market then, when controls were loosened in 1978, outperforming the market. Oil service companies such as Schlumberger and Halliburton and drilling companies such as Parker and Helmerich & Payne tookoff immediately, because their worldwide operations were not hampered by U.S. price restrictions. Investors saw lucrative contracts in the offing for Foster Wheeler and Combustion Engineering. They would build the new nuclear generating facilities for electric utilities that were switching away from oil. Reserves of coal as a competitive fuel became more valuable. Coal stocks advanced.

Lists of winners and losers could go on and on.

After 1980, when the price of oil began to slide back down, most of the winners became losers and most of the losers became winners. But in August 1990, it started all over again when Iraq seized Kuwait.

Once a change becomes widely recognized, every stockbroker in the business begins to dream up ingenious ways to make money in stocks of companies that might benefit from the change in some queer or remote way. You can be sure that during the first winter of the energy crisis, some broker out there was recommending the stock of a company that sold long john underwear.

You'll find that few brokers ever suggest stocks of well-known, major corporations, the industry leaders. Consciously or not, most brokers want their clients to see them as shrewd, imaginative fellows who do their own research—more knowledgeable than others in the business and, certainly, more knowledgeable than you. As few, small, obscure companies survive, my advice to you would be to forget about diamonds in the rough and stick with the industry leaders.

Commodity price changes in reaction to some unforeseen happening can be sudden—up or down. Disabuse yourself of any idea that you or anyone else can forecast prices. Anything that you may know, at any present time, about the supply and demand factors of, say, crude oil is known, too, by everyone who has an interest in either buying or selling crude oil. Remember that what you may know—and lots of things you don't know—already have been taken into account by every one of those buyers and sellers. What you and I know already is reflected in the present price.

You can anticipate, however, the consequences of an abnormal price change or the consequences of any other happening.

Ripple effects move out in every direction. Recognizing that change has occurred, you should set loose your imagination. Get a pencil and paper. Write down everything that comes to mind—everything, regardless of how farfetched. Maybe even go to a library to see whether an encyclopedia offers illumination of the subject. If you wait for the experts to give you their interpretations, you will have missed the boat. So-called experts, moreover, don't always know what they're talking about. You'll do better to rely upon your own imagination, your own good judgment and common sense.

As oil reserves are continuously depleted, the long-term direction of price can be only up. Higher prices, however, will bring to the surface more oil. The bigger payoff potential will take exploration to more remote, almost inaccessible areas, to deeper depths. High drilling costs will be an incentive to develop more effective methods of secondary recovery—to get out the 50% of all reserves that present, ordinary methods have left in the ground.

We can be certain that oil demand sometimes will exceed supply and the price will rise; that supply at times will exceed demand and the price will fall—even if only temporarily. And sudden, severe price swings will produce, just as during the oil crisis, winners and losers in the stock market.

CHAPTER 15

FOREIGN EXCHANGE—WINNERS AND LOSERS

In money matters, it seems to me that Europeans always have been more sophisticated than Americans. That's not to say that Europeans are any smarter. It's probably because of the obstacles they've had to overcome: their many national boundaries, many languages and many currencies.

European countries are small. France, the largest country in Western Europe, is not nearly as large as Texas. Neither the U.K. nor Germany is as large as Georgia and Alabama put together. If you travel 1,000 miles in one direction in Europe, you'll cross into three, five or more countries, each with a different language, a different currency—differences that are almost overwhelming.

Although many Europeans are bilingual or even multilingual, how many foreigners, apart from the Dutch, speak English so well that you've never had to to ask, "How's that again, monsieur?" However fluent European businessmen are in each other's languages, I'm not sure that they always understand precisely what they're trying to say to each other. And even when they do, they must be so busily converting, in their heads, German deutschemarks into French francs or Italian lira that they miss a lot of what is being said. What a mess.

In the U.S, you and I can travel more than 2,000 miles from Atlanta to Seattle, Washington, to buy salmon or to sell peanuts. There, we speak the same English, use the same dollar and need have no concern about differences of law or custom. Competing with the U.S., Europe is badly hobbled. I don't see how they do it.

Beginning in the 1970s, however, we, too—all of us—had to learn some new things about money, interest rates and inflation. Beyond just complaining about rising prices, ordinary householders became conversant with home mortgage rates, the best deal for financing the purchase of a car and even rates of return they could get in money market funds. Investors in common stocks had to learn about changes in the value of the U.S. dollar against foreign currencies—the exchange rate.

Most of our large corporations are multinational, manufacturing and selling both in the U.S. and in foreign countries. We compete against foreign companies that often do every bit as good a job of manufacturing and selling as U.S. corporations. Consequently, the value of the U.S. dollar against the currency of a foreign competitor can mean, to the U.S. corporation, either price advantage or no sale.

How much is the Yankee dollar worth? Well, that depends upon what we're talking about. If it's purchasing power within the U.S., we know that it won't buy as much as it once did. That's our domestic inflation with which we already are familiar. But when we start talking about how many yen, pesos or whatnot a dollar will buy, we're off on a different subject.

Until sometime around 1980, the worth of a dollar in exchange for foreign currencies didn't make much difference to most U.S. investors.

In 1944, toward the end of WW II, an international monetary conference at Bretton Woods, N.H., had produced an agreement fixing rates at which major currencies were exchangeable, one for another. To keep those currencies from drifting apart, the arrangement was anchored to the U.S. dollar, which, in some special circumstances could be exchanged for gold at $35 an ounce. But, it was the dollar that war-damaged countries so desperately needed for their rebuilding. As those countries recovered from the war, the dollar, over the years, lost some of its importance.

In 1971, President Nixon snipped the thin thread that tied our dollar to gold, and the many other currencies began to move away from the dollar to find their real values. Allowed to trade in a free market, the dollar, in relation to those many other currencies, started on a long decline in value. In 1973, fixed exchange rates were abandoned entirely, and currencies floated up and down in an almost free, foreign exchange market.

By the late 1970s, the rest of the world was complaining bitterly that a cheap U.S. dollar gave us an unfair competitive advantage in foreign trade. It wasn't until 1980 that the dollar finally bottomed out. (Perhaps totally unrelated, but coincidentally, it was in 1980 that commodity prices peaked and our rate of inflation started down.)

Now the shoe was on the other foot. As the value of the dollar rose against other currencies, we were just as distressed that the yen, deutschemark, pound sterling, etc., were too cheap in relation to the dollar; that we were at a disadvantage in foreign trade. From 1980 to 1985, the value of the dollar, against other major currencies, gained more than 80%. For us, that cut prices of foreign goods almost in half. For foreign buyers of our goods, that raised prices 80%.

What had made the dollar gain against other currencies? I'm not at all sure. Some reasons or easy explanations could have been:

➤ High interest rates in the U.S.

To arrest inflation, our Federal Reserve Board had restricted growth of U.S. money supply and forced up interest rates—the cost of borrowing. To invest in the U.S. at better rates of return than could be had elsewhere, foreign investors exchanged their money for dollars. That, of course, depressed the values of their own currencies and pushed up the value of the dollar.

➤ Confidence in U.S. resolve to control inflation

To have money that they viewed as gaining in value, foreign investors were selling currencies of their own countries to convert into U.S. dollars.

➤ Rising oil prices

To buy oil on the international oil market one has to have dollars. When the price of oil was zooming, buyers had to come up with more and more dollars.

➤ Worldwide drought and crop failures

The U.S. at that time was producing bumper crops of grain. Foreign buyers had to pay prices also quoted in dollars.

Many explanations, I suppose, could be given for the strong U.S. dollar. To me, the one that seemed especially persuasive at that time was stability of the U.S.A.—stability of the government, the economy—and confidence everywhere that the U.S. still would be flourishing long after many other governments disappeared.

Sharing my all-American sentiments, as I'm sure you do, you then must ask: Why, in early 1985, did the dollar go into a steep nose dive, straight down for two years? Without advancing some economic theory, I'll suggest that everything we heard in explanation of the strong dollar, now had turned 180 degrees.

Interest rates had fallen. Although rate of inflation continued low, U.S. Government borrowing had doubled the national debt causing concerns about the dollar's long-term value. Oil prices had dropped. Everywhere, food shortages had become food surpluses. And finally, the rest of the world may have been seeing the U.S. as not quite so invincible.

In Beirut, more than 200 Marines had been killed in the bombing of their barracks. Invading Grenada and bombing Libya, we became the international bully boy. Americans were kidnapped and held hostage in Lebanon. To the bad guys in Iran, our President offered military weapons as ransom. Nothing much to brag about.

A change in the rate at which two currencies are exchangeable has almost no immediate effect upon prices within either country.

Food, clothing, rent and, most importantly, wages stay about the same. If you are using the currency of one of those countries to buy anything in that other country, however, the price difference can be a shock. Depending upon which country's currency falls and which country's currency rises, someone wins and someone loses.

As an example, let's suppose that the time is mid-1978, that you're planning a trip to Germany. You read that the deutschemark, or DM, is worth 48 cents. How many DMs will you get for a dollar? You divide $1.00 by 0.48 and find that the rate is 2.08 DMs to the dollar. For each $100, you'll get 208.33 DMs. For money to spend in Germany, you decide to buy $2,000 worth of travelers checks.

If you're like most of us, it doesn't occur to you that travelers checks are available both in dollars and DMs—and certainly the bank teller never asks which you'd prefer. So your travelers checks are denominated in dollars.

Maybe it's a month or six weeks later that you arrive in Frankfurt. You hustle off to the nearest bank where you sign over $100 worth of checks. In return, you're given 192 DMs plus a few pfennigs. Wait a minute! $100 divided by 0.48? that's 208 DMs plus some pfennigs. "What is this?" you ask. "According to my calculator, I should get 208. You're gypping me out of 16 DMs—that's about seven dollars and fifty cents. What kind of skin game is this?"

Only after you've made something of a scene do you learn that the exchange rate of the dollar has dropped; that the DM, instead of being worth 48 cents is now 52 cents. Dividing $1.00 by 0.52, you get 1.92 DM per dollar and that times $100 is indeed 192 DMs.

From the time you bought your travelers checks until you cashed them, prices within West Germany probably hadn't changed a bit. In international currency transactions, however, the dollar had dropped. Now $100 was worth only 192 DMs. Although prices in Germany hadn't gone up and prices in the U.S. hadn't gone down, the weak U.S. dollar was about to make everything in Germany more expensive to you.

As a tourist, you're not likely to turn around and return home. But if that DM keeps on rising, other U.S. vacationers may decide that visiting Germany has become too expensive. They'll either go elsewhere or stay home. Tough on German tourism.

In the same way, changes of rates of exchange can be damaging to a country's foreign trade.

While the exchange rate of Germany's DM is rising, goods that a German manufacturer offers for sale—at no change in price in terms of DMs—have suddenly become more expensive to a buyer with U.S. dollars. To buy those goods in Germany, the U.S. importer first must exchange his dollars for DMs. He comes out on the short end: fewer DMs.

For the same reason that tourists may have lost their enthusiasm for traveling in Germany, a U.S. plastics manufacturer who buys chemicals by the boatload will find that Germany's prices—although unchanged in terms of DMs—are higher in terms of dollars than he has to pay in the U.S. So the plastic manufacturer now buys his chemicals at a better price in the U.S., and the U.S. chemical company begins to take business away from the German competitor. Thus a strong DM hurts Germany's foreign trade, and a weak U.S. dollar helps our foreign trade.

In theory, such disparities in exchange rates are self-correcting. Because of Germany's higher prices, fewer of their products are sold abroad and fewer DMs are needed to buy those products. As demand for the DM dries up, its value should fall, making German goods less expensive. And because of increased demand for U.S. dollars with which to buy cheaper U.S. goods, the value of the dollar should rise, and the trade advantage should disappear. That, at least, is the theory. Yet theories don't always prevail in the real world. Many other pesky things, such as politics, interfere.

Not all major currencies move together, up and down, against the U.S. dollar. From 1982 until 1985, the Canadian dollar, along with the DM, yen and pound sterling, dropped against the U.S. dollar. Yet the Canadian dollar did not recover along with those others, even though Canada is the largest trading partner of the U.S. Other waywards were Korea and Taiwan, the governments of which declared their currencies exchangeable for U.S. dollars at fixed rates.

Your investments, the prices of the stocks you own, can be hit hard by a shift in the exchange value of the U.S. dollar. Caterpillar Tractor (now Caterpillar, Inc.) was a good example.

For may years, CAT's sales of heavy earthmoving equipment were about half in the U.S. and half abroad. Until maybe 1980 or '82, almost all of its tractors and diesel engines were manufactured in the U.S. In 1981, sales, profits and the price of the stock were at all-time highs. But in '82 as the exchange value of the U.S. dollar began to climb, the company began to lose money.

As a suffering stockholder throughout the bleak years that followed, I'm somewhat an authority on Caterpillar.

I bought CAT in 1983 and 1984. The stock was not one of my winners. In fact, it was a dog. But what was my rationale for buying CAT? I still have the sales presentation that I prepared for my brokers. This was written in 1983.

The world's largest manufacturer of tractors and earthmoving equipment, CAT has been hit hard by recessions and is operating at only 30% of capacity. Earthmoving equipment wears out in about five years. The average age, nationwide, of equipment now in use is 4.6 years—the oldest in 35 years. Purchases of new equipment can't be postponed much longer. Also, the recently imposed five-cent-a-gallon Federal tax will produce $5 billion for highway construction and maintenance. For CAT, that means sales opportunity.

In the past 10 years, CAT has spent $5 billion on new, more efficient manufacturing facilities. That should mean increased profits.

CAT is being undersold by its major competitor Japan's Komatsu, which is enjoying tremendous advantage over CAT because the Japanese yen is cheap and the U.S. dollar is expensive. The exchange rate is damaging to CAT's international business. Here's how.

Say a British construction company wants to buy a bulldozer. From either Caterpillar or Komatsu, it can get about the same equipment. Having pounds sterling, the British company must convert its money into either dollars to buy from CAT or yen to buy from Komatsu. The Englishman looks at exchange rates. The pound has been weak against the dollar. It will take a lot of pounds to get the dollars that CAT is asking for its equipment. But the pound has been only slightly weak against the yen. Far fewer pounds are required to get the yen that Komatsu is asking. The British contractor thanks the CAT dealer for quoting a price and buys his bulldozer from Komatsu.

The dollar can't keep going up forever. A drop in the dollar will make CAT competitive again. The stock's a buy.

When that was written in 1983, CAT was trading in the mid-40s. But the dollar kept on going up; the yen kept on going down. The advantage to Japanese manufacturers—and disadvantage to U.S. manufacturers—became so great that Komatsu equipment, at one time, was as much as 30% cheaper than CAT's. Not surprisingly, CAT's business suffered badly. The stock fell to 29.

Along with many other U.S. manufacturers, Caterpillar began "outsourcing"—buying parts for its machinery from foreign manufacturers. The company was using high-priced dollars to buy the low-priced foreign currencies with which to pay for those parts. CAT closed many of its U.S. factories and opened factories in Europe and the U.K. where, in terms of deutschemarks, francs and pounds, costs were much lower. A splendid idea—so long as the dollar continued to gain against other currencies.

Although Caterpillar had many more problems than just the expensive U.S. dollar, it was the exchange rate that I saw as their major problem. I knew that the dollar would drop in value—some day. It did. But it took a long time.

The dollar, after a five-year advance against most of the world's major currencies, finally broke in 1985. Because so many of our large corporations are multinationals, the declining exchange rate of the U.S. dollar was good news for the stock market. Investors anticipated that prices of U.S. goods would become more competitive, that U.S. companies would recover advantages lost to foreign competitors, that both earnings and stocks would go up.

After a few months, CAT's stock began to advance. Earnings benefited but not to the extent that I had hoped and not, I must add, to the extent that Wall Street analysts had forecast. Demand in the U.S. for heavy earthmoving equipment was limited. Our infrastructure now was adequate for a population that was leveling off. In underdeveloped countries, the demand was there, but those countries were broke. Even so, CAT finally did recover nicely.

We've all seen how U.S. manufacturers can lose domestic market share to foreign imports. In the 1980s, U.S. auto makers had to admit that they were selling against a better product imported from Japan, but the strength of the dollar against the yen added to their troubles. The dollars for which a Japanese car was sold in the U.S. converted into a lot of yen to the Japanese auto maker. Not only were the Japanese selling a better car, they could sell it at a better price. (And selling within the U.S., CAT, too, was up against the same sort of price competition from Komatsu.)

When the dollar is strong, what happens to a multinational U.S. corporation that's manufacturing in a foreign country, operating profitably, through its wholly-owned, foreign subsidiary? As an example, what about a company manufacturing personal computers through its French subsidiary, selling to French buyers and receiving payments in French francs? What happens when the profits are remitted to the parent company in the U.S.? Remember, now, the dollar is strong.

The profits, in cheap francs, must be converted into expensive dollars. Lots of francs; not many dollars. To the parent company in the U.S., profits from its French subsidiary, when the franc is weak against the dollar, don't do much for the U.S. parent company's per share earnings—and don't do much for the price of its stock.

It would be a different story, however, if those French made computers were shipped to the U.S. and sold for U.S. dollars. The

U.S. parent of the French subsidiary would enjoy the same currency advantage as any French company selling its products for a strong U.S. dollar.

A strong dollar, however, isn't all bad. It puts the heat on managements of U.S. corporations. To compete, to operate profitably, they must cut expenses, gain efficiency, improve quality, sell more aggressively. And a weak dollar isn't all good. It allows management to become complacent and lazy.

In 1986 and '87, when the value of the dollar was falling, we all waited for U.S. exports to boom. The turnaround was slow in coming. To retain market share, German and Japanese manufacturers cut prices and accepted slimmer profit margins. The U.S. found that recovering lost markets wasn't easy. Even though the dollar fell to a postwar low, the U.S. continued to be plagued with tremendous trade deficits.

Athough the European Community is expected to agree upon a single European currency within the next few years, a single world currency is no near-term likelihood. Changes in exchange rates, therefore, will continue be an important consideration in your investment decisions.

After exchange rates have remained fairly stable for some time, after everyone has become pretty well adjusted to the relationships of currencies, rates lose importance to us. It's when something happens to upset those relationships, to change those rates, that the value of the dollar becomes a number that you'd better watch. Always helpful are charts that show ups and downs of currency futures. Don't believe the forecasts that you read or hear about. Just be alert to the consequences of change when you see it happening.

You and I must accept the fact that we can never forecast and, therefore, cannot anticipate a change of rates. No one can. But we will know when our dollar is gaining on other major currencies, and we will know when our dollar is losing value against other major currencies. No great analytical skills are required. When we see that the U.S. dollar converts into more yen, DMs and pounds than it did last month, we know that the dollar is gaining in value. When we see that the U.S. dollar converts into less of those currencies, we know that it's losing in value.

When the dollar is gaining in value, earnings of most U.S. corporations probably will be dragged down. Each corporation will be damaged in a different way and to a different degree.

Every U.S. company that competes in the world market is going to be hurt—directly. Hurt how much? That depends. How tough is the foreign competition? How big are foreign imports in the U.S. market? How much of the company's total revenues come from abroad? If it's only 10% or 15%, the U.S. company may not be hurt too much. If it's 50% or more, maybe it will be hurt a lot—especially if the dollar gains a lot against foreign currencies.

When the dollar has been gaining in value, a U.S. corporation, such as CAT, manufacturing in the U.S., is undersold both at home an abroad by the competitor with factories in one of the major industrial countries with a currency losing in value. The U.S. company that manufacturers in the U.S. for export and sale abroad finds that foreign currencies convert into fewer and fewer dollars. Even if profits abroad are holding up well, brought home, those profits don't convert into as many dollars. To maintain profit margins, the U.S company might raise prices, but that's at the risk of pricing itself out of the market. So to stay in business, to hold market share, the U.S. company may have to operate at a loss—temporarily, its management hopes.

And the U.S. corporation that manufactures in the U.S. and sells all its products in the U.S. may be selling against a foreign-made product imported from a country that's enjoying the advantage of a currency falling in value. To meet the price competition, the U.S. manufacturer must cut his price and accept a lower profit margin—just as U.S. automakers, at times, have had to do to sell against Japanese cars. When that happened, U.S. automakers' earnings fell, and their stocks fell.

When the dollar is gaining against other major currencies, I can't say that you ought to sell stocks of U.S. exporters and multinationals—although you might wait to see what happens before becoming a buyer. Stocks of foreign companies, however, might be attractive. Anyhow, remember that neither you nor I nor anyone else ever will know when the dollar will turn and start down or turn and start up again.

When the dollar begins to fall against other currencies, the advantage begins to flow to the U.S. manufacturer and away from the foreign manufacturer. U.S. corporations begin to get more dollars for their foreign profits. Earnings go up. Stocks go up. But in the 1980s, we found that didn't happen overnight. The advantage of a falling dollar began to pay off only after many months. The market, however, anticipated higher earnings and stocks went up.

CHAPTER 16

BUSINESS CYCLES—WINNERS AND LOSERS

A graph of business cycles tells the story of what has happened to the nation's economy, good times and bad times, ups and downs, expansions and recessions, booms and busts. What you see is a picture of changes that, in one way or another, for better or for worse, affected us all.

Some business recessions are more severe than others; some recoveries more robust than others. Whether recession or recovery, when either will begin or how long either will last, you never know. You can be sure, however, that a recession will be followed by a recovery; that the recovery will be followed by another recession.

As a business recovery progresses, everyone becomes more optimistic, more confident that the upswing will continue. Sales and profits improve. The trend, clearly, is up. Based on projections of increasing demand, surely greater production capacity will be required. Construction is begun on new plant. Profits pay for some of the expansion; borrowed money pays the rest. Why not borrow? Isn't business booming? Isn't everybody happy? Do you want our competition to walk off with the business?

As those sentiments become widely accepted, a day comes when sales drop a bit below the rate of production. Slackening demand is viewed, at first, as temporary. The high rate of production is continued. Overproduction is accumulated in inventory.

In time, excessive inventories, overexpansion and increases in debt loads cause the economy to pause and then to topple over into another recession. As pessimism takes over, the recession deepens. To work off inventories, production is cut back and prices reduced. Unemployment rises. Banks begin to tighten the screws on borrowers. Weak, inefficient businesses go broke.

A friend once told me that recessions are periods during which money returns to its rightful owners.

Recession clears away the wreckage, the excesses of the preceding era of prosperity. A foundation is uncovered for the next recovery.

From the end of WW II and into 1990, the U.S. went through eight business recessions. The stock market anticipated 10 recessions, two of which just didn't happen. As an investor, you must know, however, that the stock market has been the single, most reliable lead-indicator of change of the national economy. The stock market has been the forerunner, the herald of economic change that happened, eight out of 10 times, within a few months. It has not been the other way around. News of the economy has not told us what the stock market will do.

The picture on page 101 is of time intervals between economic recessions and recoveries; between market tops and bottoms. The solid lines link times that later were identified as economic peaks and troughs. The broken lines link times that later were identified as stock market tops and bottoms.

Do observe that I've written: later were identified. Only looking back are we able to distinguish tops and bottoms. At the time, we didn't know whether the trend—up or down—of either the economy or the market would continue or not. Only that which happened afterward told us that a change, in fact, did occur.

On the chart, the shaded areas are periods of economic recession—from the time the solid line peaks until it bottoms-out. In most of those cycles, the broken lines representing the stock market, move—both up and down—several months ahead of the solid lines representing the national economy. Whether up or down, each turn of the economy has been anticipated by the stock market. The market's two false alarms appear on the chart as lines A-B and C-D. Through both of those market sell offs, the 1961-69 economic recovery continued without interruption.

The E-F market decline was so far ahead of the 1980 recession that you must question the relationship.

During the down-drafts, the recessions, we're looking for the recovery. During the recoveries, we're looking for the next recession. Most investors are almost consumed with economic forecasts. They can quote the latest pronouncements of the most eminent economists of the day. Toward recovery tops, when the popular business periodicals are euphoric, investors are eager buyers of stocks. Toward recession bottoms, when things begin to look hopeless and the mood of every article about business and the economy ranges from concern to despair, investors want out. After going through one or two business cycles, after buying at the top and selling at the bottom, they angrily conclude that the stock market is nothing but a shell game, that buying stocks is foolishness that anyone ought to be smart enough to avoid.

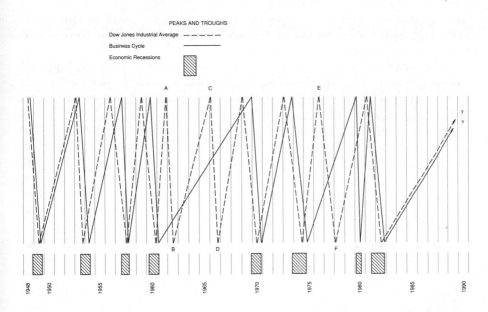

See Appendix for enlarged version of this chart

You will recognize immediately that the chart shows only time intervals, from left to right, between peaks and troughs. The up-and-down lines, obviously, do not reflect the extent of the rise or fall, only its duration. The actual peaks and troughs of the DJIA are not nearly so well defined as I have represented them on the chart. The purpose of the chart is to show you that through nine complete market cycles and seven complete economic cycles, the economy lagged the stock market by several months. Yet most of what you hear and read seems to suggest just the opposite.

Investment experts forever are examining economic tea leaves for omens of stock market direction. For calling turns of the market, economic reports and indicators seem to be about as useful as what once was described to me as a mule barometer. Take a handful of straw, tie it up at one end, set it outside on the window sill and pull down the sash to hold it in place. When the straw shakes, expect windy weather. When it's wet, rain. When it's dry and warm, fair and sunny weather.

Clearly, anyone studying economic or business statistics in hopes of finding some signal that the stock market is about to move either up or down, probably will be disappointed. Nevertheless, you will continue to hear and read that, because of some improvement or deterioration of the economy, the stock market soon will go up or go down. Just remember that the stock market, most of the time, seems to anticipate by several months changes in direction of the national economy.

Does that mean that the stock market controls the economy? Certainly not. The stock market, I believe, is so sensitive that it begins to reflect investors' changing feelings before investors themselves are conscious that their feeling are changing.

In my rationalization of the phenomenon, I can imagine a merchant who senses that fewer customers have come into his store during the week, a manufacturer who's a bit uncomfortable about how much he owes for the financing of a recent expansion, a salesman who is told of the cancellation of an order for some item that until recently has been hard to get. Now, let each one of those businessmen get a phone call from his stock broker who recommends purchase of another hot idea, a real moneymaker. Those three men, emotionally, aren't quite as optimistic as they were a few days earlier. Each is apt to say to his broker, "If you don't mind, I think I'll hold off for a while." Buyers of stocks become slightly less aggressive. The market slows down. Prices drift. The normal, everyday selling that comes in finds that bids are below last sales by somewhat larger fractions, and those bids are for somewhat smaller quantities of stock.

Investors haven't decided that the market is about to break. They're not selling out. Although scarcely conscious of it, they just don't feel quite as good about things as they did only a few days earlier. They have some vague concerns about their businesses. In the earliest stages of a recession, most businessmen, I suspect, assume that the problems are confined to their own companies: What's wrong with our advertising? How did expenses creep up on us like this? Maybe the dogs just don't like our dogfood any more. Probably, they don't even relate their business concerns to their personal investments.

The slight malaise is experienced by other folks—employees of those companies, suppliers, customers, bankers, investment bankers, investment counselors who manage their pension funds, accountants and maybe even their lawyers catch on. The unasked question is, What's happened to management's glow of confidence?

As such unspoken feelings might spread throughout the country, no one has given much thought to a break in the market. They just don't feel too enthusiastic about buying stocks. Business news continues to be good. Corporate earnings reports show gains over last year. Dividends are being increased, stocks split.

I think that's the way most down-markets begin—quietly, insidiously, a withdrawal of buying enthusiasm. A couple of months later, we look back and say, What's happened to the stock market? I've got big losses. And, sure enough, the economy now is giving clear signs of faltering. Corporate earnings estimates are reduced, and another recession is upon us.

All of that is to tell you that the stock market, usually, has started down when business never looked better, and business keeps sailing along for a few more months. Only after the economy has begun to sour do we recognize the message that the stock market was sending.

Now, both the market and the economy are falling together. The downturn in business is more than a pause or a dip. This recession is getting serious. Every item in *The Wall Street Journal* is negative. There is no good news. Who's the wise guy who says to stay fully invested? I'd rather get back half my money than see that, too, melt away.

Now, folks are getting emotional. They're scared. They sell out.

Then a funny thing begins to happen. The retailer notices that traffic through the store picked up last week. The manufacturer begins to feel that, after all, he may be able to pay the interest on his borrowing. The salesman gets his first good order in nine months. None of these fellows jumps back into the market. But if already they haven't sold out, they decide to hang on a bit longer—only because they're not quite as frightened as they were last week. Throughout the country, nobody feels good, but then again, nobody feels quite as bad as he did. There's no buying enthusiasm in the stock market. The selling pressure, however, has let up. The market levels off, and prices, here and there, pick up fractionally. Although the economic news is worse than ever—terrible—the stock market doesn't respond. Stock prices seem to be ignoring bad news. Slowly, the market rises.

That's the best I can offer to explain why the broken line of the stock market has changed directions, eight out of ten times, ahead of the solid line of the economy.

CHAPTER 17

DEMOGRAPHICS—WINNERS AND LOSERS

Former Harvard Professor Senator Daniel Patrick Moynihan once said that the most momentous economic decisions are made privately, by couples in bed—decisions to have babies or not to have babies. After World War II, young married couples in the U.S.A. seemed to have decided almost unanimously that having babies was a splendid idea. And they didn't stop with just one, two or three. Actually, enthusiasm for the idea appears to have picked up before the war.

Some changes come upon us so gradually that we don't recognize what has happened until a long time afterward when we turn around to look back.

Some years ago, I found in an almanac a table of annual numbers of live births in the U.S. (Shortly afterward, I learned that I could get those figures from the Public Health Service.) Also shown were annual numbers of births and deaths per 1,000 population—birth rates and death rates. I plotted those figures on graph paper and for several years kept them up-to-date. That's what you see on page 106. The vertical bars show for each year the numbers, in millions, of live births; and the two lines running from left to right show annual birth rates and death rates. Between the bars, the spaces you see are the years for which I could find no numbers of live births. Use the scale at left for millions of live births: one, two, three, four millions. Use the same scale for birth and death rates: 10, 20, 30, 40 per 1,000 population.

Afterward, I discovered that the U.S. Department of Commerce, Bureau of the Census, publishes annually *Statistical Abstract of the United States*. It's a 1,000-page book that costs about $20. From it, you can get current figures to update the graph. Also, it contains other statistics of almost anything that you could wish to know.

The birth rate, the number of births each year per 1,000 population, is interesting.

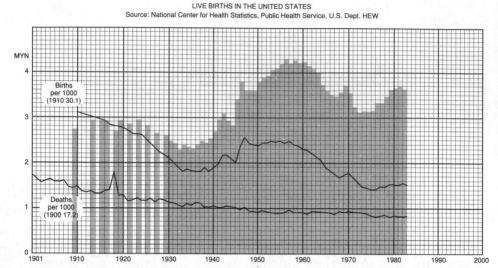

LIVE BIRTHS IN THE UNITED STATES
Source: National Center for Health Statistics, Public Health Service, U.S. Dept. HEW

See Appendix for enlarged version of this chart.

Back in 1910, I suppose that most homes still had no electric lights; so when the sun went down, home entertainment opportunities must have been somewhat limited. Births per 1,000 population were 30.1. Never since has the birth rate been that high. From 1910, the rate declined steadily and bottomed out at 18.6 in 1936, during the Great Depression when most folks thought they couldn't afford to have children. Also, there were other things to do. You could listen to the radio. And Amos 'n Andy didn't come on until nine o'clock.

During the economic recovery and into WW II, the number of births per 1,000 population started back up. In 1944 and '45 when the boys were overseas, the birth rate dipped to just above 20. But when they got home, they wasted no time. In 1947, the rate peaked at 26.5 and remained around 25 until 1958 when again it started down.

From 1975 to 1985, births were at a rate of only 15 or 16 per 1,000 population. Why? No one knows. Development of the birth control pill certainly was a factor—pregnancy became an elective.

Birth rate, however, doesn't help us too much. By itself, birth rate doesn't translate into the sale of a lot of diapers and baby food. But the absolute number of births during any year gives us a pretty good idea of the numbers of six-year-olds that we'll have six years later and the number of 16-year-olds, 16 years later.

The bar chart of live births was the first picture I'd seen of the tremendous, 25-year surge of births that began in the mid-1930s and continued until about 1960.

But that picture is history. It's static. Each year, a bar is added at the right, and birth and death rate lines are extended one, small space. Everything else on the graph will remain the same, forever. It's the past. Investing your money, you're looking in the opposite direction—looking ahead. You're trying to project your thinking into a murky future; because to invest successfully, you must anticipate change.

In 1972, I asked Bureau of the Census for a break-down of U.S. population by age. They sent me numbers, handwritten, for each age—30-year-olds out to 84. They gave me estimates for not only 1972 but for 1974, 1976, 1978 and 1980. And in 1983, the Census Bureau published *Projections of the Population of the U.S. by Age, Sex and Race: 1983 to 2080.**

The booklet was exactly what I needed. With numbers of persons of every age, zero to 84, projected out for every year for the next 100 years, I could produce a picture of what age distributions would look like in whatever future years I wished to see.

The graph on page 108 shows U.S. population, distributed by age, in 1990. Along the bottom of the graph are ages zero to 84. At left, are numbers, in millions, of persons of each age—their ages in 1990. Also on page 108 is a similiar graph that shows Census Bureau projections for 2000. Beyond 2000, my interest dwindles; so if you wish to look further into the future, you'll have to draw your own graphs.

What you see on these graphs is something of a mirror image of "Live Births," back on page 106. The difference is that these are living, moving pictures of our population, moving forward with age. On the graph, "Projection of the Population, 1990," deaths and anticipated deaths are reducing the numbers of old folks. (Placing himself on that graph, a septuagenarian sees a lot more past than future.) I should note that estimates of immigrants have been added to all ages; in the Southwest, those numbers are important. The Census Bureau, incidentally, calls all persons of the same age an age cohort.

On the graph, rising and falling waves that you see have been produced by earlier rising and falling numbers of births. In 1990, 30-year-olds were the largest age cohort. All, of course, were born in

*In case you want a copy, it's U.S. Department of Commerce, Bureau of the Census, *Population Estimates and Projections, Series P-25, No. 952.* It's based on the 1980 Census. Perhaps you know—I didn't—a census every 10 years is required under Article 1, Section 2, of the U.S. Constitution.

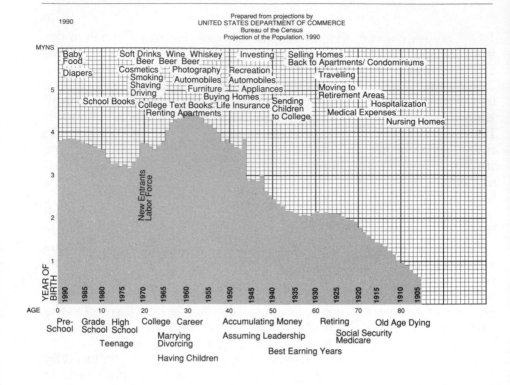

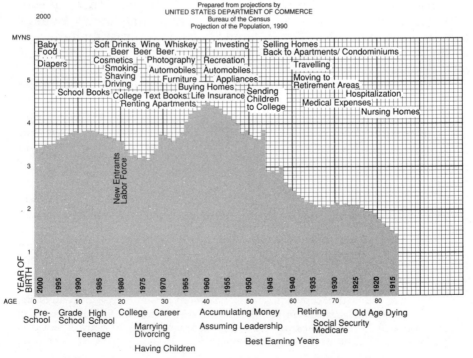

See Appendix for enlarged versions of these charts.

1960. They were the crest of the post World War II Baby Boom. In front of that big wave, the shallow trough that you see are 1990's 56-, 57-, and 58-year-olds, born during the Depression of the 1930s.

So the great population wave began to rise in 1933 and, except for 1944-45, rose almost every year for 27 or 28 years—until about 1960. Absolute numbers of births in 1932 were about 2.3 million; in 1961, 4.2 million—an increase of 82%. That's a lot of babies. The countless decisions to have those babies created a population tidal wave, moving forward in time until the last Baby Boomers grow old and die. From 1933, that rising wave of population has slowly moved forward—on the graph, one space each year.

For 27 years, the front of that advancing wave, each year, brought more and more persons into the next older age.

For the graph to be useful as an investment tool, you must visualize the wave as moving to the right, ratcheting forward, every year that passes, one space. Everything else on the graph stands still—just as you now see it. Only the waves move, finally heading down the drain as folks grow old and die. Described along the top are wants, needs and activities peculiar to particular ages; along the bottom, stages of life. None of those moves. The population waves—crests and troughs—move into and pass through the many ages and stages. Every generation repeats all of the things of the generation before it—not much change, not much improvement.

On the graph, those wants, needs, activities are the product of no scholarly study of social behavior. From what we've both seen of a walk through life, they are simply a few of the many sights and vacant lots along the way.

Distinctive interests and activities are characteristic of every age. From your own experiences and observations, what do you associate with a baby of less than one year? Apart from diapers and baby food, parents may require more living space. Indeed, the birth of a second child is supposed to trigger the decision to move from an apartment into a house. So rising numbers of births suggest greater demand for free-standing houses—with yards in which the kids can play. That should benefit stocks of building materials suppliers—unless high interest rates make homes too expensive. Other beneficiaries: furniture and household appliance manufacturers.

Life insurance salesmen know that the father of a newborn is a good prospect. An uptrend in births, therefore, could be good news for life insurance companies. And what about pictures of the baby? Eastman Kodak must love infants most of all.

The forward moving wave of Baby Boom humanity brought about change—big change and little change. Upon the economy, the rising wave of population made demands—big demands and little demands. Most of the big changes and big demands were basic requirements of an exploding population. Numbers of school buildings and classrooms, adequate in 1946 for the 2.5 million first-graders born in 1940, couldn't begin to accommodate, in 1953, the 3.8 million first-graders born in 1947—or 10 years later, the 4.3 million born in 1957.

Families needed larger houses, more bedrooms for the children. To buy larger houses, they had to move out to the suburbs. They had to have a second car. To carry the increased traffic, new streets and roads were needed. Families required more of everything—food, clothes, furniture, appliances. That meant more trucks to haul those goods.

Construction began on the Interstate Highway system. Colossal quantities of earth had to be moved, concrete poured, steel bridges errected. No facility was adequate: not enough factories, hospitals, office buildings, electric generating capacity. The list could go on and on. It was a boom time for basic, heavy industry—steel, cement, glass, aluminum, chemicals; factories in which to make tractors, airplanes and everything else.

And then, too, there were little demands and little changes. Only in 1959 did I become aware of the economic importance of Baby Boomers. We were living in Macon. In our older daughter's room, I saw lined up on the dresser eight or ten small, metal cylinders. What are all these? Lipsticks, different shades or colors. What does one cost? Almost two dollars, made by Revlon. (We're talking about 1959, mind you, when a big lunch at the Dempsey Hotel cost a buck—plus a 15-cent tip.) Although looking at lunch money for two weeks, I was immediately interested in Revlon stock. I lacked, however, one of the two ingredients of a moneymaking speculation: I had the courage, but I didn't have the capital. In the next year or two, Revlon stock was a great performer.

Coca-Cola was another. From World War II, Coke was one of the few stocks of a major corporation that had done nothing. Not that Coke wasn't aggressive. During WW II, even infantry units sometimes got Cokes, delivered right up in the line. But all those postwar kids of ours didn't start drinking Coke in a big way until they became teenagers. I'm not going to the archives for this, but I remember that in 1960 Coke split its stock 3-for-1 and increased the dividend. That signaled good business ahead. Coke stock started up and kept on going. Baby Boomers had started drinking Cokes.

As numbers of teenagers increased every year from 1960, many other corporations profited. As more boys began to shave, Gillette sold more razors and razor blades. As more girls began to menstruate, Tampax sold more tampons. College textbooks, I learned in

1961 when our older daughter entered Emory University, cost like the mischief. What company was the biggest publisher of college textbooks? McGraw-Hill. And sure enough, the stock moved. Our second daughter, two years younger, appeared with two swains distinguished by their protruding abdomens. How do they get in that shape? Drinking beer; all the boys drank beer. We bought Anheuser-Busch, and a great buy it was.

Shortly after our older daughter got married, she mentioned that her husband had bought a life insurance policy. That sounded interesting. When Baby Boomers marry, they'll buy life insurance. What better way for a husband to show his devotion? I asked the insurance analyst of our firm: What sort of policy is the most profitable to a life insurance company? Level premium, or ordinary life. What's the best company concentrating in that area? Jefferson-Pilot. Then, however, the analyst told me of several reasons for not buying any life insurance stock. Nevertheless, I did buy JP and made money. That's not to tell you how dumb the analyst was and how smart I am. The analyst's selection was excellent.

An analyst works within the narrowly restricted area of the industry in which he specializes. He can hardly do otherwise, for it take years to learn something of the complexities of just one industry. To do a good job, an analyst must specialize. Consequently, he likely will develop tunnel vision. I was interested in the spending patterns of a special segment of the population; the analyst was concerned with something more immediate in the industry. It was my decision to buy a life insurance stock; it was the analyst's job to tell me which stock to buy. I view that as the proper role of an industry analyst.

With the great bulge of population that the Baby Boom produced, I associated only purchases of consumer goods. In retrospect that's curious, for the big demands of a rapidly growing population were more dramatic: highways, buildings, airports, factories etc. That I missed.

All of that is the past. Over 12 years of anticipating wants and needs of Baby Boomers, I got five or six investment ideas—all from observing my two girls who had been born one and three years ahead of the Baby Boomers. Getting one good idea at two-year intervals is about the best you can hope for. Owing to God's mercy, we can't see into the future.

When you get a good idea, don't be talked out of it by an expert. Have the courage to risk your money. If you're convinced, the odds, likely, will be in your favor. Take the chance. Losing your money will be less disruptive to your digestion than watching your hot stock run away while you stand on the sidelines as a spectator.

After 1974, fewer children each year became teenagers. After the newborns of 1961 turned 16, Revlon, Coke, Gillette and other suppliers of teenage demands found themselves, as you can see on the chart, on the backside of the Baby Boom wave.

For me, tracking spending patterns of persons moving toward middle age was not too rewarding. I asked my older daughter to make a study of how she and her husband spent their money. We found nothing that told us to rush out to buy some stock. Maybe my daughter and her husband already had bought everything they'll ever need. Only sometime afterward, however, did I see the Baby Boom change in a different way.

Younger people, people in their 20s, 30s and 40s, are buyers of things, tangible things—houses, home furnishings, autos. Also, younger people are borrowers of money and users of credit cards. Many recklessly spend more than they can make, take on debts that they cannot repay.

Older people, people over 50, become savers. Maybe they, too, have bought everything they'll ever need. But older folks are not only savers of money, they are investors and lenders of money. That always was evident to those of us in the brokerage business. I'd guess that as much as 85% of our individual investor business was with men over 50.

The over-50 population, which had been dropping for some years, bottomed out around 1986 when people born in 1936 turned 50. Because births in the U.S. began to rise just before 1940 and continued to rise for 20 years, until just before 1960, the number of persons turning 50 increases every year until the year 2010. People born around 1940 turned 50 around 1990. They are the vanguard of a massive, rising wave. That means a huge, growing wave of savers and investors and a tremendous growth of capital to fuel the economy.

From 1940 to 1960, the growing demand was for baby diapers. Until at least 2010, the growth should be in stocks and bonds. What a great time to be in the retail brokerage business.

Around 1980, demographers with the Bureau of the Census decided that having babies was going out of style, that 25% of Baby Boom women never would have children. That proved to be a bad guess. Many of those women had children. They simply had waited a few years before starting their families. Only 15% have remained childless.

Although Baby Boom mothers were from families that averaged more than three children, their own families average less than two. But the lower birth rate was overcome by sheer numbers of Baby Boom mothers. By 1990, they were producing an almost record, 4 million babies a year. Unless the birth rate rises sharply, numbers of new babies will taper off as women of the WW II Baby Boom pass into their 40s.

Numbers of teenagers began to rise again in 1988 when babies of the 15-year Boomlet that started in 1975 turned 13. They're followed each year by somewhat larger numbers. Athough of smaller size, that wave is another that will move forward for its lifetime.

The total U.S. population is still growing, but the rate of growth has slowed. According to the Census Bureau, that rate of growth will drop to zero sometime around 2000.

My interest in writing this is to help you learn a bit sooner than you might otherwise, how to invest without losing your money—and maybe even to make some money. To do so, you must allow your imagination to range on a grander scale than just school books and soft drinks. To think on a different level, you could consider the consequences of change in rate of population growth. What about a no-growth population? What I see may give you some ideas.

The U.S. infrastructure (our military almost wore out that word during the Vietnam War)—meaning streets, highways, bridges, water and sewer systems, factories, office buildings, housing, schools, all big stuff—now is largely in place. Instead of more such facilities, ʹhe needs now are maintenance, improvement, replacement. That means no long-term revival of boom times for basic, heavy construction materials such as steel, cement, lumber, aluminium.

In 1980, numbers of 18-year-olds entering the labor force—after rising for more than 40 years—peaked out. The downtrend that began in 1981 won't bottom out and start back up until 1995. So that's a 15-year period of declining job entrants. The older Baby Boomers, meanwhile, are advancing in age, experience and job skills. As they progress and are promoted, fewer and fewer young, unskilled job entrants are coming along behind them to fill those job vacancies. Maybe it's just as well. For some years, blue-collar jobs in labor intensive industries—steel, auto, textile—have been "exported," first to Japan then on to Korea, India, Brazil.

Already shortages of skilled labor have appeared. By the mid-1980s, shortages of unskilled labor had become evident. As an example, jobs at Atlanta's fast food restaurants went begging. Minimum wage, you ask? No, almost double minimum wage, plus transportation by van from the inner city to the job sites. Our youths, we're told, do not respond to the help-wanted signs still out there.

A shortage of labor results in higher wages. To reduce costs, employers invest money in automated equipment, in robots. Manufacturers of such equipment ought to enjoy good demand.

In the U.S., fewer 18-year-olds has meant reduced unemployment. The quality of recruits into the military must be declining. Possibly we'll have to go back to the draft. The European Baby Boom, I've read, followed ours by about eight years. Perhaps they could benefit from what we've learned here about our advancing Baby Boom wave.

For many years, I used a population chart as a source of investment ideas for my brokers—so often, in fact, that distribution of the chart at our meetings produced audible groans. Kept updated, however, it can be for you a chart in a nautical sense to determine your investment course.

Change is what you're looking for. Every change opens one investment opportunity and slams shut another. To invest successfully, you must be alert to change. Have confidence in your own thinking. It's more reliable than most of the opinions you'll hear.

Your sources of investment ideas are unimportant. But it is important that you understand the rationale supporting an investment idea. Logic must convince you that the stock is going up. If you don't understand what's going to make that stock go up, don't buy it. If you can't grasp the logic behind a recommendation, be assured that the logic is either faulty or lacking. Your informed judgment is likely to be as good as that of anyone in the securities business. Don't be overwhelmed by an expert. Too, remember that once you've made an investment, that expert won't be around to hold your hand and to tell you when to sell. Only if you understand what's going to make the stock go up, will you know to get out if it comes a cropper.

Still, you must be careful not to exaggerate the importance of a change. Yes, one company will benefit and another be hurt. But will the change add significantly to the earnings of the one? wipeout the earnings of the other? To a multi-billion-dollar company with annual profits of hundreds of millions, a million-dollar loss, more or less, means little. To a small company, a million dollars, as a profit, might double the price of its stock; as a loss, might bust the company.

Around 1950, Southern Company came into existence as a holding company of four, electric generating utilities, one of which is Georgia Power Company. Georgia Power, as far back as I can remember, had owned and operated Atlanta's streetcars that ran on rails and were powered by electricity drawn down from overhead power lines by trolleys—thus, "trolley car." A year or so before WW II, the streetcars were replaced with electric buses, and asphalt was laid over the tracks—only to be pulled up when the war effort was crying for scrap steel.

Electric buses, also drawing power from overhead lines, were more satisfactory, incidentally, than the diesel buses we have now: they were noiseless, fast and pollution free. The system, however, was one, big money loser for Georgia Power. It was the Georgia Public Service Commission, I believe, that required the Power Company to continue the service.

The broker with whom I had a loose, buddy arrangement to cover for one another, had a customer who worked at Sears, Roebuck's mail order plant out on Ponce de Leon Avenue. The mail order business, I might add, seemed to make modest demand of intellect. The customer, in fact, was a nice old boy. His earlier career had been in semipro baseball. Until this moment, I'd never thought of it, but across from the Sears plant was Spiller's Field, home of the Atlanta Crackers; so he may have changed careers by simply crossing Ponce de Leon Avenue.

One day, he came in and somewhat excitedly bought some Southern Company stock. He explained that while coming to town, he'd observed that the buses were packed with people; that Georgia Power and, therefore, Southern company, must be making a killing.

Well, the customer had identified a change, but the Public Service Commission would allow no fare increase. Georgia Power was made to subsidize Atlanta's bus riders, and no profit could have derived from its bus operation. But viewed somewhat differently, the change he'd seen was important. The population of Atlanta and the Southeast was growing, and certainly the demand for electricity could have been expected to grow. Southern Company was indeed a good buy. The customer was right but for the wrong reason. You may be amused by the rest of the story.

Later, Georgia Power succeeded in unloading their bus operation by selling it publicly as an independent company. I knew of only two persons who owned the stock of what then was called Atlanta Transit Company; both were officers of the corporation.

Then for Atlanta Transit something good happened. Congress gave money to the big cities for development of rapid transit. Here in Atlanta, Metropolitan Atlanta Rapid Transit Authority, MARTA, had to get control of the bus routes for integration later with a sophisticated rail system. MARTA paid owners of Atlanta Transit a handsome price for their stock.

So what the old ballplayer had observed, the increase in numbers of bus riders, paid off. If he had stuck with his logic to its final realization—if instead of buying Southern Company, he had waited a few years until Atlanta Transit stock could have been bought in the open market—he would have been right for the right reason. Lots of ifs. Whether you're a hero or a bum depends upon when you turn around to look back.

Each year, everybody becomes one year older. Numbers of persons in each age group, therefore, are in continuous change.

Forever, persons are being born, growing older, moving into the next stages of life and dying. Babies being born today—any today—are part of some sort of population wave, rising or falling, crest or trough, that will raise or lower ships and boats all over the world. Investing your money, you should pay attention, always, to demographic phenomena—even though numbers alone don't tell all of the story.

Everything changes—customs, ethics and even religions. Fashions and hysterias spring up and, just as quickly, disappear. Social changes, too, are unpredictable, pervasive and important.

When I was a boy, wives worked outside the home only if their husbands had failed or died. Now, women workers in the U.S. constitute about half of the work force. Two-income families have more disposable income, eat at restaurants more often, spend more money for entertainment. Some working women require more expensive clothes. Every change of spending patterns means opportunity to some business.

Antibiotics to cure venereal diseases and the oral contraceptive pill brought on the sexual revolution. More casually than before, unmarried couples live together, and persons are somewhat older when they marry. More persons never marry at all. Of those who do, half opt out by divorce. So the number of single-person households is increasing. More children live in one-parent homes; their mothers work. For those children, day-care must be arranged. That's big business.

While younger couples who want larger homes move out to the suburbs where housing per square foot costs less, older persons are moving back into the cities to live in apartments and condominiums, all on one floor—in England, they say flats, no stairs to climb. They want to be close to public transportation, shopping centers, medical services, churches.

By the year 2000, the numbers of persons turning 65 will begin to grow and continue to grow until 2025 when the old folks population will have doubled. To support those oldsters, the working youngsters will have to double their efficiency; they'll be like Sinbad the Sailor carrying the jinni on his back.

I recommend that you keep up with demographic changes.

Chapter 18

Ways You Can Buy Stocks

Although you and I can recognize change and even make some pretty good guesses as to consequences, selecting a stock to buy is beyond the competence of most of us—and beyond the competence of the broker who tells you, "I do my own research." The job of analyzing the outlook for an industry, the prospects of a corporation and its financial condition is for full-time, experienced professionals.

I doubt that either you or I could be both a securities analyst and, at the same time, a successful investor. An analyst, as a specialist, must concentrate, necessarily, on his own, narrow area of study. As investors, you and I must watch continuously the wide spectrum of events for an appearance of change. Identifying a change, you then should turn to the analyst for his recommendations of the best stocks in the area of your interest. Here, however, most investors will be disillusioned.

Few investors have enough capital to get much attention from a competent, experienced, successful broker with a leading brokerage firm—and through him, his firm's research. It's just a fact of life. Brokers can't afford to waste time with clients of limited means.

How much investment capital must the individual investor have for a broker to see him as a worthwhile prospect? That depends, of course, upon the broker.

The less successful broker tends to be passsive. He's something of a schnook. He responds to whatever demands clients make upon him and allows persons with little money to consume his time. He may understand investments, but he's not much of a businessman.

An outstandingly successful broker—producing, in 1990, more than $1 million—is looking for the prospective client with a lot of investment capital. How much? I'd say $1 million. In 1970, I'd have said, something more than $100,000. In 1980, probably more than $500,000. The investment capital that a broker is looking for might be the rough equivalent of that broker's annual production. The million-dollar broker is looking for the million-dollar client. And, as another fact of life, the million-dollar broker gets first call on his firm's research and every other service.

Nine out of ten investors—the small investors—find themselves assigned either to successful brokers who ignore them or to less-than-successful brokers who offer them only aimless conversation. To get a firm's research, most of us have to ask our brokers for specific information—for a print-out of the analyst's comments and opinion on a stock, for a list of investment quality stocks recommended for purchase. Few clients get the information and direction that they must have. And even with that information and direction, few investors have any luck making their own decisions to buy and sell stocks.

Within the population, a person emotionally equipped to make rational investment decisions occurs with about the same frequency as an albino. And I'm not even sure that I'm one—emotionally equipped, that is. But for right now, I'd like to skip over the emotional stuff. Until we return to that subject, please accept that most persons tend to take market action more on emotion than on good investment judgment; that emotional decisions seldom are good decisions.

So how do we go about investing in stocks? For most of us, three alternatives seem to me practical.

Managing Your Own Common Stock Investments

First, we can buy Stocks of a few, big-name corporations that, financially, are among the soundest, the industry leaders. That's what I do. As I buy only the highest, investment quality stocks, I feel safe enough with a large part of my money in each of only a few stocks. The quality of the stocks I own gives me safety. Therefore, I don't need wide diversification. If I were more speculatively inclined—that is, younger and dumber—my money would have to be spread around among a lot of cats and dogs to cushion me against the calamity of one or two dropping dead. That's one reason for diversification, to distribute risk.

By diversifying, you also enhance your odds of hitting upon a big winner. But the more widely you're diversified, the smaller your position in any one stock, so a big winner contributes little to your overall profits. I prefer to rely on careful stock selection. I find, moreover, that I can feel confident about no more than maybe half a dozen stocks, and I believe that I can keep up with no more than 10 corporations.

I buy a stock to hold for the corporation's long-term growth of earnings. Trading, switching out of one stock and into another, rarely has improved my results. So long as the corporation continues to prosper, I now keep the stock.

You may be one of the few persons who has the time and temperament to become competent in the management of your own common stock investments. If so, I'd encourage your doing so. I enjoy the excitement of investing my own money. I can't say pleasure, because I buy my share of losers and sell my share of winners—and being wrong is not pleasant. Win or lose, it is exciting.

Direct investing in stocks is for emotionally stable persons who are willing to work at it.

Hiring an Investment Counselor

The second possiblity is to engage an investment counselor to manage your stock and bond investments. Now, you mustn't confuse investment counselors with financial planners. Further along, we'll come to different conclusions about financial planners.

Both banks and brokerage firms offer investment counseling, but for a clear picture, let's look first at firms that do nothing but investment counseling.

For the service, you pay an annual fee that is some small percentage of your funds that you have placed under management. Independent investment counselors will not hold stock certificates and bonds, will not touch your money. For those custodial services, you must go to the trust department of a bank.

Almost every investment counselor will require that you give him full discretionary authority to enter orders to buy and sell securities in your behalf. He won't call you to discuss transactions he's about to make. He doesn't make recommendations for you to approve or disapprove. He simply enters the orders. Otherwise, counselor and client would be engaged in an Indian hand-wrestling contest over each transaction. That won't do. First, the counselor hasn't the time—nor the patience. Second, investment decisions made by committee, by consensus, are poor decisions, poor compromises.

Quarterly, counselors report to their clients on investment results—both overall gain or loss and performance in relation to the entire stock and bond markets.

Some smaller investment counseling firms offer their services to private investors. Most, however, are out after the large pension funds of corporations, cities, counties, states. That's because their fees are based on asset size. Big funds pay big fees. The more successful investment counselors want only the multimillion-dollar accounts. And why not?

To an investment counselor, the private investor as a client can be time consuming and, therefore, frightfully expensive. Still, some counselors are willing to work with private investors. Maybe you can find a qualified portfolio manager or money manager—as they sometimes call themselves—in a one- or two-man shop. Starting out in business, some will take on the individual client until they can break into the pension fund business. A good investment counselor, however, probably won't take an individual account of less than $1 or $2 million.

Probably, you'd have no conflict of interests with an investment counselor. Although brokerage firms will provide computer services and other favors for him in return for the business that he directs to them, a counselor does not participate in the brokerage commissions that you pay. Both you and the counselor want only good investment results. You want your capital to grow; he wants to earn a reputation for getting those good results.

As any business person, an investment counselor must be an effective salesman. Otherwise, he'd never land a client. He'll tell you of his successes, but don't expect to be shown an accurate record of his investment performance. Understandably, counselors present themselves in the most favorable way. Even though major counseling firms are quite ethical, many counselors display only their best performing accounts and, for results, select a period of time beginning with the trough of a market cycle and ending at the crest. One counselor, I've heard, shows what he calls his model account—what he would have done. How about that? What I would have done. It sounds like booking bets on yesterday's horse races.

How would you go about identifying a good counselor? That's not easy. Your retail broker won't be of much help. The counselor to whom he might try to steer you could be some inexperienced or unsuccessful guy who's promised to direct commission business to brokers for sending clients to him. But if you just happen to know an institutional broker, he might be able to tell you who in town does the best job. But you can forget about your banker. He'll try to sell you on the counseling service of his trust department.

To find an investment counselor, you probably will have to depend upon the experiences of your friends and business associates. Even then, you later may find that you've hired, not the best investment man, but the best salesman.

Both brokerage firms and trust departments of larger banks offer investment counseling services. They, too, are looking for the big pension fund accounts. Most trust departments will accept individuals accounts of some minimum size. So there's no harm in asking. But a bank would rather invest your money, along with that of other individual accounts, in their common fund of stocks. That gives their investment department ease of management—a single investment decision can be made for all the clients who have their money in the fund. To the bank, the cost of managing a separate account for a client with limited means can exceed the amount of the fee charged.

Either way, common fund or separate account, how good a job do banks do? Their reputation is not great. But that's not a fair statement. Only a professional who does investment performance analysis could know which banks do a good job and which don't. In my limited experience as a trustee of several funds here in Atlanta, I've observed that Trust Company of Georgia gets good investment results. Few banks, however, will pay the salaries that it takes to attract and keep the best talent.

The major brokerage firms also offer counseling services to private investors, but again the salaries they pay are not too competitive. They do get the advantage of immediate access to a large securities research staff, as their money managers usually are located in New York. Your contact with the portfolio manager is through a broker in their local office.

Some brokerage firms charge an annual fee for making the investment decisions and, additionally, charge your account for the commissions on those trades. Some firms will give you the option of paying a larger fee that includes the cost of executing transactions for your account.

Whether with an independent counseling firm or a bank or a brokerage firm, most investment counselors concentrate their efforts on the management of common stock portfolios. Managing a bond portfolio is viewed as somewhat pedestrian, as, in fact, it is.

In their selling efforts, investment counselors often identify themselves with some fad currently popular within their profession. In the late 1960s, it was owning only those stocks that would go up 20% every year. A pretty good idea, wouldn't you think?

In the 1972 market, when the big blue chip stocks alone were enjoying a spectacular advance, fearless, 23-year-old money managers who had never seen a down market, told us of their discovery: the one-decision stock—once convinced that you've found the best stock in the world, make one decision, buy; then hold it forever. From that developed the Favorite 50, the stocks that every money manager, at that time, felt compelled to buy in every portfolio he managed. But nothing's forever. The fortunes of those companies were changing. And from the concentrated buying, those institutional favorites became overpriced.

About the time all the institutions were fully invested in the Favorite 50, the stock market, in anticipation of a business recession, headed down. When the selling started, those dauntless young money managers all were trying to get out through the same door at the same time. Losses were staggering.

Even though its popularity sometimes ebbs, the stock picking fad is always with us. In the late 1960s and early '70s, brokerage firms hired recent graduates of fashionable business schools as institutional salesmen. Selling their firm's hot stock ideas, they called upon bank trust departments and investment counselors.

The 1974 market drop had little respect for the brilliance of those recommendations. Thereupon, investment counselors became—as they styled themselves—market timers. That means that they sell-out to go into cash when the market starts down and become fully invested when the market starts back up. After the big break in the late summer of 1974, all of them were telling the world, "In our accounts, we're 100% in cash."

That sounded convincing enough—except for two facts. First, they had sold-out at the bottom of the market. Second, after the market ran away on the upside in early 1975 and again in early 1976, many of them still were sitting on cash, waiting for the buying opportunity.

You might ask, does anyone at any time ever know that the market is starting down or starting up? The answer is no, never. As something of an anomaly, big pension funds and other institutions found themselves paying large fees to their market timing investment counselors for not investing.

Market timing is market forecasting. I used to tell my rookie brokers that only one man ever had a capability of forecasting the market—that he was a carpenter who lived 2,000 years ago.

Withal, the next time you hear someone explaining why the stock market soon will go up or go down, you'll find yourself listening and—just as I—halfway believing.

We can be certain that other fads for investing will come along. Each new method or scheme will sound plausible. You'll be saying to yourself, By George, this young chap may be on to something. At that moment, remember what I've just told you about the carpenter.

As a service to pension fund trustees, some larger brokerage firms analyze and measure performances of investment counselors. Results are compared with Standard & Poor's 500 Composite Stock Index. A report is prepared for the trustees; a copy is given to the counselor. If ever you consider employing an investment counselor, you might ask to see a recent performance measurement report on one of his accounts. If his results have been good, he'll be happy to show it to you.

Beware. Anyone can become registered as an investment counselor. No education, no experience required. Just fill out a

Securities and Exchange Commission registration form, pay their $25 or $30 fee and you're registered. In the Yellow Pages, under Investment Advisory Services, you can find a long list of persons who have paid the fee to call themselves investment counselors.

Most of the established, reputable investment counseling firms do a reasonably good job, but few investment counselors outperform the market.

Investment counselors are for the rich who don't want the bother of investing their own money.

Investing in Common Stock Funds

The third alternative is a common stock fund that manages investors' money in a common pool. The most widely held are the mutual funds. You've probably heard them called open-end funds. That's because new shares are offered continuously at net asset value—the cash value that would be received for each outstanding share if the fund were completely liquidated. If you own shares and want to sell them, you can do so only by surrendering your shares back to the fund in exchange for the net asset value. You do have the comfort of knowing that you're getting a fair price.

Several hundred open-end mutual funds are available to the public. An open-end fund is in continuous registration with the SEC and is offered as represented by a current prospectus that the SEC has reviewed for completeness of disclosure.

Most open-end mutual funds are sold through brokerage firms that are paid a commission or load—thus load fund. Buying a load fund, you pay net asset value plus a load that can be as high as 8 1/2% for an order below, say, $20,000. On larger orders, that rate drops to maybe 2% or 3% on a single order of $100,000 or $200,000.

Some open-end mutual funds can be bought without having to pay a commission. As you'd suppose, those are called no-load funds. They are sold mostly by media advertising and direct mail, sort of mail order funds.

The second type of fund is an investment company or, as probably you've heard, a closed-end fund. It's a corporation as any other corporation with a fixed number of shares of common stock. Its only business is the managed investment of its capital. However, a closed-end fund—just as an open-end mutual fund—is exempt of corporate income tax, because almost all profits and income, each year, are paid out to the shareholders. The stock of a closed-end fund trades publicly. Several are listed on the New York Stock Exchange. In each Monday's *Wall Street Journal*, you can find the closed-end funds listed in a small box that's headed, Publicly Traded Funds.

In the secondary market—on the NYSE, American Stock

Exchange or Over-the-Counter—buying or selling the stock of a publicly traded, closed-end investment company, you'd pay the same commission that you'd be charged for a transaction in any other stock.

No more than about a dozen of those closed-end funds invest in the broad stock market. About 30 invest their capital in specialized areas, such as stocks of a single foreign country—examples are Japan Fund, Italy Fund, Korea Fund. Specialized funds, both open-end mutual funds and closed-end investment companies, come into existence to appeal to investor appetite for some stock group that's been having a spectacular run. But once that big play is over, the group can go dead for 10 years. I wouldn't buy a fund that's restricted in its investments to some single industry or some narrow area.

Most of the time, stocks of closed-end investment companies sell at prices well below their net asset values—at discounts sometimes greater than 25%. Investing in a closed-end fund, you'd hope, of course, to buy at an historically deep discount. But that's the same as saying that you'd hope to buy near the bottom of a down market, because in a rising market those discounts narrow and, toward the top, almost disappear.

Also at the top of a market, you can expect initial public offerings (IPOs) of stocks of new investment companies. Seeing the public willing to pay close to net asset values for existing closed-end funds, brokerage firms are quick to take advantage of the enthusiasm by creating new closed-end funds to sell publicly. The mark-up, as on any new issue, is at least two times regular commission. And the sponsoring brokerage firms become investment managers of their new closed-end funds and receive forever nice management fees.

I wouldn't buy a closed-end investment company on an IPO. Why pay full price for unproven investment performance when, in the secondary market, you can buy—at a discount—a seasoned fund with an established record of investment results?

And watch out for gimmick funds. As an example, you'll see quoted two funds with the same name. One is called the Capital Fund; the other, the Income Fund. From the same portfolio of securities, the Capital Fund gets all the profits when the fund is terminated at some specified, future date; the Income Fund, meanwhile, pays all the expenses and gets all the dividends and interest. One may prove to be a great buy and the other a dud. The only way to make a choice is to flip a coin. That's not the best way to invest your money.

Wall Street spends a lot of time figuring out new packaging for plain old stocks and bonds to make them look like something different from stocks and bonds. In a fancy wrapping, the new product then can be marked up in price and sold at a nice profit to the brokerage firm.

Occasionally, an investment manager is widely publicized for his success in selection of stocks that are market leaders. He acquires an overnight reputation as a great stock picker. Sometimes he'll become the manager of a brand new personality fund—maybe even with his name in the title. All that makes for persuasive sales presentation, but you'll do better to stick with a fund that has a proven record. I wouldn't buy a new mutual fund. Again, there are enough seasoned funds from which to chose.

A good salesman can make a convincing argument for the purchase of an open-end load-fund, but you must remember that no-load funds pay him no sales commission. Sometimes, new, open-end mutual funds, offered for the first time, claim to be without sales charge. Be careful. You may find that you must pay a penalty if you want your money back within the first five years. Other funds, to pay the salesmen, take money from your principal over some number of years.

If your broker is trying to get you to buy a fund, you can bet that he's getting paid for making the sale. And what he's paid comes out of your money. A salesman, I believe, earns his commissions and is entitled to whatever he's paid for making a sale. I object only to an effort to disguise or conceal the commission. Nothing's for nothing.

I can't tell you that an open-end fund will give you better results than a closed-end investment company; that an open-end load fund will outperform an open-end no-load fund. As that's getting into the future, I don't know. It's apparent, nevertheless, that the sales charge or load that you pay reduces the amount of your investment—the money that you will have working for you.

Both mutual funds and investment companies are single pools of money. Their managements' only job is to get best investment results. To be successful, to enhance their reputations, to earn higher salaries and bigger bonuses, managements strive to outperform not only the market but other funds as well. All of their energies, skills and talents are directed to the management of one, single pool of assets. Their selfish interests correspond to the selfish interests of their shareholders. Owning a fund, you know that your investment dollar gets the same attention as the dollar of every other shareholder. You're paying for that, of course—somewhere between 0.5% and 1% of your investment every year.

Some open-end mutual funds you'll see described as stock funds, others as balanced funds. Stock funds invest only in common stocks. Balanced funds invest in both stocks and bonds. Because it's your decision as to what part of your capital, what amount of your money, should be invested in stocks and what part of your money in bonds, you should buy a stock fund if you're investing for profit. If you need investment income from bonds and don't want to make direct purchases of bonds, you could consider a bond fund.

Mutual fund distributors such as American Funds Group, Fidelity Distributors Corporation, Massachusetts Financial Services and many more, market a "family" of funds—stock funds, balanced funds, bond funds, etc. Within the family, you are allowed to switch, once or twice a year, from one fund to another at a cost of only $5 or $10. That could be a useful service. If you own a stock fund and need more investment income, you might wish to switch a part of your investment to the distributor's bond fund. Although you might switch one way or the other during some rare market extreme, don't fool yourself to believe that switching funds is a way to trade the market. No one can trade the market, because no one can forecast the market.

I wouldn't ask my broker for his recommendation or his firm's recommendation of a fund to buy. Few brokers know that much about past performances of funds. And as most large brokerage firms have their own in-house funds, any recommendation that you get will be biased. Most brokers get enthusiastic about a fund only when their firms might be in the midst of a selling campaign— usually offerings, IPOs, of new funds.

In their September issue, *Forbes* magazine, for many years, has featured a special section on performances of funds of all types. Before buying a fund, I'd study that edition. You and I can understand what we read. We don't need expert interpretation.

The only indication of competence of a fund's investment management is that fund's record of past performance. The record is no guarantee of future performance, but management that's done an outstanding job over the past 10 years and the past five years probably will do well in future years. Also, I'd be interested in what it's going to cost me to buy, own and sell that fund.

What's the load? Although that depends upon the size of your order, a sales charge of 5% seems high to me. Buying $10,000 of a fund and paying a 5% load, $9,524 is invested for you; the difference, $476, goes to the selling brokerage firm. That, probably, is more than the dividends you'll receive from a common stock fund in two years.

How about the expense of running the fund? In 1980, the SEC gave us Rule 12b-1 which allows funds to dip into the assets of the fund, to use your money, to pay for marketing and distribution. I'd be suspect of a fund that has total annual expenses of more than 1% of assets.

And what about undisclosed charges? In 1982, the SEC approved "exit" fees. You pay no load to buy the fund, but if you want out you can lose as much as 6%. Typically, the fee is reduced each year that the fund is held until, after five years, no fee is charged. Investors have complained that such funds have been represented to them as no-load funds.

I must admit that buying a stock and seeing it go up is ego gratifying. For many of us, being right is as important as making money—until later when we look back, almost with disbelief, upon our several small profits and our one or two disastrous losses.

Of investors I've known, nine out of ten never should have made direct purchases of stocks. A good mutual fund would have served their interests much better—not only better investment performance but reduced anxiety as well.

Mutual funds are for most people with money to invest for profit.

However you decide to invest in common stocks, you will require professional help. And whether you're charged commissions or fees, you will have to pay for the help you get.

The only basis for selecting professional help is past performance. Selecting a brokerage firm, you must rely entirely upon the firms' reputation, because quality of service isn't measurable. If you're considering an investment counselor, he may be willing to show you an outside audit of one or more of his accounts. If you'd rather buy a mutual fund, its performance is public information.

As an investor, you've got to own common stocks. Your only choice is how you go about it.

Chapter 19

Emotional Signals and Time Bombs

Most people are afflicted with unreasoned fear of the stock market. In fact, most investors that I know are scared stiff of the stock market—most of the time. Most of the time? Yes, but not all of the time. As the market approaches a long-term top, most investors become fearless buyers of stocks.

Why would anyone be so witless as to buy stocks only when prices are high? I don't know. Maybe it's some sort of psychosis.

As the market rises, more and more stories circulate about persons of uncanny foresight who bought stocks last month or last year and who now are sitting on nice profits. Sitting pretty, you might hear. Wives begin to ask their husbands, "Why don't we own any stocks? Charlie Smith has cleaned up. Why don't we get into the market?"

That's about all it takes: a little greed, a little ego. You and I are just as smart as Charlie Smith. And the higher prices go, the more Charlie Smiths we hear about—until finally, everyone in the world who's heard about a Charlie Smith has spent all of his money buying stocks.

Then on the following day at the opening of the market, a funny thing happens. No more enthusiasts are out there on the floor buying. They've got no more money. Sellers, who recently have had a field day hitting those eager bids, begin to find that now they must take a little less for their stocks. Buyers aren't coming to them. Sellers have got to attract buyers. They drop their offering prices, but bids come in below the market and for only a few hundred shares. Now it's the sellers who become aggressive, competing with one another to get out.

The Charlie Smiths and all of their disciples are confident that prices will turn back up. They're wrong. They overstay the market, see their profits melt away and finally sell out, desperate to salvage what little is left. Forget the cheese, let me out of the trap.

Something like that seems to happen to almost every generation. The public is attracted to common stocks only toward the end of a long bull market when everyone has become convinced that stocks will continue up forever. Then when the market breaks, that whole generation wants nothing more to do with stocks.

Because the stock market in the 1920s had become a national mania, the Crash of 1929 had the broadest impact. And because the Crash was seen as a cause of the Great Depression, the stock market became politicians' whipping boy for several decades. Even people who had owned no stocks—and probably never would have, anyway—resolved never to invest in the market.

When I began selling securities in 1947, almost every person I called on wanted to talk about the '29 Crash—still terrified after 18 years. Yet anyone who bought stocks in 1947, and stayed invested, made a fortune. And how much more one could have made if he'd had money to invest in 1932 and '33.

When the market has gone up so much that ratios of prices to earnings and prices to book values have become historically high, you'd expect investors, logically, to begin thinking about selling, taking profits. Instead, all of us are eager to believe that something peculiar to this advance makes it an exception to all of the old rules; that if we don't jump in, we'll miss out on a great buying opportunity.

At the bottom of a market, what you see is the mirror image.

When the market has gone down so far that prices in relation to earnings, dividends, book values, or anything else are historically low, we become so despairing that it's easy to conclude that stocks never again can have value. The logical decision would be to buy. But the emotional decision is to sell.

In 1984, aboard a cruise ship, my wife and I were seated for dinner one evening with three other couples. One of the men, about 35 years old, told us that he was the owner of a computer company. We gathered that he was quite successful. Upon learning that I once had been a stockbroker, the young man began to tell us of his misfortune, two years earlier, as an investor. From the conversation, I assumed he had invested a whole lot of money in the market. And it was evident, almost immediately, that he had been right and the market, somehow, had been wrong.

The 1981-82 recession was the most severe in 50 years. At mid-1982, the market, had done nothing for a year but slide slowly, sickeningly from about 1,000 to 800. The outlook for the U.S. economy was worsening. And our dinner companion remembered it all. He recited to us the succession of frightening news items that had filled every day's *Wall Street Journal*—no silver linings, only lowering clouds of an approaching storm. Convinced that the country was headed down the drain, he had made the decision. He had sold everything.

As you might have expected, the stock market started up. The advance, in fact, was one of the strongest of many years. From a low of 776 in 1982, the DJIA was back above 1,000 at year end and almost 1,300 at the end of 1983.

Well, why wouldn't the man have been upset to have sold out just before that explosion? to have watched the stocks he had owned double in price? Who wouldn't have felt sorry for the poor guy? Yet listening to his story, I had to ask myself two questions.

First, was this man the only person in the world who knew about all that bad economic news? A silly question? Yes, but the answer is that the fellow had no privileged, inside information. Faithfully, *The Wall Street Journal* had reported it all. Everyone knew what our investor knew. Some persons may have known even more.

The second question: Was he the first one to realize that bad economic news would become bad earnings news? bad stock market news? No, all of that was last year's bird nest. That's why the DJIA already was down from 1,000 a year earlier, to something below 800, more than 20%. For some months, the prescient, cautious or just plain scared had been selling—had been selling at much higher prices. Now sellers were beginning to act out of something akin to panic. Emotion had become a stronger force than reason.

And how about the other side of the market? Sometimes we forget that no sale can be made without a willing buyer.

At the beginning of the decline, buyers—to have been buyers— must have dismissed the sell-off as just a correction, nothing too serious. Down below 800, however, buyers must have been the stout of heart, not just willing, but able to hang on. They were buying when the news was at its worst. On their part, reason, probably, was a stronger force than emotion.

Our dinner companion had sold into the final liquidation—not a panic such as we saw in October of '87, but an exhaustion, the sort of emotional climax that creates a bottom for the market. He had joined the crowd. And I'm sure that he, too, had to told himself, I'll never invest in stocks again.

A long-term market cycle takes us through two extremes, from bottom to top and from the top back into another bottom—from wild enthusiasm at the very top to black despair at the very bottom. Toward a market top, buying becomes reckless and finally a head-long stampede. Toward the bottom, selling becomes panic. In a small way, all of us contribute to the emotionalism; in a great way, all of us are affected or even driven by it. That's why investors tend to buy at the top and sell at the bottom.

But short-term or intermediate run-ups and sell-offs also produce in us emotional jolts to which we react, buying or selling, out of greed or fear. During a four-week period, just a 5% swing of the market is enough spark an urge to chase the trend. So it's not just the long-term tops and bottoms that set off within us emotional storms. As investors, we're all slightly, mildly, to violently manic-depressive.

If you know how your own emotional signals can lead you off in wrong directions, you're more likely to slow down enough to apply your good sense before taking market action.

When the market's been going up almost every day for six months, buying stock is an easy decision. Your past fears, clearly, were foolish; you've overcome your skepticism and now at last you've become a believer. You're convinced. But you must remember, you and I are awfully average persons. If we're convinced, let's not forget that probably everyone is convinced. Many persons became convinced before we did, so maybe we're late for the show. Buying now is an easy decision but not nearly as good a decision as it would have been six months earlier. Although this may not be the top, that top certainly is closer—in time, closer by six months; in price, closer by whatever the advance, so far, has been. Time is running out. Some part of what was the profit potential, already has been realized. Risks, consequently, are greater. Still enthusiasm, emotion—maybe even greed and ego—crowd out good judgment.

Surely with no intent ever of doing so, the news media often identify major tops and bottoms of the market. During a single week of early January, 1975, five national magazines had cover pictures of vicious looking bears, symbol of stock market calamity—the bear market. Our astute manager in Chattanooga made photocopies that he sent to me. In each of those magazines, the cover story was the same: Stock prices were way down, everything looked bad, everything was about to get worse. Five national magazine editors had heard Chicken Little. All agreed. The sky, indeed, was falling. That very week marked the low of the market for more than 15 years.

Looking back, it's all so funny. At the time, it wasn't funny at all. Everybody was scared. Rationally, however, applying common sense, you'd had to have said to yourself, If the sky's falling, why not buy stocks? What have I got to lose? That would have been the tough decision—to buy when you're scared. That would have been the right decision.

During a down market, we all go from confidence to concern, to distress and finally to panic. In the early stages of a sell-off, the stocks that you bought with such confidence now are down with everything else. You tell yourself, The market will come back, and anyway, I'm an investor, not a speculator. But as prices continue to slide, you want to kick yourself, How was I ever dumb enough to let that broker talk me into this? You're disgusted but not yet scared. Soon you're reading nothing but bad news about business and the economy. With every jarring news item that comes across on the wire, the market drops further. At last, you just can't take anymore: If I wait any longer, I'll have nothing left. Selling now is the easy decision—selling when you're scared. And selling now is the wrong decision. You can be sure that we're at or near the bottom of the market.

The tough decision is to sell into a market that's running away on the upside. Perhaps the weekly news magazines will give us the sell signal. Cover pictures of snorting bulls could suggest that the top is at hand.

Emotionally, you and I and everyone else react to rising markets and falling markets in exactly the same way. Whether fearless at the top or frightened at the bottom, we can be sure that the stronger our emotional feelings, the greater the probability of our being wrong.

Surely by now, you're beginning to believe that the market has a malevolent life of its own, that it's some malicious dragon. But it's not. The dragon is within us, our own emotions, our driving greed at the beginning, our paralyzing fear toward the end. Once anyone allows himself to be controlled by emotion instead of reason, whatever he does will be wrong. He buys at the top; he sells at the bottom. The market doesn't know that he's bought and then turn down, or know that he's sold and then turn up. It's the investor, not the market. He buys almost at the moment that everyone finally has become convinced that the market will continue up. Everyone's money then has been invested. He sells after a long decline, just when the last scaredy-cat gets spooked out. Now the selling is over.

Becoming an investor, you enter into a highly charged, emotional marketplace in which you can be swept along with the crowd and sucked down into the vortex. You will be lost unless you can identify and control your own driving feelings of fear and greed, unless you have the courage to go exactly, 180 degrees in the opposite direction. Only then do you control your investments. Only then does the stock market not seize control of you. It can go up or it can go down without wrecking your life.

I learned, a long time ago, that the marketplace is tough enough without burdening myself with additional emotional baggage.

As manager of a brokerage office, I got all the customer complaints—for 25 years. Seldom did I hear from a happy investor.

The only calls I got were from clients who had lost their money. Hence my job was more pleasant in up-markets than in down-markets. As the tide goes out, the rocks begin to appear. And my phone would begin to ring.

A client complaining of his loses has but one reason for calling. He wants his money back. Most would protest, "It's not the money; it's the principle." But the conversations never got around to principles; it was always about money.

To complain, an investor, first, must convince himself that unfair advantage has been taken of him, that his trust in his broker was misplaced, that he's entitled to compensation for his loss. Sometimes the investor was right, and we paid off. Sometimes the investor, out to make a quick killing, had gotten himself into trouble. When the loss was his, I refused to accept any part of it. In other cases, client and broker shared responsibility. Whether the fault was 90%-10% or 10%-90%, I had to arrive at some fair settlement without giving away the store. In making that judgment, I relied heavily upon the confidence I had in my broker's integrity—over time, I weeded out brokers in whom I did not have complete confidence.

As investors, most of us get ourselves into whatever trouble we find ourselves. Perhaps aggressive brokers encourage our follies, but we have to be at least a little greedy to fall for the crackpot ideas of unprincipled brokers.

If ever you find that you've gotten yourself in the soup, don't entertain any hope that the market will fetch you out. The stock market never accommodates. It's always perverse. That tells you to anticipate trouble so that you can avoid emotional crises and time bombs.

Most folks somehow have learned to control their physical responses to the emotional surges that we all experience. Otherwise, we'd still be having temper tantrums on the floor. Also, we've learned to avoid encounters that can lead to emotional crises. As an example, you may get upset with the driver of another automobile and call him an s.o.b., but as a pedestrian, you don't speak that way to a passer-by on the sidewalk. That's because drivers rarely come out of their cars to get at one another, but on the sidewalk, you'd be inviting a fist fight, a crisis to avoid.

Over the years, I saw how investors and speculators got themselves into trouble. Often I had to preside over final liquidations of their ill-advised adventures. Each time, the person had entered into the type of transaction that predictably led him into an emotional crisis just at the time when he needed clearheaded judgment to deal with his losses. From those experiences, I learned to avoid time bombs that I know will detonate when I'm least prepared to deal with a crisis. For myself:

1. I invest only that money for which I have no foreseeable need.
2. I borrow no money to buy securities.
3. I never sell short.

Why activate time bombs?

1. Invest only the money that you won't need.

Who'd be crazy enough to take a chance with money that he knows he's going to need? Well, lots of folks. It goes something like this:

Let's say that you and your spouse have just sold your home. We'll assume that you're building a house that won't be ready for occupancy for a year-and-a-half and that temporarily you're living in an apartment. Having just closed the sale of you old house, you've got the check in your hand. You say to yourself, Gee, the way the stock market's been moving . . . everybody else is making money. . . .

So you phone a brokerage firm and find yourself talking with some friendly young man who has a convincing recommendation—the stock of some company you've never heard of but which is doing marvelous things in some advanced technical area that you don't understand. You invest the proceeds from the sale of your house—the money for the new house. You buy that hot stock.

Almost immediately you have a loss, maybe just a small loss, but a loss. You're philosophical, Prices always fluctuate. So you turn to more important things. But the stock keeps on sliding, and before you know it, a year has passed. In six months, you've got to come up with the money for that new house, and you say to yourself, If I can come close to breaking even, I've got to get out. But in the next couple of months, the market falls apart, and suddenly you hear yourself saying, I'm not going to be able to pay for that new house. In panic, you sell out to recover what's left. You sell of course, on the low, and immediately the market turns back up.

I don't know why it works out that way. It just does, always. Do I believe in hexes? No, I'm just telling you what I've seen, so many, many times.

Before you made that investment, as long as you kept your cash, you controlled your own affairs. Once you bought that stock, the moment you bet your money that great good fortune would befall you, you allowed yourself to be driven in whichever direction the winds might blow. And time was against you. You had only 18 months. Every month that passed reduced your odds and added to your anxiety. Less time remained for something good to happen. No longer was the choice yours. You were forced to sell—at the wrong time.

You can find yourself in the same trap if you overextend yourself and leave no cushion for emergencies.

Frantic persons have no emotional control. That's why I'd never invest money for which I had foreseeable need. I'd keep it in Treasury bills, the bank or a money-market fund.

2. Don't invest borrowed money.

Don't invest borrowed money? Of course you wouldn't. Who'd go out and borrow money to play the stock market? Lots of people, I'm afraid. But they wouldn't call it borrowing money to speculate. More likely you'd hear someone speak of having a margin account or trading on margin. Even better, how about "taking advantage of leverage"?—as you may read in the literature of a brokerage firm.

In the securities business, we have cash accounts and margin accounts. A cash account can be cash-and-carry—pay in full for the stocks and bonds you buy and get certificates for your securities. That's what I do. Too well I remember 1974 when it looked like some brokerage firms would go under. If the firm that holds your securities goes broke, you could find yourself tied up in the messy business of trying to recover what you own. As a service, however, most brokerage firms will hold securities in cash accounts for their better clients.

A margin account is comparable to having a collateral loan with a bank. For your security purchases, you pay only a part of the cost. Most of the time, the Federal Reserve Board, the Fed, has required that you pay at least 50%. The brokerage firm lends to you the rest and holds your securities as collateral. You pay interest on what you owe. So long as your collateral is adequate, the brokerage firm will continue your loan—your debit balance—indefinitely.

Margin accounts confuse most clients—and some brokers. Although the Fed's Regulation T requires that you put up enough money to pay for half the cost of your purchases, the initial margin requirement, once you've put up the money to meet the Reg-T call, the Fed has no further interest in your account. The brokerage firm, however, has its own continuing maintenance requirement: your equity cannot drop below 30% of current market value. Let's see how that works.

Suppose you have $25,000 that you invest in stocks—or in just one stock. A price advance of 40% means that your market value went from $25,000 to $35,000, a profit of $10,000. So you say to yourself, "If I'd gone on margin, I could have made twice that much, $20,000." And so you could have. You could have bought $50,000 of the stock, put up your $25,000 to meet the Fed's initial margin, or Reg-T, requirement and borrowed the remaining $25,000 from the brokerage firm. On that $50,000 investment, the 40% price advance would have made for you a profit of $20,000. On your own $25,000, you would have made a profit, not of 40%, but 80%.

Is it, you ask, just that easy? It sure is. If the market goes up. Shall we see what happens with a price decline of 40%?

That's a big drop, you say? Yes, but it happens. Here's the arithmetic.

In a cash account, the $25,000 of stock that you bought and paid for in full is worth only $15,000. You've got a loss of $10,000—40%.

In a margin account, your $50,000 of stock, against which you owe $25,000, now is worth only $30,000. You've got a loss of $20,000—40% of the $50,000 market value. But of your own $25,000, 80% is gone. You have left an equity of only $5,000—only 20% of your original $25,000.

Leverage, you see, cuts both ways.

Actually, your brokerage firm never would have allowed your equity to drop down as low as $5,000. This is where the firm's maintenance requirement comes in. Most firms require their margin clients to maintain equity at no less than 30% of current market value. It works like this:

You bought $50,000 worth of stock. You put up $25,000 to meet the Fed's initial margin requirement. The brokerage firm lent you $25,000. At that moment, your equity—your $25,000—was, of course, 50% of market value. If that market value now goes up, your equity goes up, dollar for dollar; if the market value goes down, your equity goes down, dollar-for-dollar. Whether the market value goes up or down, however, your debit balance remains the same; you still owe the brokerage firm the $25,000 you borrowed. Observe that profits, as well as losses, are yours and not those of the brokerage firm. They're not about to become your partner in speculation.

The firm is comfortable with your account so long as your equity is greater than 30% of current market value. If a market decline carries your equity below 30% of current market value, you'll get a maintenance call. You then must deposit enough cash or other, fully paid-for securities to bring your equity back above 30%. And what happens if you don't? Remember, as collateral, the firm holds your stocks. To protect itself against the possibility of loss, the firm will sell whatever is necessary to reduce your debit balance to 70% of remaining market value—that brings your equity back up to 30%.

How far down can your market value go before you get a

maintenance call? Well, if your equity can't go below 30%, that means your debit balance can't go above 70% of market value. But we can't work from your equity, because it's continually changing along with market value. As your debit balance, what you owe the brokerage firm, remains constant, we'll have to work from that— work backward.

To determine the lowest market value that can support your $25,000 debit, divide your $25,000 debit balance by 70%, the maximum debit: $25,000 divided by 0.70 = $35,715 market value. Put the other way around, when your market value might drop to $35,715, your $25,000 debit is 70% of that market value. So a market value of $35,715 is the critical point. Your account would look like this:

Debit balance	$25,000	70%	(what you owe)
Equity	+ $10,715	30%	(your money)
Market value	$35,715	100%	(total)

A market value of $35,715 is as far down as the firm will carry your $25,000 debit. If it drops below that, you'll start getting maintenance calls.

Let's suppose that on the following day your market value drops to $30,000. Pretty rough day. Remember now, your $25,000 debit remains unchanged. Your account would look like this:

Debit balance	$25,000	83%	(what you owe)
Equity	+ $5,000	17%	(your money)
Market value	$30,000	100%	(total)

and the firm would require you to deposit immediately enough money to bring your equity up to 30% of market value: $30,000 market value X 30% or 0.30 = $9,000. As your equity is down to $5,000, you'd get a maintenance call for $4,000 to get it back up to $9,000. Once deposited, that $4,000, of course, would reduce your $25,000 debit balance to $21,000—which is the maximum, 70% of your $30,000 current market value.

Watching his equity go down the drain, a client begins to see that he can lose a lot of money. Reeling from the shock of his first maintenance call, he has a vision of pouring money down a rat hole. And he's right. It's a rat hole.

Is it, you ask, just that dangerous? It sure is. If the market goes down.

Brokerage firms insist upon a minimum equity of 30% as a cushion to protect themselves against losses in a precipitate drop of prices. Because sell-outs aren't automatic, maintenance calls are a bad time for everyone. The client stalls his broker. The broker doesn't want to offend his client. The office manager wants to continue happy relations with the broker. The firm's New York office wants to appear stern without offending the office manager.

The broker plays along with the client and tells his manager what a swell guy the client is. The manager plays along with the broker and reassures the New York office. And everyone is hoping for a market recovery. But as the market continues to decline, that maintenance call becomes one of dozens of calls within the office, one of hundreds within the firm, and the New York office enters sell-out orders to cover all delinquent maintenance calls.

I never could feel too sorry for the speculator who was getting maintenance calls. Few speculators can blame anyone but themselves. Yes, brokers sometimes encourage their clients to become overextended. Getting a client to go on margin and double his buying power, the broker can double his business from that client. But for that to happen, the client must be wishy-washy, greedy or a bit of both; the broker must be too lazy to get outside to find more clients.

To begin with, most speculators put more money in the market than they can afford. On top of that, they go on margin. That allows them to take on positions that are more than twice what they can afford. When the market goes with them, great; they make twice as much money. When the market goes against them, they lose twice as much money.

Here's the way it goes, again and again:

The margin client's first indication of trouble is a phone call from his broker. Following an exchange of pleasantries, the broker says, "Oh, by the way, Mr. Client, you've got a maintenance call for $4,000."

That moment is important in the client's investment life. He's about to learn, only now, about maintenance calls.

When the client asks, "What's the hell are you talking about?" he finds the broker's explanation somewhat disconcerting, not for any difficulty of understanding but because—as the client puts it—"Why didn't you tell me, when you got me into this, that I'd need more money?" Not a bad question.

Maybe not the smartest guy in the world, the client nevertheless senses that the broker is on the defensive. And you must remember that the broker is a salesman, afraid that he might lose the client. For openers, the client says, "It's not convenient for me to add more money to my account just now." The broker explains that if he doesn't deposit the $4,000, some callous person in New York will sell enough of the client's stocks to reduce the debit balance to 70% of remaining market value. The client argues that the firm doesn't have that authority. The broker reminds him of the Margin Agreement that he perfunctorily signed to go on margin.

The client doesn't have the $4,000, so the best thing for him to do is what most clients in such circumstances do: scream. Into the broker's ear comes a torrent of abuse—some of which the broker deserves, all of which he suffers for fear of losing a client.

The client expresses his concern that he was drawn into a scheme that served only the broker's interests, that the broker ever allowed him to jeopardize the financial security of his family, that the brokerage firm permits its clients to assume risks unsuitable to their circumstances.

Somewhere in that tirade, another possibility enters the client's mind: *"Suppose the market turns around and starts back up and those rascals already have sold me out at the bottom?"* All greed is not dead. With that, the client becomes reassuring, "Give me a couple of days to get a check to you."

Beginning the following day, the client's heart drops every time his phone rings: *"It's that broker dunning me again . . . When's the market ever going to stop going down?"* Another dismaying prospect, that of his wife's questions: "Why didn't you ask . . . ? Who told you . . . ? Where are you going to get $4,000?"

When the second day dawns—after a sleepless night—there's nothing left to do but lie. And sure enough, the phone rings and, of course, it's that broker again. Assuming a tone of annoyance, the client curtly tells him, "I'm putting the check in the mail today." The broker tells his manager that the check is in the mail. The manager wires his New York office, CIM.

Next day, no check. Again, the client's phone rings, polite question, curt answer and everyone agrees that the postal service is abominable. Another day gets us into the weekend. Monday brings no surprises. No check; no market recovery. A call to the client produces only a snarl and the threat, "If you sell my stocks, I'll write my Congressman." The brokerage firm sells out the account. But by that time, proceeds of sales won't cover the client's debit balance. The brokerage firm is left holding the bag for several thousand dollars. Maybe they'll sue; maybe they won't.

Through all that name-calling turmoil, how do you suppose the client could have exercised rational investment judgment? Impossible. He'd gotten himself into such a highly charged, emotional situation that his only way out was to get sold out.

It's weak brokers and weak managers who make possible that familiar story of a maintenance call. Ironically, many firms, after such an experience as that, will continue to do business with the client. Some brokers are just about as greedy as some clients, so everybody gets pretty much what he deserves.

In the 1929 Crash, my father lost everything he had. A speculator, he had bought as heavily as the 10% margin of that time would allow. Buying, say, $1 million worth of stock, he could borrow from the brokerage firm $900,000 and put up, of his own money, only $100,000. So in the Crash, the first 10% of the market's decline wiped out his entire equity, and the brokerage firm sold out his stocks to recoup its 90% loan. As you might guess, I've never bought on margin.

3. Don't sell short.

Hoping to buy-in at a lower price, a short-seller sells stock that he doesn't own. On the other side of the trade, the buyer has no way of knowing that he's buying from a short-seller—and doesn't care. The seller's brokerage firm, under Stock Exchange rules, is responsible for making delivery on settlement date, five business days following the trade. To make delivery, the firm must borrow stock. The big firms borrow from accounts of their own margin customers who have authorized such use of their stock by signing a Lending Agreement—which is a part of the Margin Agreement. Once borrowed stock has been delivered against the short sale and the buyer's brokerage firm has paid for the purchase, that buyer and the borrowed stock are gone. Buyer and short-seller have no further relation with one another. Now it's between just borrower and lender.

As collateral to guarantee return of the borrowed stock by purchase in the open market, the short-seller's brokerage firm holds the proceeds of his sale—the money that the buyer paid for the stock. Additionally, the short-seller must deposit as margin an amount equal to 50% of the proceeds. (The Fed can raise or lower that 50% as part of its job of regulating the nation's credit.) The seller's brokerage firm holds the 50% margin, along with the full proceeds of the sale, to ensure that the short position can be bought in at no loss to the firm.

Large brokerage firms that have a plentiful supply of lendable stock are happy to carry short positions. Without interest cost, they have use of the short seller's money, both proceeds of the sale and the 50% margin deposit. If the short seller's brokerage firm hasn't the stock to lend and must borrow from another firm, the two firms share in use of the money.

An example may be helpful.

A speculator who is convinced that a stock at, say, 65 is too high, decides to go short. He sells short 100 shares at 65. To make settlement, his brokerage firm borrows 100 shares, delivers it to the buyer and is paid $6,500. The brokerage firm holds that $6,500 and also calls the short seller for the 50% margin requirement. The short seller deposits 50% of $6,500 or $3,250. The seller's account now has a credit balance of $9,750 and a short position of 100 shares.

Let's say that the stock goes down and the seller buys in at 55. Of the $9,750 balance, $5,500 is paid out for the purchase of stock to return to the lender. That leaves $4,250, so the speculator has made $1,000 on the trade. However, stocks also can go up. If the short seller buys in at 75, he has a loss, of course, of $1,000.

As long as a short position is open, any dividend that the company pays become the obligation of the short seller to pay to the lender—the lender's stock, remember, is long gone, so he is receiving no dividends from the company. Thus to a short seller, his short position is producing, not income, but outgo.

As a broker in Atlanta in the 1950s, I had a client who was a major stockholder of E.L. Bruce, a Memphis company that produced hardwood flooring. (I believe it still does but as a subsidiary of another company.) For whatever reason, Empire Millwork—or something like that—decided to buy out Bruce. I don't know why, for all this is from my recollections of 30 years or more ago.

The Bruce family opposed sale of the company to Empire, which was run by some upstate New York character named Gilbert. The contest for control was widely publicized, and the stock of E.L. Bruce had advanced from the 20s to the low 30s.

Although the largest outside stockholder, my client did not know the patriarch of the Bruce family. Nevertheless, he went to Memphis to offer his support in fending off the raider. My client's block of stock was large enough to ensure continued control by the Bruce family. Oddly enough, however, he was not graciously received. Bruce not only declined my client's offer of assistance, he so offended him that my client sent to me his E.L. Bruce stock certificates with instructions to tender—to sell out—to Empire Millwork. With that stock, Empire would have close to 50%. Meanwhile, the Bruce family, too, had close to 50%. The small, publicly held, floating supply of stock, therefore, would become critical to control.

That's how things stood when I developed laryngitis. I remained at home on the following day.

Returning to work, I saw that another client, whom I'll call Abe, had sold short 100 shares of E.L. Bruce at about 33. Having watched Bruce run up sharply, Abe had decided that it was overpriced.

Without violating the confidence of my other client, I told Abe that he should immediately buy in to cover his short, that the risk was too great. Abe wasn't especially impressed. Perhaps other advice I'd given him hadn't been the best. A few days later, Bruce dropped a couple of points, and Abe knew he had a winner.

Gilbert then must have announced that Empire District had

acquired almost 50%. Both Empire and the Bruce family began to buy up the few remaining shares. They bid aggressively against each other. Speculators, too, began buying, and anyone short the stock must have scrambled to buy in. Almost nothing was offered for sale. The price was going up several points a day. Each morning, I was calling Abe for more margin—enough to buy in 100 shares at the price of the previous close plus 30% maintenance margin to protect us against loss should the stock continue up and Abe run out of money.

Because so little stock remained in public hands, the American Stock Exchange removed E.L. Bruce from the list of stocks approved for trading on its Floor. Trading then moved to the Over-the-Counter market—OTC. It was a thin market; few transactions, but skyrocketing.

Abe finally covered at around 125. His loss was about $10,000, certainly no fortune but as much as this young broker made in a whole year in the early 1950s.

The Bruce family lost control of their company to Empire and Mr. Gilbert. Afterward, Gilbert was convicted on some criminal charge. He fled the country and lived as a fugitive in Brazil. After some years, he returned to the U.S.A. to serve his term in jail.

That's an example of selling short because you're convinced the price is too high, can go no further and, logically, must start down as soon as you get off your short sale. Selling short a stock that's outrunning the market requires a good bit of ego, if not arrogance. Time and your money may run out before the trend reverses. Still, that's one school of thought among short sellers, sell at the high— as though anyone ever could know that a stock is at its high.

If ever you feel compelled to sell short a stock that's having a big move, be patient, wait for a sharp break, then continue to wait for the recovery—don't worry, it probably will come. Watch for the recovery to run out of gas somewhat shy of its earlier peak. If it stalls without making a new high, then make your short sale. With luck, you may be selling on a failed resumption of the advance. You might have a chance.

Instead of trying to sell at the top, some speculators prefer selling into weakness. Identifying a downtrend in its early stages, they hope for more bad news and accelerated downside momentum. I remember aanother short seller in the 1950s, who sold into weakness. It was during an economic recession. Steel demand was way down, mills were being closed and the stock market, of course, also was down. The stock of U.S. Steel had come down probably more than the market.

The client—how about Charley?—came in and explained to me

that U.S. Steel was going out of business. (Some 30 years later, that wouldn't have been a bad guess.) He instructed me to sell short 300 shares at around 35. Before entering the order, I remember asking, conscientiously, all the questions a good broker is supposed to ask of a client about to make a short sale. How much of a loss was he willing to take on the trade? He told me that he expected to lose nothing. Would he cover—buy in—and take his loss if Steel got to 50? Charley said that he'd get out long before that. I suggested an order—what we call a stop order—that automatically would buy him in should Steel trade as high as 45. Charley said that wasn't necessary, because he came in every day to watch the tape.

Although the recession continued and the economic news got worse, the market leveled off and began a slow, laborious recovery— up a bit one day, down a bit another, but quietly inching up. Charley finally covered at 70.

That's an example of selling short because you see how bad things are and assume that the downtrend never will reverse itself. But if you've gotten that confident, perhaps it's the bottom of the market—the wrong time to be selling.

That's the second school of thought among short sellers, selling into weakness.

A couple of things about short selling are worth noting.

In the early stages of a rising market, the advance is slow and gradual, just eighths and quarters of a point. If you're short, no single day causes you great alarm, so you're not apt to be panicked out. The unexciting uptrend, however, in insidious. Only after some time, when you might subtract your sale price from the current price, do you discover that you are in trouble.

The second thing is your risk/reward ratio. In neither of those two short-selling examples did the speculator have a chance of making more than five points, but their upside risks were more than three times that. Their risk/reward ratio was upside-down. To risk $1, they should have had a reward potential of at least $3.

Short selling can become rather expensive. Time, as you can see, is against the short seller. The longer he has the open short position, the more expensive it becomes—opportunity loss, no re-turn on his money, and paying out dividends. The short seller's got to make it fast or suffer the Chinese water torture. Now, let the price of the stock advance. The short seller's imagination becomes active. He can see the price rising to the moon and, to him, a ruinous loss.

Yes, speculators can make money shorting stock. Although I've never seen one walk off with a bundle, maybe it's because not many speculators sell short. But I wouldn't recommend it to you. What-ever money you might make on the short side wouldn't be worth the anguish you'd have to endure. If you must bet on the downside, you can limit your risks with put options, which we'll get into later on.

Simply buying and owning stock can produce enough emotional stress for most of us. Investing money that you know you'll need for something else, buying stocks on margin or selling short—all are emotional time bombs that surely will blow up just when you already have more trouble than you need.

And you mustn't count on your broker to lead you through the mine fields. He's there to do business. If you want to take a chance with next week's grocery money or go on margin or sell short, he won't refuse your order. So don't blame him for your losses. After all, it's your money.

>   >   >

Corners on the market have been rare in this century. In 1901, Jacob Schiff, of Kuhn, Loeb & Co., and E. H. Harriman, of the Union Pacific Railroad, began buying stock of the Northern Pacific to gain control of its majority interest in the Chicago, Burlington & Quincy Railroad. They were up against J. P. Morgan who was in Europe when he found out what was going on. Morgan viewed the Northern Pacific as his own railroad. But as neither Schiff nor Morgan owned 50% of Northern Pacific, they began bidding against each other in the open market. During one week, they drove up the price from 100 to 1,000. The shorts got trampled. Morgan and Schiff finally let them off the hook at $150 a share to avoid a national financial panic. And Morgan kept his railroad.

Thirty-six years before the E. L. Bruce battle, another corner on a stock had come out of Memphis. A local boy Clarence Saunders founded Piggly Wiggly Stores in 1919. Forerunner of supermarket chains, it was a great success and, in 1922, the stock was listed on the NYSE. Within about a month, a group of Floor traders launched a bear raid—first going short a whole lot of stock and then, to drive down the price, spreading rumors that Piggly Wiggly was about to collapse. Saunders, with the help of Jesse L. Livermore, proceeded to buy up all the floating supply of the stock to put the squeeze on the shorts. He succeeded so admirably that the NYSE Governing Committee stopped trading in Piggly Wiggly and suspended its rule requiring sellers to deliver the stock against their sales—"until further action by this Committee." That just about busted Saunders who ended up peddling Piggly Wiggly stock through local newspaper ads. Among the sights shown to visitors to Memphis is Saunders' home, the Pink Castle.

CHAPTER 20

WHEN THE MARKET GOES CRAZY

Hearing what sounds like a freight train passing through your backyard, seeing trees rise out of the ground and into the air, you know that you're in the midst of a tornado. That's not forecasting the weather. Hearing pandemonium from the Floor of the Exchange, seeing stock prices go crazy, you know that you're in the midst of panic or frenzy. That's not forecasting the market.

Although market extremes, even major market extremes, are not quite that dramatic, you know, nevertheless, that something extraordinary is happening.

Market extremes are recognizable. Whether panic at the bottom or frenzy at the top, you know that you're witnessing something climactic. At the bottom of the market, the shock that you suffer along with everyone else, and at the top of a market, the delirium that you enjoy along with everyone else—those feelings are unmistakable signals that you, too, are being swept along with a wild mob that has gone too far in the wrong direction.

Maybe you've been through it before. Maybe you've learned, the hard way, that your strong emotional reactions are treacherous, pushing you along with the crowd, in the wrong direction. If the crowd and your own emotions are carrying you headlong in the wrong direction, then the opposite direction must be the right direction.

But your emotional reactions to extremes are bad only if you allow yourself to be pushed along with the crowd. Your own reactions, recognized for what they are, can be useful to you as unfailing signals to stop, to apply common sense, to turn around, to go in the opposite direction—the right direction.

I'm not suggesting that you and I go against our emotions just to be different or perverse. Instead, you and I are admitting that we react in a fairly average way to what we hear and read of business and economic happenings. Everyone else who hears and reads is reacting to those same events at the same time and in much the same way. At the bottom of the market, we all agree that the worst is yet to come—and maybe it is—but most investors who want out already have done their selling. Who's left to sell? to push the market any lower? At the top, we all agree that the best is yet to come—maybe so —but most investors who want to get in already have done their buying. Who's left to buy? to push the market any higher?

During either panic or frenzy, you find yourself, emotionally, swept along in the direction that the market's moving. Everything that you hear or read is someone's attempt to provide a logical explanation of the illogical, to convince you that the present extreme now has become the new normal, the new standard—and all for the best of reasons.

Our own emotional extremes always occur at market extremes. If you're strong enough to go in the direction that is the very opposite of that to which you feel yourself pushed, you have a good chance of making money.

In the years of our lives when we are active investors, we get only three or four of the priceless opportunities provided by market extremes. I've seen four.

From 1946 to 1949, highest quality stocks were selling at P/Es of less than seven, dividends yielding more than 7%. For three years, an investor could have bought bargains. A dollar invested in 1947 was worth more than $16 at the 1987 peak—plus a 40-year flow of dividend income. But at the time, none of that could have had any meaning to me. I was too new to the business to recognize the extreme or to understand the rare opportunity. I believed all of those rational explanations of the irrational. But even if I could have understood what was going on, I had no money.

In 1949, the DJIA, at 162, started up and kept on going for 17 years, until 1966, just short of 1,000.

Another period of excess was in 1972 and '73 when blue chip stocks went out of sight. The market didn't follow. The excess was confined to that relatively small group of highest quality stocks, the Favorite 50 described earlier (Chapter 18, Ways You Can Buy Stocks). Young money managers, recently graduated from prestigious business schools, had discovered growth—growth of revenues, earnings and . . . stock prices. Growth stocks. With their yet untarnished MBAs, they confidently applied the new investment logic: buy stocks of companies that never will have a year of down earnings—only growth, forever. Price was of no concern. Their buying was so concentrated that prices and P/Es of the Favorite 50 soared. Sears Roebuck traded at nearly 30-times earnings. IBM, above 35-times. Eastman Kodak, close to 40-times.

What a wonderful time—fully invested, gloating over your profits. What a better time it would have been to have sold into the extreme.

The break came in 1973. And breaks come fast. Suddenly you're bagged. It's too late to get out—or so you think. Then it gets worse. From the 1973 top to the 1974 low, Sears dropped from 61 to 21—65%. IBM, from 91 to 38—58%. Eastman Kodak, from 67 to 26—61%. I owned all three and got out somewhere on the way down.

The third major market extreme was year end 1974. From a high of 1,052 in 1973, The DJIA bottomed out at 577 in 1974—back to the extremes of 7- or 8-times earnings, dividend yields of 6%, 7%. Nixon had been driven out of the Presidency, corporate earnings were falling, the country was in a recesion, OPEC had set off the first oil crisis, President Ford wore a lapel button with bold letters, WIN—Whip Inflation Now. What a dreadful time to own stocks and be faced with growing loses. What a wonderful time, therefore, to have bought stocks. From 577 in 1974, the DJIA topped out in 1987 at 2,700—and at 3,000 in 1990.

The fourth major extreme that I experienced was that 1987 top.

Except for my sketchy recollections of the late 1920s when my father was a full-time trader, I've never seen stock market speculation become a national mania attracting almost everyone with enough money to get into the game. The 1987 Crash, too, resulted probably from mania, but the players were mostly professionals investing the money of pension funds, mutual funds—and brokerage firms dumb enough to risk their own capital. Big volume also came from "risk arbitrageurs," buying and selling on inside information, and from "program trading." Yet the public had not come into the market.

Through the first nine months of 1987, stock prices zoomed, P/E ratios approached historical highs, dividend yields got dangerously low and book values were left in the dust. But for most companies, earnings estimates for 1988 and 1989, were up. Too, the investing public had yet to be drawn in. Reckless public buying almost always had signaled major market tops. But in 1986 and early '87, individual investors had shown little interest in stocks. Perhaps professional money managers had become the surrogates of a gullible public. I continued fully invested through the disaster of Monday, October 19.

The slide began from a high of 2,722. From mid-September, the DJIA dropped 200 points then recovered in early October. But the rally failed. From Wednesday, October 14, to the close Friday, October 16, the DJIA lost 261 points. In a single day, Monday, October 19, it fell 508 points to 1,738—almost 1,000 points, or 36%

from the high.

In the two months from August 21, the market value of my stocks dropped 25%. But what I lost was the profit I'd made during the preceding 12 months. Reflecting back, I'd been happy enough a year earlier, so for me the Crash was no major disaster.

I've earned no citations for meritorious conduct during market extremes. Yet I didn't sell out on the 1974 bottom, and I didn't go on margin to double up during the spike move of 1986-87. So I guess I could have done worse.

In the months before the top of the 1987 market, I would have become increasingly skeptical except for my fear that I would be getting myself into market forecasting. That's to say, I didn't differentiate between market forecasting and identifying a market extreme. Next time, I hope to do better.

A doctor friend once explained the difference between major surgery and minor surgery. Minor surgery is done on other folks. Major surgery is done on you—or me. And so, I suppose, an intermediate break in the market is when other folks lose money. A major crash is when you or I lose money. Minor or major, market extremes have the same characteristics.

Market cycles pass through somewhat predictable stages, blurring from one stage into another. Investor attitudes move across the entire spectrum, from pessimism or even panic at the low to optimism or even frenzy at the high. At a major bottom the P/E is eight or seven, dividend yields 6% or 7%, the DJIA below book value, the volume all but dried up, the news all bad. Having been mauled and clawed in the bear market, investors are wary. Conviction and confidence are gone. Many say to themselves, Never again. They take the pledge.

Starting back up, the market attracts little interest. Small daily advances go unnoticed. Prices begin to recover, not because of more aggressive buying, but because of less aggressive selling. Recoveries are slow and tedious. Only afterward, when we look back, can we see that possibly a bottom was made. Only after recovery is evident do investors begin to straggle back and, even then, only slowly, cautiously. Coming back into the market after a big break, they're looking only for a reasonable return on their money. Why take chances again?

As the market rises, investors begin to tell themselves, It wasn't all that bad; maybe I can make back some of what I lost.

Because of nagging skepticism, market gains, for a while, are suspect. We hear that the only way to make money is to trade, to take profits when you can. As time passes and prices improve, investors take a more long-term view: good stocks are bought to hold. Logical explanations are advanced to justify high prices, high P/Es. Speculative interest develops in stocks of small, obscure companies. Now is the time for investment bankers to bring to market stocks of new companies identified with whatever businesses or industries are in vogue at the moment. Every day, two or three new issues, IPOs, are snapped up by eager investors.

As a young broker during the 1950s, in the late, speculative stages of an advancing market, I remember telling a client to buy some new offering, a stock with a strange name. He instructed me to buy double the number of shares I'd mentioned and then, when I called back to report the trade, he said to me, "Tell me again. What's the name of that stock?"

That was alarming. Even at the time. Even to me. Something like that tells you that we're nearing the top. Sentiment has moved from fear to skepticism, to hope, then confidence—all the way from fear to greed.

At a major top, the DJIA P/E is above 20, dividends yield 3% or less, the Average is more than 2-times its book value, the volume is a source of great joy in Wall Street, news is all good—front page stories of new highs of the market. What then follows can be called a correction, a break or a crash. Whether a sudden drop or a long period of price erosion, the cycle is completed when everyone finally gives up hope of ever making money in stocks.

No one can forecast the market. And yet we can recognize market extremes, whether long-term bottoms or long-term tops. Extremes are products of public emotionalism, deep despair at the bottom, wild enthusiasm at the top—when all of us finally have become convinced that market direction will never change. We can recognize that sanity has given way to panic or mania.

I hope that I've convinced you that no one can forecast the market. Now, with the next breath, I'm telling you that you can know when the market is at an extreme. That's not a contradiction. Forecasting is the useless effort to penetrate the future, the unknown. Identifying an extreme is seeing and feeling the excitement, going on right now, all about you and recognizing the panic or frenzy as irrationality.

An investor once told me that whenever he had felt so pleased with his investment results that he patted himself on the back, he always could expect to have a sprained arm. That's a way of telling you that your most reliable gauge of excess in the stock market is your own emotional feeling. On the upside, making money seems easy. You want to lean back and let the good times roll. Your own feeling of euphoria is an early warning.

At other times, things can look so bad that only two possibilities remain: either the world's coming to an end or it's an opportunity to buy with every dollar you can rake up. It's so bad that if you lost all your money, that money would be worthless anyway. Yet if the country staggers back, if the world continues to rotate, you've hit it big. It's a time at which the risk/reward ratio is so favorable, so compelling that you must go against all of your instincts, all of your emotions and take your chances—little or nothing to lose, everything to gain. The time of greatest fear also is the time of greatest oppportunity.

Although occurring at intervals of sometimes many years, market extremes are recognizable. Perhaps you can profit from one of those rare opportunities—if you have the courage and the money. Surely, you can avoid the mistake of acting upon your own emotional inclinations. Periods of panic are not the time to sell. Periods of frenzy are not the time to buy. The rules of the game don't change: buy low, sell high.

CHAPTER 21

LEARNING THE HARD WAY

Hanging around the local farmers' market for a few weeks, you and I probably would learn a good bit about how produce is bought and sold, how some buyers and sellers make more money than others and how some get taken and others don't. In any marketplace, the practicalities of moving merchandise in and out result in customs peculiar to that market. But with no experience at a farmers' market and unfamiliar with the practices, you and I soon would discover that we were buying and selling fruits and vegetables at not the best prices. Although I can only suppose that's true of a produce market, I know it's true of the stock market.

Buying and selling stocks for myself, I apply a few practical lessons that I learned from hanging around the marketplace. Maybe some of what I've learned can be useful to you.

Large Orders

Anyone would know that the larger an order—the greater number of shares of a single stock bought or sold on the same order—the more likely that order will be executed at a price that's not quite as good as the preceding trade. The only trouble with that morsel of wisdom, however, is the word large. What's large?

In your newspaper, look at yesterday's 10 or 15 most active stocks. Whether buying or selling, a single order of several thousand shares of any one of those stocks probably wouldn't move the price more than a eighth of a point, 12 1/2 cents a share. Yet a single order, buy or sell, of the same size but in an inactive stock could be executed more than half a point or 50 cents a share away from the last transaction. That's just a fact of life. Large, therefore is relative. In any stock, a buy or sell order for maybe 5% or 10% of yesterday's volume is large.

On the other side of your large trade, most of the time, will be a market-maker, either a Stock Exchange specialist or an Over-the-Counter, OTC, dealer. When you buy, he sells; when you sell, he buys. The market-maker is out there to make money for himself. He's trying to make the spread, trying to buy on his fractionally lower bid and then sell on his fractionally higher offer. He'd like to make a nice, fat spread on every in-and-out. Supervision by the Stock Exchange or, in the OTC market, competition, limits that opportunity, however, and keeps market-makers reasonably honest, tends to narrow the spreads and protect you and me from bad executions—not always, just most of the time.

Limit Orders and Market Orders

Because I try to own no more than half-a-dozen stocks, usually of major corporations that are active traders, my orders are somewhat large. But I've never entered a limit order. That is, I've never specified the only price at which, or better than which, I'm willing to trade. Instead, I always instruct the broker (and I trade only with a large, reputable firm) to enter my order for execution at the best possible price. That's called a market order.

If I've made up my mind either to buy or to sell, why quibble over a fraction? Limiting the broker, when buying, to some maximum price, I might miss out on a big winner. And if I didn't think the stock's a big winner, why am I buying it in the first place? Limiting him, when selling, to some minimum price, I might be left, high and dry, with a loser. And if I didn't think the stock's a loser, why am I selling? Whether buying or selling, maybe I could get a better price by waiting, but I don't know that. I do know that I've made up my mind. So what am I waiting for?

Most clients enter orders only at limit prices, limit orders. Perhaps they're too concerned with paying up an eighth or a quarter and forget that stocks are bought to double one's money—not overnight, but in time; not always, but that's our hope.

GTC Orders

Some clients enter limit orders away from the market and good-till-cancelled. To me, that suggests they'll buy only if something bad happens and the stock collapses, and sell only if something good happens and the stock takes off. They must want to buy losers and sell winners. I prefer market orders. But remember, I deal only with a large firm with a reputation for good executions.

Entering Orders at the Opening, at the Close

Throughout the day, most stocks trade in orderly fashion. Rising or falling, prices move in small fractions, small steps up or down. On the New York Stock Exchange, the specialist, who's the market-maker, is required by Exchange rules to make "a fair and

orderly market." Between trades, if the price change seems excessive, a Floor official almost immediately appears to require of him
an explanation. In spite of an occasional gripe I'd get about the price
of an execution, I seldom felt that the client had been treated shab-
bily.

It's at the opening of a stock, the first trade of the day, that the
price can be at a wide gap from the previous close—even though
subsequent trading sometimes will fill that gap. I always suspected
that the specialist was allowed to get away with more at an opening,
that he exaggerated the effect of maybe a small imbalance of buy and
sell orders and whined to the Floor official about having to step up
to take the opposite side of the unmatched orders. Buying or selling
for myself, I avoid entering orders for execution on the opening. I
prefer that my trades be among the more orderly succession of
trades throughout the day.

Also, I avoid entering orders toward the close. In the rush to get
off trades during the final 20, 10, five minutes, lots of wild things can
happen.

Probably you have been wondering, why enter a large sell order
all at once? why not feed it out in small pieces? Because the
persistence of your selling would cause the market-maker to become
nervous. Not knowing how much stock he's about to be hit with, he'll
drop his bid after each trade. And if you're entering buy orders, one
after another, the market-maker will begin to wonder whether a
large buy interest is about to push the stock way up—remember, if
you're buying, he's got to sell, even if he must go short. He starts
raising his offering price after each of your trades.

Stop Orders

Around 1955, some professional dancer—yes, a dancer—wrote
a best seller on how he'd made millions trading stocks. According to
his story, he had beat the market by use of stop orders to limit his
losses and protect his profits—to take him out at the earliest
beginnings of price reversals.

Sounds great, you say. So what's a stop order? you ask.

Assume that you own 100 shares of stock trading on the NYSE
at 50. Let's say you just bought it at 50. You think it's a good speculation, but you don't want to lose more than 10%. That's five points
or $500. Or maybe you've owned the stock for some time, you have
a nice profit, but you don't want to see it drop back more than five
points. Whether limiting a loss or protecting a profit, you'd enter an
order, good-till-canceled, to sell at 45 stop. Your brokerage firm
gives that order to the NYSE specialist to whom the stock is
assigned. In his "book," under the price of 45, he records your order

as a contingency which says to him, "The first time this stock trades at or below 45, sell me out, on the very next trade, at the market."

That makes a lot of sense, you say. So what's the hitch? you ask.

If your stop is too close to the current price, if you're a bit too cheap or a bit too clever, you're within the trading range, within the area that any stock moves up and down during a week or a month in which nothing special happens. And that normal price fluctuation triggers, or "elects," your stop and takes you out. Getting the stop too close, you won't give your stock a chance to go up.

But if your stop is down at the level that would suggest a reversal and the beginning of a down trend, it's probably so far below the market that you'll be risking more than you're willing to lose. You might as well just sell out now and forget it.

Place stops too close and you get whipsawed; place stops far enough down to be outside the trading range and you get no protection. And then too, stops sometimes don't work. A stock can gap down, through and way below the stop—usually overnight, from yesterday's close to today's opening. Here's what can happen.

Again, assume that you entered a sell stop at 45, that the price has drifted but never has touched 45, that last night's close was 46. Before the opening, the company discloses that it's in default on its bonds, close to bankruptcy. Before the opening, a flood of sell orders hits the Floor, and the specialist opens the stock at 38, down eight points. That trade elects your stop at 45. You're sold out on the next trade, which might be even lower than the 38 opening.

The dancer's book, nevertheless, popularized the use of stop orders, and specialists' books became filled with sell stops at every fraction of a point below the market. In some stocks, minor price dips would set off stops that, in turn, would set off stops at the next fraction down, like a package of Chinese firecrackers.

To provide for orderly markets, specialists had to be buyers, even though they could see more stops on their books, all the way down. On the American Stock Exchange, a rule was adopted to permit entry of only stop-limit orders. A stop-limit provides almost no protection, because when elected, the sell order is entered, not at the market, but at a limit price the same as that of the stop. If bids are all below that limit and dropping, the stop never gets off.

A few years after his book appeared, the dancer admitted that the only money he'd ever made was either as a hoofer or as an author; that he'd never made money in the stock market.

Buy stops, too, are used. Speculators, who believe that charts of past price movement can be used to foretell the future, place stops above the market to buy at some level they've identified as a breakout on the upside.

Stops may be okay for traders. How they lose their money makes little difference, for lose they surely will. And anyone dumb enough to sell short ought to enter a buy stop to limit his loss. Otherwise, I'd use no stops.

Cycles

The stock market moves in cycles, up and down. A lot of time has been spent and, probably, a lot of money lost by persons who have tried to find in those repetitive ups and downs, a method of forecasting the market. Their efforts always have been, and always will be, frustrated by the duration of the next cycle and the extent of its swing, from top to bottom to top. No one can predict how long a cycle will last, how high it will go, how low it will go. Cycle theories, therefore, have been useless in market forecasting.

Reaction to News

News can impact the market in ways that sometimes seem perverse. Occasionally, you can read in the morning's paper an announcement of a big increase of a corporation's earnings. You own the stock. Pleased to be holding a winner, you eagerly turn to yesterday's stock market prices. Although the market was up a bit, your stock was down on the day. Hell fire, what kind of game is this anyway?

The explanation is reasonable. That big improvement of earnings had been widely anticipated. For several months, analysts had been raising their earnings estimates. Management had been confirming those higher estimates. Buying in the stock had been aggressive. The price had run up. Now comes the earnings announcement that you read. Some stockholders who had wanted to sell, for whatever reasons, had been holding off. Some speculators who had bought into strength saw nice profits. Those folks sold on the news. The stock dropped a fraction.

In the same way, the market can go up with the announcement of bad news that's been widely anticipated.

News that comes as a surprise is a different story.

From Denver, on Saturday, September 24, 1955, a spokesman for the Eisenhower Administration told the press corps that the President had become ill. A few hours later, the nation was told that Eisenhower had suffered a heart attack. Investors, most of whom, always, are Republicans, saw that as bad news—not because of their affection for Ike, but because of what they feared would happen to the economy and the stock market. Responding, not to throbs of the heart, but throbs of the pocketbook, investor thinking ran like this:

A Republican Administration is good for the economy and the stock market. A Democratic Administration is bad. [Stocks, however, had doubled during the Truman Administration, not too bad.] *Democrats control Congress. Apart from Eisenhower as a candidate to succeed himself, no attractive Republican hopeful is waiting on the bench.* [Vice President Nixon, interestingly, was not seen as Presidential quality.] *If Ike can't run for a second term, Republicans haven't a chance, the economy will falter, and the market can go only down.*

For two days, Saturday and Sunday, with the market closed, every investor had opportunity to reflect upon the news and those implications. Almost unanimously, they arrived at the same decision: sell out before the crowd panics. Individually, independently, everyone made his decision to get out at the opening on Monday.

On Monday, around 8 a.m. when I got to the office, phones were ringing. Sell. Getting their orders in early, the sellers assumed that they'd come out at prices around Friday's close; that other investors wouldn't wise up until the market began to fall. A great idea, except that everyone was doing the same thing at the same time—500,000 sellers trying to get through the same door. (That, incidentally, was one of the rare times when a seller should have entered a limit order, naming the minimum price he was willing to to take.)

On the other side of the market, about the only buyers were the NYSE specialists, some with limited capital. In those days, no institutional buyers were out there with bushels of pension fund money.

At 10 a.m., the market opened, but openings were delayed in many stocks. Specialists, trying to attract buyers to help them out, were announcing the sizes of order imbalances on the sell side. As they began to see the huge quantities of stocks they'd have to buy, many specialists left the Floor to scurry around the Street in search of bank loans. They came back to argue with Floor officials about the prices at which they'd open their stocks—the prices they'd be paying for the stock they'd have to buy for their own accounts. As buyers, they wanted to open their stocks at prices way below Friday's closes. Many openings were down five points or more. Some specialists didn't open their stocks until a minute before the close—hoping, I suppose, that fears would subside overnight. Some specialists couldn't open their stocks at all on that Monday.

Tuesday, although not quite so hectic, was a repeat of Monday. Afterward, we learned that many specialists at the close Tuesday had committed all their capital and had exhausted all their credit; that another down day would have put them out of business. That would have crippled the Exchange and the entire securities market. At the opening Wednesday, however, the storm had abated, and in the weeks that followed, the market recovered.

The moral of that story is that investors who sell with the crowd probably will come out at the bottom—or who buy with crowd, will get in at the top.

Now, let's review the situation of the NYSE specialist, the stalwart who was buying all that stock. He did pretty good for himself. Do note, however, that he was the guy who set the price at which he would open his stock—the price at which he would buy. He fought for approval to open at as low a price as he could. He was out there to make money. Yes, he took big risks, but the lower he could open his stock, the greater his opportunity for profit.

So the rule is, don't sell with the crowd. The corollary of that rule is, go with, not against, the NYSE specialist. If he's forced to buy, he'll open his stock—he'll be a buyer—at a price that he thinks will be low enough to let him out in a few days at a profit. If it's on the upside, he'll open his stock—he'll be a seller—at a price high enough to let him buy in his short position in a few days at a lower price, at a profit.

On November 22, 1963, it happened again. It was during market hours, on a Friday. President Kennedy was assassinated in Dallas. During the week before, right wing Dallas crowds had spit on Adlai Stevenson, the despised liberal. Was the assassination part of a plot to take over the Government?

Sell orders flooded the Floor. More responsible specialists got permission to stop trading, but some dropped their bids to unconscionable levels to buy in stock being sold out of panic. The specialist in RCA, I remember, allowed the price to drop from something like 21 down to maybe 14, where he bought. Monday was a day of National Mourning. Exchanges were closed. On Tuesday, those stocks that had been allowed to sell down so drastically reopened at prices right back up where they had been trading before the news flashes on Friday. The NYSE slapped a few wrists, but offending specialists kept their profits.

Stock prices adjust gradually to news anticipated over a long period of time. Prices react violently to the unexpected. Don't get caught in the crush.

Crashes

Stock market crashes are different. Behind the dam of investor confidence, the level of stock prices rises until pressure ruptures the dam to release the deluge. Market excesses preceded the Crashes of both 1929 and 1987. In '29, individual investors, frantic to get aboard for the ride that would put them on easy street, had borrowed as much as 90% of the cost of purchases and pushed up stocks to prices that never could have been supported by even the wildest expectations of earnings gains. Rational persons who took the risks of buying probably were telling themselves, The price I'm paying makes no sense. But next week or next month, someone even more reckless will pay even more, and I can get out with a profit. That's what Bob Farrell* calls "the greater fool theory."

When the '29 break came, brokerage firms had to protect their own capital. They were in hock to the banks from which they'd borrowed money to finance margin lending to their clients. Clients whose accounts were under water got calls, maintenance calls, for immediate deposits of additional funds. Few could come up with the money. Most were sold out. Those forced liquidations added to selling pressures, setting off something like the chain reaction of a latter-day nuclear explosion.

Before the '87 break, corporate raiders, financed by sales of junk bonds, had bought out entire companies, paying twice going market values. Often in collusion with the raiders and their investment bankers, "risk arbitrageurs," as they generously described themselves, jumped in early. Takeover targets and rumored takeover targets were bid up further by public speculators. Adding to volatility was "program trading," which we'll get into along with futures trading.

Neither the Crash of '29 nor that of '87 was triggered by a single, momentous happening. The Crash of '29 seems to have been the precursor of the Great Depression of the 1930s. In 1987, that association of Crash with Depression was frightening to the public, most of whom never owned a stock, and to political leaders, some of whom couldn't have gotten reelected had the economy turned sour. Was the market sending out the same signal in 1987 that it did in 1929? It had happened before. Could it happen again? More fearful than market losses was foreboding anxiety. What is the market telling us? Depression? Deflation? Elimination of debt by inflation? by repudiation? Two years afterward, most of those fears were forgotten, and the market recovered its losses.

Although only 10 years old in 1929, I can remember the Crash. I knew that my father was trading on a 10% margin, that he was taking big risks. I knew that he had weathered the first day, that he was sold out on the second. He told my brother and me that he was broke. At our house, the Depression started early.

On October 19, 1987, I was 68 years old. I owed no money. I was unhappy about the Crash but not distressed.

---

*Robert J. Farrell, the super-star market technician of Wall Street.

Although many clients got sold out, margin liquidation in 1987 had nothing like the snowballing effect that it did in '29. The initial margin requirement, for some years, had been 50%. Yet, the Federal Reserve Board's Regulation T allows many artificial credits to buying power, and many clients were down to the 30% maintenance level. On the days following the break, some of those clients were sold out. Unsecured debits in some of those accounts could not or would not be paid off, and brokerage firms had to take the hit. The big losses, however, were in accounts of trusting souls who had let their brokers get them short put options. And in '87, heavy selling came from "program trading" of big brokerage firms and pension funds that sold stocks and simultaneously bought index futures. Later on, we'll get into all of that in some detail.

In the '87 Crash, on Monday, the bad day, NYSE stocks closed down five, ten, 15 points—and more. But there was a market. Sellers could sell.

How about the OTC market? Well . . . that was something else again. In an active OTC stock, dozens of dealers make a market. Their bid and ask prices appear on the NASDAQ* screen. National Association of Securities Dealers rules require market-makers in an OTC stock to continuously display their quotations, the prices at which they are committed to buy or sell a minimum, in those days, of only 100 shares. In the Crash, some dealers, according to newspaper stories, simply let their phones ring. Others withdrew their quotations and accepted the NASD penalty of having to remain out of the market in those stocks for 48 hours. Those dealers, you may be sure, were laughing up their sleeves. Afterward, I was told, that apart from two large brokerage firms, few dealers maintained continuous bids. Some probably would argue that it was impossible, that the system wasn't working, that they hadn't the personnel to answer their phones. Well, maybe not.

The NYSE did somewhat better. About half the specialists, market-makers, were out there on the Floor throughout the day, books in hand, buying the stock being thrown at them and paying something, even though down several points from Friday's close and gapping down on successive trades. Those specialists took the gas. And when prices bounced back on Tuesday, surely some got out okay. I hope they made money. Remember that on Monday, when often they were the only buyers in a panic market, those specialists

---

*National Association of Securities Dealers Automated Quotations system to which all dealer members subscribe and from which they trade OTC stocks among themselves.

didn't know that prices would be up on Tuesday. They bought, they supported the market, they took their chances.

The other half of the specialist cadre, however, earned no medals for gallantry in action. During the day of the Crash, about one third of NYSE specialists sold more stock than they bought. And some ended the day with net short positions. Instead of maintaining fair and orderly markets, those guys were tossing kerosene on the fire.

The NYSE, nevertheless, congratulated itself on having done a splendid job under trying circumstances.

Although the NYSE specialist system worked, it's an anachronism dating back to the 1920s and earlier. The system might operate more effectively if at least two competing specialists were assigned to make the market in each stock on the Exchange. And whatever capital the NYSE requires specialists to maintain, it probably is not nearly enough. Perhaps the big, well-heeled brokerage firms ought to be out there making markets, but the employee of a corporation is no risk taker. Specialists get the job done because they're buying and selling with their own money. They survive only by their wits. They take risks, of course, but only for the opportunity to profit. However selfish their drive of personal gain, they serve a public need. They are buyers of last resort, the flimsy safety net beneath public ownership of U.S corporations.

If you're in the market when a Crash comes, there's no getting out. Reported prices lag transactions by as much as an hour or two. You don't know whether your stocks are going up or down. The price at which your market order might be executed could put you in shock. If you're a believer in the Crash and Depression sequence, you've got to hang on, scared as you will be, to wait for the bounce back, to sell into strength. You can only hope, meanwhile, that the specialist system continues to function.

In the summer before the 1987 Crash, I took comfort from the low, 3% or 4% rate of inflation, the absence of broad public speculation and the strong estimates of earnings for the coming two years. Although the current P/E of the DJIA was about 20, estimates of 1988 earnings of individual companies, almost across the board, were up 25-to-30%—and for '89, another 25-to-30%. Even with stock prices at record levels, earnings gains of that magnitude would pull down those lofty P/Es to bargain levels. But it was the drop in stock prices that first cut the P/E—down to 14 after October 19. Although I couldn't have known whether a Depression would follow, whether earnings would disappear, I did feel that 75% of the damage was behind us and that I could ride out the remaining 25%.

Before the Crash, I was betting that the major trend would

continue up. Was I forecasting the market? Not really. I just didn't believe that all the elements of excess had developed.

Several months after the Crash, in 1988, I began to wonder whether the market was telling us something. I decided that, for me at age 69, making a lot of money was not as important as the possibility of losing a lot of money. For me, it wasn't a good risk/reward ratio. I sold off about two-thirds of the stocks I owned. If we were going to have another Depression, I wanted to have enough money to see me through. I hadn't forgotten the 1930s.

Those earning estimates for 1988 and '89 did prove accurate. Earnings rose about 75%. Even with stock prices at new alltime highs, soaring earnings in 1989 brought down the DJIA P/E to 13. And so I participated in the recovery only in a modest way.

Avoiding the Obvious

As a broker, I learned that the toughest stock to sell to our clients often was the best buy, that the easiest sale often was a loser. Last year's big market leader always was easy to sell. If oil stocks had been the big gainers, recommending an oil was the easy way to do business. Yet, once a group has been widely exploited in the market, once the party's over, that group can be dead for years.

Too, a stock that had come down after a big run up always was easy to push: "Just last year, this stock was selling at double today's price." Investors are eager to believe in a repeat performance. It just doesn't happen.

It's also easy to recommend the stock of a secondary company that's in the same business as the booming industry leader. Investors always were ready to jump on "another IBM" in its heyday. There was no other IBM.

You'll hear obvious stories that make it easy for you to buy obvious stocks. Seldom will those stocks be good buys. Stocks that are colorless, of companies that are colorless, are tough to get excited about. Yet sometimes among those stocks you find your best buys.

Discretion

It is my opinion that any investor who allows his broker to exercise discretion has lost his mind.

So what is discretion?

For your account, your broker, as your agent, can enter buy and sell orders only as you specifically direct. You must tell him, buy or sell, what stock, number of shares and whether at a price limit or at the market.   Straightforward—your stock, your money. As an exception to that, NYSE rules allow a client to authorize his broker to exercise discretion, to take market action on his judgment alone, to buy and sell without the client's instructions to do so. The client signs the brokerage firm's form which, in effect, turns over to his broker complete control of his account and absolves the firm of any responsibility, any liability for losses. To provide some sort of oversight, Stock Exchange rules require that an officer of the firm, before the end of the day, initial every discretionary order that has been executed—after the close, after the fact, after the damage has been done.

Most discretionary orders, however, are entered without that written authorization. The broker and his client have some loose, oral understanding. Not that it makes much difference, for with or without written authorization, the client's money probably will be lost. The signed form serves only to protect the brokerage firm against suit for damages.

Every month or so the NYSE publishes a summary of disciplinary actions taken against members and member firms, their officers, registered representatives (brokers) and employees. Most of those actions are against brokers for misbehavior. Most of the misbehavior is the unauthorized entry of orders (discretion) and excessive trading (churning). Brokers guilty of unauthorized discretion and churning have siphoned off their client's money by over-trading to generate commissions.

To be given discretionary authority, a broker must convince the client that he will make money for him. Yet that broker is not paid for making money for his clients. He's paid for the volume of commission business he can generate. The selfish interests of the broker collide with the selfish interests of the client.

When a broker decides to enter a discretionary order to buy or sell in the account of his client, whose interest does he serve? Sure, he doesn't want his client to lose money. And sure, he'd like for his client to make money. But that broker has got to do business. If he doesn't do business, he doesn't get paid. Don't you suppose it's easier for that broker to find a reason for entering the order than to find a reason for not entering the order?

I must ask, furthermore, what's so urgent that the broker can't phone his client to get approval before entering an order? For my own account, I've never had a transaction that I couldn't have executed one week earlier or one week later with just as good results.

Years ago in Macon, a client asked one of my brokers, "Why is it necessary for you to call me before every transaction? I always go along with your suggestions."

The broker's answer was illuminating. He said, "Before calling you on a recommendation, I make notes from which to explain the reasoning behind my conclusion. In having to do that, I sometimes discover that the reasoning doesn't support the conclusion. That's the call you don't get from me, the transaction you don't make. If instead, I were to take market action entirely on my own, I'd lose the discipline of having to prepare a logical presentation. Then I'd find myself making knee jerk decisions."

During my 25 years as an office manager, I never allowed a discretionary account. That's not to say that none of my brokers ever took unauthorized discretion. I'm sure that some did. In the few instances that turned up, I fired the broker.

Clients, however, can be the bad guys in cases of unauthorized discretion. Some clients are unprincipled. They encourage the broker to exercise discretion and, to recover any losses, make him the fall guy. Annually, I spoke to my brokers about discretion. This is the talk I gave.

> Never does a year pass but what I hear almost the same story of a broker's being released for entering orders not authorized by his client. Probably, you're aghast, and properly so, that a a broker could be so witless as to jeopardize his career by entering discretionary orders. Never has he anything to gain. Always he has everything to lose. Each of those tragedies has a seemingly innocent beginning. A client tells his broker to sell a stock during the day at a time of his own choosing, to "watch out for things" during the client's absence of two or three days, or "Why didn't you go ahead and buy it anyway? you know it would have been all right with me." The client feeds the broker's ego. It's so easy but so insidious. The broker enters a few discretionary orders and suddenly finds himself responsible for the account. He's trapped. The client begins to confront the broker, accusingly, for not making trades, and activity in the account picks up as the frantic broker tries to hit a winner. But losses increase. Finally, the client, who from the very beginning wished to avoid responsibility for his own decisions, now seeks to transfer responsibility for his losses. Heads, he wins; tails, we lose. He goes to the office manager or writes to our New York office. His profession of shock with respect to his losses is exceeded only by his disbelief that his broker, without authority, could have entered orders for his account. What about the confirmations mailed to him on the day following every trade? Oh, those. Why, he never saw them. His secretary forwards them, unopened, to his

accountant. And the monthly statements? Also forwarded unopened to the accountant. Yes, the client's a crook, but the broker takes the gas. The broker is discharged, and a record of wrongdoing plagues him for the rest of his life. As for the client, he collects from us his losses. That's what he had in mind all along.

Discretion is the exercise of your own judgment with respect to any portion of an order.

Security: The client must decide what he wants to buy or sell. Quantity: The client must specify the exact quantity. Price: The client must give you either a limit order or a market order. Time: You must enter the order immediately.

And all of that applies to the cancellation of an order. You cannot take it upon yourself to cancel an order. The client must give you instructions to do so. Either you have an order or you don't have an order. There's nothing in between. As you receive an order, write it out, directly on an order form. Read it back to the client. Check his account on your CRT screen to ensure that we have his money for a buy, his stock for a sell. Enter the order immediately. When you receive a report of execution, promptly call the client to report the trade, promptly post the trade to the client's holdings record. Here, you will catch any error or misunderstanding, and we can take immediate corrective action. A broker who enters a discretionary order is subject to immediate dismissal.

In some rare instances, market action must be taken without instructions from the client. Say you're in the midst of a switch from one security to another when prices change abruptly, a judgment must be made about the order, but you canot contact your client. When you may find yourself in the dilemma of being unable to serve your client's best interests without exercising discretion, bring to me your hot potato. With you, I'll try to determine your client's probable wishes. If I'm reasonably confident of his intent, I'll instruct you to act accordingly and initial your order. If a dispute arises, I am the responsible person—not you. You are completely insulated from any criticism or blame. Any loss that we may have to take is my loss, not yours. As a broker, you can't ask for a better deal than that. You're not paid to worry. I am. Let me do the worrying. You do the business. Never enter a discretionary order.

Discretion is bad business for everyone. I'd suggest that you have a clear understanding with your broker: before entry, every order must be authorized by you. Ask your broker to read back your orders. If ever your broker enters for your account an unauthorized order, go immediately, in person, to the manager of that office. Demand that the transaction be taken out of your account. Ask that your account be assigned to another broker. And if the manager seems less than shocked over the incident, take your account to another firm. A broker who exercises unauthorized discretion is either a fool or a crook.

Errors

Brokerage firms make their brokers pay for the costs of their errors. Although I can imagine that a weak manager, at the demand of one of his big producers, will make an occasional exception, an error comes right out of the pocket of the responsible broker. For you, that's important to know.

A few years after I retired, I was visiting with a friend. His phone rang. He picked it up. Sitting there in his office, I had to overhear, whether I wanted to or not, his side of the conversation.

"Ben Evans . . ." Pause.

"Yeh, great, Mike. How 'bout you?" Pause.

"You mean we bought more ABC than my cash balance will cover? Uh-huh . . . Well, you know, it's in my retirement account, and I've already contributed as much as I'm allowed for this year." Pause.

"Well, I guess you're right, we'll have to sell something. But I hate to let go of XYZ. It's been my only winner." Pause.

"Yeh, Can't go broke taking a profit. Okay, sell the XYZ. That'll pay for the ABC." Pause.

"Yeh . . . yeh. You, too."

Hearing just the client's side of that conversation, any broker could tell you what was going on and, during each one of those pauses, what was being said on the other end of the line. Would you like to hear both sides of that conversation? Although this, of course, is all surmise, I can tell you, almost exactly, what happened. First, let's go back several days earlier.

My friend's broker must have heard something about ABC. Maybe nothing sensational but, at least, an idea. To do business, we all need ideas. He flips through his loose-leaf book of clients, sees the holdings page of my friend's account and phones him.

After hearing the story and the suggestion that he buy probably 1,000 shares, my friend may have said that he didn't have the money just now. The broker then must have noticed the next holdings page, that of my friend's retirement account.

"Ben, I hate to see you miss out on this one. Why don't we buy it in your retirement account? . . . Aw'right, I'll pickup just a couple of hundred." And to himself, *Not much of a ticket, but just like bad breath—better than no breath at all.*

As it's noontime, Mike gets up from his desk to go to lunch and, over his shoulder, says to his sales assistant, "Buy 200 ABC in Ben Evans' retirement account." So much for that.

Five days later, two days before settlement date, Mike gets a notice from the cashier. Ben's account needs $6,500 to pay for the ABC purchase. *Rats,* or some other four letter word, *I've over-bought—and in that damned retirement account. What was the stock again? Oh, yes, ABC. What's it trading at?* Hits it up on the quote machine. *Down two points. Wouldn't you know. Why didn't I check the balance in that account before I entered the order?* What follows is the broker's review of the situation.

If only it were up two points . . . I could tell the manager that it's my error, let him transfer the trade to the firm's error account and sell it out. That'd give me a $400 credit against my cost of errors for the month. However . . . it's down two points, and I'll get stuck $400 for an error on a stinking 200-share trade. Maybe I can get Ben Evans to sell something else out of that account to pay for the ABC. If he asks about ABC, I can tell him that two points don't matter when we're in for the long haul. I hope he doesn't squawk too much . . . and for me, another commission—not much, but not bad.

Mike the broker then calls Ben the client. Now, we'll hear both sides of that conversation.

Ben: "Ben Evans . . . "

Mike: "Hello, Ben, this is Mike. We've got a big market going here today." *Up a point on the Dow, but better than down a point.* "How're you doing?"

Ben: "Yeh, great, Mike. How 'bout you?"

Mike: "Nothing like a bull market. Oh, by the way, you know that 200 ABC we bought? I just heard that we need $6,500."

Ben: "You mean we bought more ABC than my cash balance will cover? Uh-huh . . . Well, you know, it's in my retirement account, and I've already contributed as much as I'm allowed for this year."

Mike: "That's okay, I can handle it. We should have sold your XYZ anyway. I don't like the way it's been acting. At today's price, it will more than cover the $6,500."

Ben: "Well, I guess you're right, we'll have to sell something. But I hate to let go of XYZ. It's been my only winner."

Mike: "We can't let ourselves fall in love with a stock. Besides, nobody ever went broke taking a profit."

Ben: "Yeh. Can't go broke taking a profit. Okay, sell the XYZ. That'll pay for the ABC."

Mike: "Nice to talk with you, Ben. So long."

Ben: "Yeh . . . yeh, you too."

Mike hangs up the phone and to himself says, *Whew, I wiggled out of that one.*

Ben doesn't know it but that foolishness just cost him $400 and, if XYZ keeps on going up, maybe a lot more.

The blame and responsibility for a market loss error are either yours or those of your broker. If it was your fault—wrong quantity, wrong stock, wrong price, buy for sell, sell for buy—you'll be required to enter an order to correct your error. The loss, and the commissions, will be charged against your account.

If an error was your broker's fault, he must pay the cost. After all, he's supposed to be the pro. If he tries to hang the cost of his error on you, he's dishonest. Get another broker.

Sell recommendations

In 1949 when I transferred from Corpus Christi to Atlanta, I found myself working for a Southern gentleman, humped at the shoulders, one leg shorter than the other, jowls that could quiver with indignation—a delightful old rascal who managed the office.

He and half the sales staff were survivors of the 1929 Crash and the '32 Depression. Their way of doing business was to ingratiate themselves with the client, talk nonsense until they were able to determine that the client inclined toward either buying or selling, and then gently pushing him in whichever direction he was leaning.

We young boys had been junior officers in WW II, had been trained in New York for six months and would have been affronted to have been called salesmen. In fact, brokers were called account executives, which was okay. We answered the phone and tried to sound knowledgeable.

Doc, our manager, had sales talent, not too polished but nonetheless effective.

In those days, the firm occasionally would offer a block of stock to be priced and sold after the close—a secondary offering. The announcement of a secondary would be made sometime during the day, and we'd begin phoning our clients to suggest purchase. In talking to the prospective buyer, the advantage that we'd emphasize was that he wouldn't have to pay a commission, that he could buy at a net price.

As it turned out, of course, any good stock at that time was the investment opportunity of a lifetime. Through those years, however, everyone was afraid of the market, and it took a lot of phone calls to move 100 shares of stock. That, on top of our poor salesmanship, put some of the burden on Doc, who was concerned with the sales performance of the office.

Seeing that we weren't doing such a hot job on an offering, Doc would prowl the boardroom, seize some sitter by his lapels and tell him, "George, I got a money-maker for you. It's a stock you gotta own. I'm gonna put you down for a couple hundred shares." And sure enough, a few sitters would find themselves buyers.

Every now and then one of our offerings would take a temporary beating in the aftermarket, and one of those boardroom buyers would walk up to Doc to voice his complaint. Doc would listen only long enough to learn that he was about to be called to account. Then, as though distracted by some more important matter, he'd stare right through the client to a distant horizon, lift his right shoulder, turn to the left and, without a word, limp on off.

You could see Doc leading the buyer down to the shore, helping him into the boat, giving the boat a shove out to the middle of the lake and then walking away. How the buyer ever got out of the boat was entirely his own business. And 35 years later, I found that still descriptive of the brokerage business.

Almost everything we hear and read about stocks is buying. What to buy, when to buy. Seldom do we get a recommendation supported by reasoned logic to sell.

Often the sell recommendation that an investor does get comes from a weak broker who is calling, not to save his client from loss, but to offer another investment. The broker, probably a bit more interested in making a commission for himself than making money for his client, anticipates that the client may not have cash immediatley available to buy more stock, so he takes it upon himself to find the money. How? Before calling, he goes through his list of the client's holdings, mumbling to himself, "What can I get this guy to sell?" Among the stocks that the client already owns, he's looking for one about which he can say something negative. He finds it and phones the client.

"Mr. Alston, you know that EFG we've got? It looks to me like it's getting ready to top out. I think we should take our profit and run. And by the way, our people in New York have come up with a great idea, JKL Corporation. Maybe you've heard of it. I really like JKL. I think we ought to sell your EFG and buy JKL." (You couldn't know how many times I heard a broker's side of that conversation.)

The only reasons for selling EFG is to buy JKL. The client, therefore is taking, not one, but two risks. The stock he buys may go down, the stock he sells may go up. Switching from one stock to another is good business for the broker, risky business for the client. A decision to sell one stock and a decision to buy another ought to be taken separately. Each decision ought to made on its own merits.

In more casual conversations with investors, I've heard, many times, "My broker tells me when to buy but never tells me when to sell." And that's a valid complaint, not only against brokers but anyone who thinks he's some sort of investment professional. One explanation may be that most of us tend to be optimistic and want to believe that a bad situation will get better—even though experience teaches that bad situations usually get worse. Furthermore, a broker, just as anyone else, would prefer to be the bearer of glad tidings, rather than bad news.

Another explanation is that brokers, in their dealings with investors, learn early in their careers that the surest way to lose a client is to sell him out of a stock just before it starts up. Investors can handle a drop in price after they've bought. In fact, they seem almost to expect it. But after they've sold, if the price goes up, the broker is never forgiven. As a small investor myself during the early 1950s, I had such an experience. As I was my own broker, however, I had no one to blame but myself.

I had bought 100 shares of McDonnell Aircraft (later, McDonnell Douglas) which looked like it might get a big Air Forces contract for a fighter aircraft. Shortly afterward when the stock had advanced a few points, the Federal Reserve Board raised the margin requirement for all stock purchases. Great market forecaster that I was, I was certain that the market would sell off on that news. I thought it would be smart to get out of McDonnell, let the market pull back, then buy back at a lower price. I sold my stock. The market, however, didn't do what I wanted it to, and McDonnell never dropped even a fraction. So I was left standing there, money in hand, waiting for the pull back that never came. Every day, watching McDonnell go higher, I developed a digestive disorder from hydrochloric acid pumping into my stomach. If I had sold on the recommendation of a broker, I never would have done business with him again.

Suffering the wrath of a few clients because of his sell recommendations, a broker soon decides that his remaining clients will have to come to their own decisions to sell. During the rising market of the 1950s and '60s, almost every sale of a stock later proved to have been a mistake. Finally, all of us, brokers as well as investors, were convinced that nothing, ever should be sold. That, of course, marked the top of the market.

Apart from having to raise money, a decision to sell—an investment decision—is made because of an adverse change of the company's fortunes or because the price of the stock has gotten unreasonably high or because the entire market has gone crazy.

An early warning of a company's business reversal can be the stock's price—not the absolute price, such as down two dollars on the day, but the price of the stock relative to the entire market. Whether the market is going up or down, how is the stock performing in relation to the market? If my stock is up 2% but the market is up 7%, I must ask myself, Why isn't my stock participating in the market's advance? is anything wrong? If my stock is down 2% but the market is down 7%, the price decline of my stock is not a reason to become distressed. In fact, my stock is looking pretty good in a bad market.

That's called relative strength, how a stock did in relation to the entire market.

I determine relative strengths of stocks I own by comparing end of week prices with prices of six weeks earlier. Every Saturday morning, I divide the closing price of each stock by its price of six weeks back. That gives me a percentage figure. If it's over 100%, the stock, of course, has advanced since six weeks ago; under 100%, the stock has declined. I do the same thing with Standard & Poor's 500 Stock Index—last week's close divided by that of six weeks earlier. That percentage figure tells me how much the entire market changed during the six-week period.

Then I list my stocks in descending order of six-week price performance—best performer at the top, poorest performer at the bottom. To see which outperformed the market and which underperformed, I draw a line between those with a percentage figure higher than the S&P and those with a percentage figure lower. The entire exercise takes only 10 or 15 minutes.

In anticipation of good news, a stock goes up; and in anticipation of bad news, it goes down. Price, therefore, can be the earliest indication that some buyers or some sellers believe that some change of the company's fortunes is in the offing. That's not to say that it's always the insiders taking advantage of non-public information, although that does happen. More often, somebody out there believes he knows something not yet appreciated in the marketplace and not yet reflected in the price.

Relative strength tells us that some persons are taking aggressive action in response to something they see or think they see happening. That aggressive action almost always is obscured, however, by the price action of the entire market. Comparing percentage figures of each stock with that of the S&P 500, you get relative performance: against the entire market, how did my stock fare? better than the market? or worse than the market?

With respect to each stock below the S&P percentage, I ask myself, "Why has this stock fallen behind the market during the past six weeks?" Each stock above the the S&P, "What's causing this stock to outperform the market?" Reasonable explanations, most of the time, come to mind. But sometimes I have no answer. If the stock has dropped below the S&P, I suspect undiagnosed disease. What do I do?

I'd ask my broker's assistant to fetch up on her CRT screen the firm's research opinion of the stock and read it to me. Research opinions, however, can lag the news. Maybe the analyst is out of town or hasn't decided whether the news is good or bad. Next I'd ask the assistant to punch up news retrieval for latest company happenings that might tell me something I didn't know.

Whatever I might learn, I'd ask myself, Why did I buy this dog? What looked so good about the company? Do my reasons for having bought it still make good sense? What's the analyst's earnings estimate? his projection for earnings growth for the next five years? What's the P/E based on estimated earnings for next year? How does that compare with the P/E of the S&P 500? If I didn't own this stock but instead had money in my hand, would I buy it now? If yes, okay. If no, maybe I should sell it. And if so, should I bail out now or wait, hoping for a bounce back? What does the firm's technician say?

To get relative strength figures, I could subscribe to some sort of service. Computer services will show relative strengths graphically, charts of stock prices as moving averages for 27 days, 93 days or just about anything you want. The cost of such a service might be reasonable in relation to the value of one's stocks. But writing down prices, looking back to prices of earlier weeks, dividing prices on my $6 calculator and ranking the stocks as to performance allows me to reflect upon one stock at a time. What happened? Why? I make no conscious effort to concentrate, but I do. Doing small things yourself, for yourself, has some magic value that doesn't come with the service you may buy, regardless of how expensive or sophisticated.

When it comes to selling a stock, you're pretty much on your own. Nothing too frightening about that, so long as you're not expecting someone else to give you the sell signal.

➢   ➢   ➢

In any marketplace, you see people shouting, running, haggling or just sitting or standing, appearing totally indifferent—people who are there only to make money. Although not above making money off one another, the regulars of a marketplace are there to make money off visiting buyers and sellers. As visitors of the marketplace, you and I ought to know enough about the trading practices to keep the regulars from making too much money on our infrequent trades.

CHAPTER 22

SPECULATING AND TRADING

Speculating

A few days after Billy P. died, in the mid-1960s, his broker, who had been my partner in earlier years, was anxious that Billy's family be told about his account with us. We were holding big positions in eight or 10 stocks against which was a sizable debit balance. Billy always had been heavily margined. After he discovered that he was stricken with cancer, however, he had sold off a good bit of his position to cut back on what he owed. Still, he owed a lot of money.

I doubt that many persons knew that Billy was rich, that he had made it speculating. Upon Billy's death, my old partner hoped to get the executor of his estate qualified without delay to become responsible for the account. Not to upset the widow or daughter, he phoned the daughter's husband to suggest that their attorney be instructed to move things along as quickly as possible. He explained, "The reason for urgency is the size of Billy's debit balance. He owes us two million dollars."

Long pause.

Then the broker realized that unwittingly he had scared hell out of the poor son-in-law. He apologized for not first having told him that the market value was more than $7 million, that the equity was over $5 million—lots of money, especially in the mid-1960s.

Billy was a salesman for Blue Plate mayonnaise. He was good. You have to be good to sell mayonnaise. But you don't get rich selling mayonnaise.

He once told me that he and his wife, as a young married couple during the Depression, were able to save a few bucks every month and had kept currency, $5 and $10 bills, squirreled away between the pages of some books around the house. I don't know how he became interested in the stock market. But he said that when he first decided to buy a stock, he shook those books by their covers to let the money fall out and took off for some brokerage office. Afterward, when his wife found out about it, she wasn't too pleased. He was on his way, however, in a parallel career that eclipsed his success as a mayonnaise salesman.

One of my earlier recollections of Billy was in 1949. He'd made an arrangement with one of our boardmarkers to save for him the Standard & Poor sheets that she otherwise would have discarded when new, updated sheets came in. That S&P service consists of several loose-leaf volumes of sheets describing the companies that trade on the NYSE and the American Exchange. On each company, there's a single sheet: on the front, comments on current company happenings; on the back, a description of the business, its capitalization, and a 10-year statistical history of sales, expenses, profits and so on—lots of numbers.

What did Billy want with a handful of out-of-date statistical sheets? He was looking for something. And he knew what it was. He had reasoned that a marginally profitable company with relatively large dollar sales or revenues and with a relatively small number of shares of common stock stood a chance of making a lot of money— a big jump in profits. It works this way. Large dollar sales divided by a small number of shares, results in large dollar sales per share. But poor profit margins produce per share earnings that are little better than break-even. And yet if that profit margin—the percentage of sales that the company retains as earnings—can be improved only slightly, the profit on those large dollar sales, of course, would improve. A big jump in earnings per share could result in an enormous rise in the price of the stock.

A good example was the stock of Armour & Company that Billy loaded up on during the late 1940s. My figures are approximate, or worse. But as neither of us could benefit from a search of records several decades back, let's just say that my figures are hypothetical.

Armour slaughtered beef cattle and sold carcasses, a business that must require little technical or managerial skill. To get into the business, no great capital investment would be necessary, so local slaughterhouses must have given Armour stiff competition. Armour, nevertheless, did a dollar volume of business that, for the time, was large. Let's say that annual sales were $300 million. Assume that its number of outstanding common shares was 600,000. Dividing sales of $300 million by number of shares, 600,000, you get $500 worth of sales for each share of stock. The stock sold somewhere around $5.

That was what Billy was looking for, large per share sales and a low profit margin. On its per share sales of $500, Armour's per share earnings were only 50 cents. That's only one tenth of one percent on every sales dollar. Wretched results.

Calling on grocers and going into stores, Billy saw that Armour was beginning to sell cuts of meats in convenient, attractively wrapped packages for which housewives were willing to pay premium prices. He saw, too, the profit potential.

Even with no increase of sales, if Armour could improve its profit margin by only one tenth of one percent to two tenths of one percent of sales, earnings per share would double from 50 cents to a dollar; that if profits on sales of $500 per share could ever get up to just one percent, earnings would be $5 a share, which could push up the price of the stock to maybe $40 or $50—again, even with no increase in sales of $300 million. Not too much to ask of fortune.

How about that for securities analysis? Could anything be more simple? And the real beauty of Billy's logic was that it worked. He made a killing in Armour. He sold out when Wall Street analysts were discovering what a great buy Armour was. That's when Billy began accumulating stock of some other company with a bleak outlook.

Perhaps you'll argure that Billy wasn't speculating, that he was investing. As it worked out for him, Armour was a successful investment. But when he bought it, a down-and-out company barely profitable, he'd have told you that he was speculating.

The last time I saw Billy, I had come from Macon to Atlanta for the weekend and went by to see him at Crawford Long Hospital. Lying in bed, he was thin and gaunt, but his eyes sparkled with excitement as he told me of some stock he had been studying. Suddenly, he sat upright on the edge of the bed, his legs dangling over the side and, with a great big smile, told me, "This is probably the best long-term buy on the New York Stock Exchange." He died about a week later.

Certainly, there's nothing wrong with speculating—if you know what you're doing. Billy P. had applied simple logic to his selection of stocks. He took big chances, but he could see the even bigger profit potentials. He used his common sense. I recall how patiently and respectfully he would listen to anyone's opinions. He bought and sold, however, only on the basis of his own reasoned judgment.

Yes, other persons can give you useful information and, sometimes, well supported opinions, but your reliance can be only upon your own convictions. It's your money. No one else can be as concerned about your money and your investments as you.

Another speculator I knew during the 1950s was David G. Retired, he had been a salesman of various products to independent drugstores. Of druggists whom he knew around the city, he made continuing inquiries as to which prescription drugs seemed to be catching on with the doctors, and he asked about new drugs that were being developed or tested. During that time, antibiotics were being sought for the many types of viral infection. For a drug manufacturer, a new antibiotic could mean a sudden surge of sales and profits. The stock market, of course, anticipated any jump of earnings, and David did his best to anticipate the stock market. He, too, applied simple logic. He was observant and self-reliant. He believed what he saw and had the courage to take market action.

David never had the patience to hold a stock long enough for the big move that comes once a significant change is widely recognized. Each time, something that looked a little better would come along, and he couldn't resist switching. When occasionally I'd chide him for selling a good stock to buy something else, David would say, "If you want to make an omelet, you've got to crack a few eggs."

He was one of the most delightfully funny men I've ever known. Simply for your amusement, let me relate a story of one of David's trading capers. It was back in the mid-1950s, a different world, when a day's trading volume rarely exceed two or three million shares.

For whatever reason, David had become enamoured of Superior Oil of California. The NYSE symbol was SOC. The trading range had been, roughly, from $400 to $700 a share. I believe it was the highest priced stock at that time on the Exchange. David loved high priced stocks. For himself, he had bought 100 SOC and had urged his wife's brother, a well-to-do shoe merchant in St. Louis, to buy 100. Sitting at my desk, David called Sam, his brother-in-law, and talked him into buying it. So that I would have instructions direct from the client, Sam, David handed the phone to me. Sam said, "Buy me 100 shares at whatever price David tells you to pay."

In those days, you could get a quote, bid and asked prices, only by sending a request by teletype to New York. But in this thinly traded, high price stock, I needed to know, too, the size—how many shares were bid-for and how many offered. So on a quote pad, I wrote, "QS SOC 756 AT." That meant, "Give me both quote and size on Superior Oil of California." The 756 identified me as the broker; AT, the Atlanta office. To get the size, one of our floor brokers had to go out on the NYSE Floor to the Post at which SOC traded to make inquiry of the specialist who made the market.

The exact prices, I don't remember, but the spread between the bid and ask was more than 100 points, $100 a share. So let's say that it was 490 bid and offered at 600. The size, I do recall, was only 100 shares on each side—100 shares bid-for, 100 offered.

For his own stock, you should know, David had paid something less than the current 490 bid.

David said to me, "Buy one hundred shares of Superior Oil of

California at five hundred dollars a share." He said it just loud enough for everyone in the boardroom to hear. David enjoyed the attention of the sitters who came in to watch the tape. By upping the prevailing, 490 bid to 500, David was hoping to attract a seller. I entered the order.

At that moment, then, SOC should have been 500 bid-offered at 600, our bid.

Waiting about five minutes, we asked for another quote-size. The bid, to our surprise, was not our 500, it was 510. Another buyer was in the market. He'd jumped our bid by 10 points. For David, the chase now was on. He called out to me—and to him I was always General, several grades higher that I'd ever held in the Army— "General, bid five hundred and twenty dollars for one hundred shares of Superior Oil of California." Again, we waited a few minutes and, again, got a quote and size. Again, our bid had been topped by 10 points. Now, it was 530 bid, still offered at 600, 100 and 100.

We went to 540. The other bidder immediately went to 550. We bid 560.

By this time, we had attracted around us something of an audience. The quote came back 570-600. We bid 580 and once more asked for a quote. It was 590-600, 100 to buy and 100 to sell. The 590 was the other guy's bid.

David's voice dropped almost to a whisper. "Maybe I shouldn't do this, but for my account, General, *sell* a hundred SOC at the market."

David's own sell order hit the competing, 590 bid. He cancelled Sam's buy order for 100 at 580, and went home several thousand dollars ahead. His parting remark: "Hardest money a union man ever made."

I still wonder whether that other bidder, after paying 590 for David's stock, quoted the market. I would have bet that it was back to 490 bid-offered at 600, 100 and 100.

What is speculating? From what I saw over the years in the marketplace, speculating to one person can be investing to another. Even though they might buy the same stock on the same day at the same price, if the one person commits more money than he can afford, he's speculating; if the other commits only a reasonable part of the money for which he has no foreseeable need, he might view himself, and properly so, as investing.

The distinction probably goes beyond what a person can afford in terms of money. To say that a person is speculating or investing, I'd have to know what the person can afford emotionally. To some persons, the mere thought of owning stocks is upsetting. To them, owning any stock, any quantity, any quality, would be speculating.

So who is a speculator? Each person probably would have to answer that for himself, about himself. If he's comfortable with the securities he owns, if he has confidence in those securities and can tolerate the ups and downs, I'd say that he's an investor. If he's overextended, hoping for a large profit in a short period of time, I'd say he's a speculator. But again, I must believe that whether one is a speculator or an investor depends upon one's own view of himself.

And what is a speculation? Once more, there's no satisfactory answer. An executive with a small, struggling, obscure company may have put every dime he's got into the stock of that company and feel that he has provided for the security of his children and grandchildren. Perhaps he has. Anyhow, he sees the stock as a safe investment. You and I, however, might see it as too risky a speculation, even in a modest quantity, for us.

Do speculators buy high risk, low quality stocks? Not necessarily. Often blue chips outperform the market. A major company can be in the early stages of an earnings turnaround, attracting the buying interests of large institutions. The stock may have broken out on the upside of a trading range of many months past, attracting the interests of speculators. Although investors could be buying as a long term holding, speculators could be buying with hopes of a quick run up. To speculate, you don't have to buy garbage. Probably most speculators do, but I'd prefer to stick with the blue chips.

Do speculators buy just low priced stocks? No, but again, probably most speculators do. A speculator with any sense, however, is more interested in the potential for percentage gain on his money than the number of shares he owns.

Do speculators always buy on margin? Most do, but not always. Borrowing half the cost of a purchase doubles the possible gain— and doubles the possible loss.

Do speculators trade actively, in and out? Smart speculators don't. As I see it, speculating can be both rational and profitable. Trading is neither.

Speculators may be just aggressive investors. And I'm sure you've heard the cynical definition of a speculation: it's an investment turned sour. Speculating, in my view, is deliberately accepting higher risk for what appears to be a reasonable chance of extraordinary profit.

Most would-be speculators that I watched were one-time buyers of hot tips they'd gotten—usually hearsay—from some self-styled wizard, a boss two levels up, a friend's rich uncle. Although I never saw one make money, they really weren't speculating. They were hoping to hit the bug—as some folks down here refer to the numbers racket.

Trading

Speculating is not trading. Some speculators make money. Nobody can make money trading. Trying to catch near-term market moves is impossible. Traders buy and sell on emotion, which means they buy high and sell low. On every trade, moreover, they lose the spread, the difference betwen the bid and ask. And unless they're members of the Exchange, they must pay a commission on each transaction, buy and sell.

Here, probably you are asking, "Don't Floor traders on the Exchanges make money?" They answer is that they do, but they aren't really traders. They're more like market-makers.

On every Exchange where stocks or options or futures are traded, market-makers and traders are on the Floor ready to take the other side of public orders to buy and sell—bids and offers made by open outcry by Floor brokers of wire houses, or commission houses, acting on behalf of their public clients. As you know, the NYSE calls its market-makers specialists. On the Chicago Mercantile Exchange and the Chicago Board of Trade, the traders are called locals. Over-the-counter (OTC), every trader is a market-maker.

By whatever name, market-makers and traders, all day long, are out there, willing to buy at a fraction below the last sale and willing to sell at a fraction above the last sale. On every in-and-out transaction, they're trying to make the spread, the difference between the bid and asked prices. To keep from getting caught on the wrong side of an abrupt change of market direction, they're in-and-out rather quicky. Some try to leave each day with no open position—neither long nor short.

Competition among Floor traders tends to make bids a bit higher, offers a bit lower. Although they have the single purpose of making money for themselves, their buying and selling produce incidental benefits to the investing and speculating public. Their trading narrows those spreads, cushions sudden price fluctuations and results in more orderly advances and declines. Your orders and mine, in consequence, are executed at prices nearer the last sale. I'm not telling you that traders and market-makers are a bunch of swell fellows, only that their scalping activity enhances liquidity of the market, an unintended benefit, as grazing cattle fertilize a pasture.

Making the spread is not trading. It's shooting fish in a barrel.

Trading—guessing what's going to happen next, trying to beat the market—is no way to make money. Any good retail broker who's been through a complete market cycle, who's seen clients trying to trade, knows that they never had a chance and never will.

The great mayor of Atlanta during the 1930s, '40s and '50s, William B. Hartsfield, for whom the airport is named, had a realistic view of trading. Occasionally, he'd come into our office down on Pryor Street to talk with his broker Jack M., a portly gentleman who, incidentally, had been a WW I pilot. Knowing that Jack was somewhat sensitive, the mayor, sitting at Jack's desk one day, said just loud enough to be heard by everyone in the boardroom, "Hellfire, Jack, I'm not asking for much. If I could just break even, I'd think I'd made a killing."

Our traders never made money. Not the little guy who traded odd lots (less than the 100-share trading unit); not the well-heeled fellow who traded 1,000-share multiples. It was hopeless. Neither client stayed with us for long.

Yet many banks and brokerage firms will trade markets with their own capital. In whatever market—money-market instruments, foreign currencies, bonds or stocks—the more volatile it gets, the more attractive the trading opportunity appears. In a way, I can understand that a banker might feel the need of diverting excitement, for banking is such a drab business. But brokers . . . ? With all their other, uninvited, daily calamities?

You would think that some banker or broker with an adult mind would ask whether, elsewhere, at any time in the past, in any of the markets, money ever has been made trading.

Why do firms engage in such foolishness? Ego, I suspect. The CEO, probably as naive as any odd-lotter, feels his machismo image enhanced when he can talk about "our trading account."

So what happens? Same old story. If an individual can't make money trading, how can a brokerage firm, trading for its own account, improve its gambling odds by increasing the size of its bets?

A firm will give trading authority to some fast talking flash and turn over to him millions of dollars of its capital. The young man— and he's always a young man, inexperienced and fearless—is told that he will get a cut of the profits. But he does not share in the losses. He's encouraged to be reckless. He exceeds the dollar limits that the firm has set, loses enough to hurt the firm badly and gets the blame for the poor judgment of the firm's management.

Having seen and talked with some of those traders, I've asked myself the question, Would I let this guy trade with my money? Not on your life.

Except crooks who pay bribes for inside information, anyone who thinks he can make money trading is a simpleton.

CHAPTER 23

THE OPTIONS MARKET

For you and me, stock options, whether puts or calls, long or short, covered or uncovered, can do nothing good. Stopping here, both of us could save a lot of time. Knowing something about options, however, you may be less susceptible to the suggestion of some broker that he can make you rich with puts and calls.

Almost everyone is familiar with an option on real estate. You've heard, "He's got an option to buy that property." Although the prospective buyer and the property owner have agreed upon price—$500,000, let's say—the buyer wants to delay closing until he's certain of being able to go forward with his plan for development. Perhaps he must arrange for financing or acquire contiguous land. He needs time. But he can't let the key piece of property get away from him. Would the seller allow him time to put it all together? Ninety days?

Well, at the price, the owner is ready to sell. Yet, to be tied up for 90 days? What if, meantime, someone else is willing to buy the property with no strings attached? And even pay more? Suppose a new commercial development for the area is announced?

"No," he says. "I can't tie myself up for three months. You've got to make up your mind."

So the prospective buyer offers the owner possibly $10,000 for a 90-day option. The owner reckons his chances of getting a better bid and the length of time his property will be off the market. He concludes that even if the sale falls through, he'll be ahead the $10,000 and still have his property. He accepts.

Within those 90 days, whenever the buyer may wish to close, the owner must sell at the agreed upon price—even if the value of the property has doubled. The prospective buyer, however, is not obliged to close. If he wishes to buy, the price to him is guaranteed for 90 days, after which his option expires and becomes worthless. If he decides not to buy, he can walk away, forfeiting his $10,000.

That's an option to buy real estate. It's just about the same as an option, a call option, to buy 100 shares of stock. In the securities business, we'd refer to the $500,000 as the "strike price," the $10,000 as the "premium" paid for the option, and we'd call the seller of that option—the property owner—the "writer."

With call options on stocks, you can be a buyer, betting that the underlying stock will go up; you can be the writer of a call, betting that the stock will remain below the strike price—so that the option you've sold will have no value, will expire without being exercised, and so that you can keep your stock as well as the premium.

As the stock underlying a call option goes up above the price at which the call can be exercised—above, that is, the strike price—the call gains in value. As an example:

If you own a call with a strike price of 30 and the stock is at 35, you can exercise the call to require the writer to sell to you 100 shares at 30. Then you can turn around and, in the open market, sell that stock at 35 for a profit of five points or $500, less commissions— and don't ever forget commissions.

Instead of exercising, you could sell the call itself, probably for more than $500, which would be a price of 5. The longer the remaining life of the call, the more it's worth, because there's more time for something good to happen to the stock. In the price of that call, anything above the intrinsic value of 5 represents the time-value—what buyers are willing to pay for the chance that the underlying stock might go higher than 35 before the call expires.

A put option is the mirror image of a call option. Whereas the buyer of a call can require the seller or writer to sell the stock to him at the strike price, the buyer of a put can require the seller or writer to buy the stock from him at the strike price. As the stock underlying a put option might go down below the price at which the put can be exercised—below the strike price—the put gains in value. As an example:

If you own a put with a strike price of 30 and the stock is at 25, you can exercise the put to require the writer to buy from you 100 shares at 30. If already you don't own the stock, you either can buy 100 shares at 25 to deliver or instruct your broker to borrow the stock and go short the 100 shares with the view of buying-in later. That put option, therefore, has an intrinsic value of 5 or $500, less commissions.

Just as with a call, instead of exercising the put, you could sell the put itself—probably for more than 5. And again, the longer its remaining life, the more the put is worth, because there's more time for something bad to happen to the stock. In the price of that put, anything above its intrinsic value of 5 represents the time-value— what buyers are willing to pay for the chance that the underlying stock might go lower than 25.

Speculators trade in options in the same way they trade in anything else. They buy with the hope that the price will go up, and they sell with the hope that the price will go down. Reacting to their emotional peaks and troughs, options traders, as any other traders, buy at the tops and sell at the bottoms. In the options markets, the only consistent winners are the Floor traders who take the other side, buying and selling to make the spreads, and the brokers and brokerage firms that collect the commissions.

That's enough to know about options, until . . .

Your phone rings. You answer. Some young man who identifies himself as an options specialist with some brokerage firm asks for a few minutes of your time to explain how he can guarantee you a return of 15%. Because you're not quick enough to say no thanks and hang up, you begin to hear something about a program for writing covered call options on stocks—a low-risk strategy developed by his firm.

When you hear "program," you are on notice that you are about to be led into a scheme that, automatically, creates in your account a large number of transactions that generate a handsome volume of commissions for that young man. Whenever you hear "strategy," you may expect a glib explanation of a brand-new, risk-free method of making a lot of money, something for nothing.

You know better, but your greed is aroused, and you say to yourself, No harm in listening. Don't be so sure. That young man's presentation anticipates every question. It sounds so good that you want to be convinced. And you never ask yourself, "Why isn't everybody participating? Why have I been selected for this rare opportunity?" Instead, you ask, "What's a covered call writing program?"

Within the hour, that young broker is sitting in your office. After a brief exchange of pleasantries, he gets right down to business.

Broker As I mentioned to you on the phone, my firm has developed a covered, call option writing program with a proven record of giving our clients a return on their money of 15%, every year, year after year. The only risks they take are the ordinary risks of investing in stocks. A study dating back to 1926 has shown that the annual return from owning stocks has been only 10%—and that's both dividend income and price appreciation. [True, by the way.] Compared with that, the risk- free 15% of our program sounds pretty interesting, don't you think? [Get the prospect moving his head up and down.]

Prospect I suppose so.

Broker We both know that the price of a stock can do only three things. It can go up. It can go down. It can remain the same. Right?

Prospect Right.

Broker Well, our strategy lets you make money no matter what the price does.

Prospect Sure 'nuff?

Broker Assume you own 100 XYZ. At last night's close, XYZ was 52. An option to buy 100 XYZ at 55 closed at 2 1/2. That option expires in October, three months from now. As an option to buy, it's a call. We speak of it as the October 55 call. At any time during the next three months, the trader who paid $250 for that call can require the seller, the writer, of that call to sell to him 100 XYZ at 55. Suppose you were the writer. You would have been paid $250 to sell your stock at 55, three points higher than XYZ closed. Wouldn't you be willing to sell stock $300 above the market?

Prospect You bet.

Broker Well, that's what happens when your stock goes up. Your 100 XYZ is called at 55. You're paid $5,500, a $300 profit. And for the privilege of calling your stock at 55, remember, the buyer of that call paid you, up front, $250. Writing just that one call, you've made $550. Not bad, huh?

Prospect Dynamite. Then what?

Broker We immediately buy back the 100 XYZ and against it sell another call. But now let's see what happens if XYZ either goes down or stays the same. As before, we sell an October 55 call. For that call to have any intrinsic value—for that call to be exercised against you—XYZ has to be trading above 55. If XYZ stays below 55, the call you've sold will not be exercised and will expire worthless. We keep the $250 premium and write another call, take in another premium. So no matter what XYZ does, we keep on writing calls and keep on pulling in that premium income.

Prospect But who would pay $250 for the call?

Broker Oh, traders and speculators who think they're getting a nice ride without putting up the cost of the stock or who don't have $5,200 to buy 100 XYZ.

Prospect How do I know what stocks to buy, to sell calls against?

Broker   Now . . . that's one of the attractive features of our program. You just put up cash, $50,000 or $100,000. Our research department tells us what stocks to buy—their list of winners. [Why not just buy those red hot winners, keep the stocks and forget the options?] Another way, is to deposit with us stocks you now own. Probably, we can write against them.

Prospect   What about dividends on the stocks?

Broker   Hey, that's the good part. You keep all the dividends. The buyer of your call gets no dividends.

Prospect   Suppose the stock market keeps on going up. What happens?

Broker   Sometimes we may have to buy-back calls at a small loss, but we turn right around and sell another. We roll up. We buy-back the 55 call and immediately sell a 60 or 65 call. And in a rising market, the premiums get wider. Instead of $250, you'll find yourself being paid $400 and $500 for that call. The most important thing to remember is that you must stick with the program. You can't let a few small losses scare you out. That'd be just the time when we start making money. Our clients who are successful in the program are those sophisticated enough to stick with it. They're willing to accept that 15% return. We call it getting rich slow. [I'm about to sell myself on this.]

All buyers of options, however, aren't dummies. They'll pay a pretty good premium for a call exercisable at a price close to the current market. They'll pay only peanuts for a call exercisable at a price, say, 15% or more above the market. So to get worthwhile premium income, the writer must be willing to get called—to sell his stock—only a point or two above the market. Also, he must realize that commission expense eats up premium income and profit on sales of stock. Commissions are charged to sell the call and to buy it back before expiration, to buy the stock and, if called away, to deliver the stock.

In a rising market, a writer of calls can expect to make only a fraction of what he'd have made if he'd never heard of covered call writing. In a rising market, a writer of calls is standing on the sidelines. He's out of the market. He's not a player, he's a spectator. Only after he's missed the market does he catch on.

In a falling market, a writer of calls participates fully. The stocks he owns fall in price along with all the others. And as call buyers lose interest in trading, writers see premiums shrink. Premium income does little to cushion losses in stocks owned.

To me, it appears that a call writing program will deny you the opportunity to make money in a rising market but leave you fully exposed to losses in a falling market.

Moreover, a program of selling calls against a diversified portfolio of stocks can produce, in time, disastrous investment results. Whenever one of those stocks might begin a strong, extended advance it's called away, and the writer has little enthusiasm for buying back that stock at a price much higher than the strike price at which it was called, and sold. To buy back that stock requires more money, the equivalent of the profit he would have made had he never written a call. To himself, the writer says, "But why dwell upon that?" And to his broker, "Let's stick with the program okay, but let's buy some other stock that won't require more money."

Persisting in a covered call writing program, you'll discover that you've gradually gotten out of every stock that showed promise but continued to own and continued to write calls against every stock that lagged.

Sell the winners and keep the losers? Isn't that the reverse of what we should be doing? Yes, in time, you would own stocks of only troubled companies. Your market losses on the stock portfolio would exceed all of the call premiums and small profits.

The bad news doesn't stop there. Somewhere along in the program, the broker tells you that ratio writing would double the premium income you're taking in. Ratio writing? Yes, instead of selling just one call against 100 shares, you can sell two calls, or even three—one covered, one or two uncovered.

Why not? That's why we got into this, to produce income—and commissions for the broker.

So against your 100 XYZ trading at 52, you sell not one call but three, strike price 55. Overnight, XYZ announces that it has agreed to be bought out by another company. XYZ stockholders will receive $70 a share. All three of your short calls are exercised. Against one call, you deliver your 100 shares of stock and receive, not $7,000 but $5,500—100 shares times the 55 strike price. To deliver 200 shares against your remaining two, uncovered or naked calls, you must buy stock in the open market. Only now do you understand that all along, in effect, you've been short 200 shares of XYZ. To buy in the stock costs you 200 times $70 which is $14,000. But when you deliver those 200 shares against the two naked calls, you receive only $11,000—200 shares times $55, the strike price. Loss, $3,000—and commissions.

Thus if you had written no calls but simply kept your 100 XYZ at 52 and sold it at 70 on the buy out, you now would have a profit of $1,800. Instead, you took in premiums of $750 on the three calls you sold at 2 1/2 and lost $3,000 buying in 200 shares at 70. Total loss, $2,250, plus lots of commissions to your deserving broker. Ratio writing. Some program. Some strategy.

Another way of earning premium income is to sell calls against stock that you own as almost a permanent investment. A business associate once told me of his having engaged in a program of selling covered calls against stock of the firm for which we both worked.

After a big move to 46 in 1972, the stock had dropped to 6 1/4 in 1974. For the next seven years, it had traded between 12 and 44. From 40 in 1980, it had drifted and in 1982 was back to 21 or 22. During that decline, my friend had been selling calls against his stock and picking up premium income as the calls had expired worthless. At Thanksgiving, 1982, when I saw him at Sea Island, the stock was around 40. He'd just thrown in the towel, bought back the calls he had sold, lost more than all of the premiums he'd ever taken in and was hanging on to his stock. Lucky that he did.

In mid-1983, the stock hit 106, up about five times over in 12 months. If he'd kept on with the call writing program, he'd have made nothing as he watched his stock climb to 106.

It's easy for a broker to persuade you to believe that you're foolish to sit on a stock that's going nowhere. Why not rent it out and get paid the premiums? Enticing, but when you do, you're out of the market. What you would have made on the advance of your stock, you lost as it was called away at prices way below the market or when, at big losses, you bought back the calls that you'd sold. And how the hell did that smart young man know that your stock was going nowhere?

The reason for owning stocks is to make money. Why own stocks then deny yourself the opportunity for profit if the market goes up? If you decide for any reason that the market is too dangerous for you, just sell your stocks and get out.

From 1982 to 1987, the DJIA more than tripled—from about 800 to 2,700. As the market rose, clients in covered call writing programs found themselves looking on from the sidelines. Patience with their brokers was wearing thin. For options strategists, it was a time of crisis. The clients were not sticking with the program. A change of strategy was indicated.

> *Broker*   [Phone rings] Options specialist.
> *Client*   [Prospect in earlier conversation] Everybody's making money in this market except me. Why the hell am I fooling around with this call writing?

Broker Uh, I was just getting ready to, uh, call you. Our people in New York are recommending, uh, modification of our, you know, strategy. Instead of, I mean, writing calls, we're beginning to see very good opportunities in puts. Writing, you know, puts. Our people project 3,500 on the Dow by year end. The public's still scared of the market—they're always wrong—and they've become buyers of puts as insurance against a sell-off. The buyer of a put pays a nice premium to be able to sell his stock below the market. What we'll be doing is writing (selling) puts and collecting those nice premiums. In this market, puts are expiring worthless every month. It's like taking candy from a baby. Even if you do have to buy stock on an occasional put that's exercised, you're getting stock way below the market. Basically, it's the same as entering a good-till-canceled order to buy at a limit price several points below the market and having someone pay you for entering that order.

Client You told me that our call writing was covered and that we couldn't get hurt. Will we be writing covered puts?

Broker Well, uh, not exactly. Basically, they'll be covered in the sense that you'll have margin up—the money, you know, in your account to cover 50% of the cost of, I mean, buying the stock if it's put to you.

Client Well, okay. But I don't want to take any big risks.

Broker Don't worry about that. Basically, you can't lose money buying stock below the market. But remember, you've got to stick with the program. Our clients who are successful in this program are those sophisticated enough to stick with it. They're willing to accept a 15% return. We call it getting rich slow.

Client [To himself] Haven't I heard that somewhere before?

During the spectacular market advance of the first half of 1987, writing (selling) put options looked like a sure thing. Premiums that buyers of puts were willing to pay were not sensational, because not many puts were winners in that rising market, and most puts had been expiring worthless. But premium income for writing puts was easy pickings. The possibility of having to buy a few hundred shares of stock during a temporary price correction was the worst that could happen. Brokerage firms saw little risks for themselves and cut their margin requirements to allow put writers to do more business, to write more puts.

The market started down in August. I guess that some put buyers saw themselves making a bit of money. And some put writers saw themselves losing money. Recovery came in September, and for the writers the outlook brightened.

When the Crash came on October 19, put writers were bagged. There they were, short puts requiring them to buy stock at, say, 50 when now that stock was down to 35. Such a put with a strike price of 50, worth nothing a few days earlier, now had an intrinsic value of 15 or $1,500. For every short put, the writer had an over-the-weekend, $1,500 loss. Multiply that by 25, 50, 100 puts or more. As puts were exercised against the writers, they found themselves owning more stock than they'd ever dreamed of—stocks that could be sold-out only at staggering losses. Writers couldn't come up with the money to pay for the stocks being put to them. Brokerage firms, to protect their capital, sold out the stocks—or bought in the puts, creating in clients' accounts uncollectable, five- and six-figure debit balances. That's where the brokerage firms took the hit big: unsecured debits in accounts of put writers whose brokers had led them out into the deep water. Buyers of puts, on the other hand, had collected on their insurance.

For dribbles of premium income, writers of puts took risks that they couldn't have understood and lost more money than many of them ever could repay.

Well, what do you think of that program? That strategy?

That's about all you need to know to avoid the options market. Listen to no clever strategies. Enter into no programs. If you need investment income, see what high grade bonds are paying. If you want to make money, to profit, buy high quality common stocks for the long-term.

Chapter 24

The Futures Market

I was introduced to gambling at an early age. When my brother and I were about eight and six, our father showed us how to play dice. And at the high school dances in the 1930s, most of us boys shot craps. For many years as manager of a brokerage office, moreover, I weighed risks, accepted reasonable risks and—when the choice was mine—often declined business to avoid excessive risks. I was accustomed to taking my chances.

Upon my first visit to Las Vegas, I was surprised at my reactions to the place. Although the bare breasted girls were great, the gambling, strangely, aroused in me no interest. I believe it was because I had seen so much speculation in futures. Gambling in Las Vegas, by comparison, seemed small potatoes. I dropped not a nickel in a slot machine.

I found myself fascinated, however, just watching players at blackjack, roulette, dice. Their odds had to be pretty poor. Throwing dice, a gambler was supporting a casino employee at each end of the table, a third man who raked in the chips and, I'd have to guess, someone overhead watching, through the mirrored ceiling, both players and other employees. Shooting craps at a casino, you have to meet a big payroll.

Gambling, I suppose, can be fun, but I'd have to decide first how much I wanted to spend for entertainment and, when that's gone, quit. Anyone who gets in deeper exposes some personality flaw.

Trading futures can get you into a lot more trouble than gambling. Trading anything is foolish enough. Trading futures is especially dangerous. Futures markets are different from other markets.

First, margin requirements are but a small fraction of the value of whatever buyers and sellers are contracting to buy and sell. Low margins tend to attract traders, and trading activity is what Exchange members want. Members can set Exchange margins, because the members are the Exchange. That's why margins are only

15%, 10% or less. The chain reaction that 10% margins set off on the New York Stock Exchange in 1929 can happen on futures Exchanges any day of the week.

The second difference: limits on daily price fluctuations are peculiar to futures Exchanges. On the New York Cotton Exchange, as an example, the daily limit is two cents a pound or 200 points. From the day's high, the market can go down no more than 200 points; from the day's low, the market can go up no more than 200 points. Once the price has moved, up or down, the permissible daily limit, transactions at prices beyond that limit are not allowed. Trading comes to a halt. Sometimes the price will back off from the limit, and trading can resume. Sometimes it doesn't, and trading stops for the rest of the day. Again on the following day at the opening, contracts can be offered down the limit with no buyers—or bid up the limit with no sellers—and again, no trading for that day. Although it doesn't happen often, that can go on for several days.

The daily limit is a device intended to dampen volatility, to allow buyers and sellers an overnight opportunity to cool off. However, the effect, as I saw it, was quite different. The daily limit seems to intensify the wildness of futures trading. With the market moving against him, a speculator can get locked in, unable to liquidate, helplessly watching his losses mount at each morning's opening. After a few sleepless nights, he's no longer his collected self.

Whether at a gaming table or in a brokerage office, whether trying to appear important or yielding to some complusion, gamblers and futures traders can be pathetic. Yet most traders have a good sense of humor. If they didn't, they probably couldn't keep on trading.

In the 1950s, an old boy up in Ball Ground, Georgia, who had been on the wrong side of the market with one contract of cotton, sent a Western Union telegram to Joe McC., his broker here in Atlanta: WHY DON'T YOU CALL ME UP AND GET ME OUT OF WHAT YOU CALLED ME UP AND GOT ME IN.

Down in Macon, a fine old gentleman told me of relying on prayer to carry him through a bad cotton market that had consumed all of the money that he could put up to meet maintenance calls. Laughing, his considerable abdomen bounced up and down in his lap as he pulled back one foot to suggest kneeling to pray: "Dear Lord, if just this one time you let me make back my money and get me out of this wicked market—just this one more time—I promise you that I'll . . . uh, uh . . . that I'll get right back in."

When I was a young broker, futures trading was a large part of my business. Several of my clients were commodities speculators. None was a winner.

In 1947, a cotton speculator who had his account with our Houston office called me at our Corpus Christi office. He was down in McAllen in a tourist court—what we now call a motel. Although it was early in the morning, I could hear party noise in the background. He asked me to enter a market order to buy 10 contracts of cotton—1,000 bales, 500 pounds each, 500,000 pounds of cotton. Why he called our office instead of Houston, I didn't ask. I entered the order, got a report of excecution and called him back with the price. Almost immediately, cotton broke and fell the permissible, daily limit of 200 points or two cents a pound from the day's high, about where we'd bought.

In each of several conversations throughout the morning, the client was getting a little drunker—girls laughing, lots of fun. Finally, he told me to try to get him out, which I did. We sold on the low. Loss, $10,000.

Meanwhile, the client had been talking with his regular Houston broker, who had received an advisory report of execution of my earlier buy order and assumed that the client was still long 10 contracts. Neither of us knowing that the other was talking with the client, the Houston broker accepted a second order to sell 10 contracts. That, too, was executed at the low. So now, the client had sold not only the 10 contracts long through me, he was short 10 contracts sold through Houston. Thereupon, the market turned and went up the limit. Once the Houston broker discovered what had happened, he and the client decided to cover the short. They bought-in at the high, for another 200-point loss, another $10,000. Total loss, $20,000. And that was 20,000, 1947 dollars, enough to drill a South Texas oil well.

We used to speak of commodities markets, but in more recent years trading has begun in many things that are not commodities, such as Standard & Poor's 500 Stock Index, major foreign currencies, U.S. Treasury bonds. It is now more accurate, therefore, to say futures markets rather than commodities markets.

Futures trading is possible in almost anything in free supply and free demand, with buying and selling broad enough that price cannot be manipulated. Whether the commodity, or whatever, happens to be wheat, gold, live cattle, orange juice or anything else, futures trading is all the same.

Dealers in the actual article—variously called the cash commodity, actuals or, if cotton, spots—want a futures market that continuously and accurately reflects the present and future prices of their actuals. Speculators want an active market in which price fluctuates widely enough to allow for opportunity to profit.

In most respects, a futures contract is a lot like any other contract to buy and sell. Buyers and sellers are represented by their agents or brokers. To facilitate trading, the futures contract has been standardized and simplified. The Exchange upon which the transaction takes place has rules that describe precisely the quantity and quality of the commodity—or whatnot—and specifies the places at which the seller can elect to make delivery. The only thing left for the buyer and seller to haggle about is price. That's not too different than any other buy-sell negotiation.

What distinguishes a futures contract—and the reason we call it a futures contract—is that delivery and payment are not made immediately. Instead, buyer and seller have chosen for settlement, some future month, usually no further out than 18 months. Although buyer and seller have agreed upon the price at which they will buy and sell, although, in fact, they have entered into a contract, delivery and payment won't be made until that future month. Only then must the seller deliver the commodity—or whatever—and the buyer pay the price upon which, earlier, they agreed.

At settlement, when delivery and payment are made, the price may be much higher or much lower than the price at which they entered into their contract.

The whole business, really, is idiot's delight, requiring no great intellect. A bit about simple mechanics:

In the business, we say that someone who has bought a futures contract now has an open long position; that someone who has sold a futures contract now has an open short position. But once a buyer and a seller have agreed upon price and entered into the contract, they have no further, direct relationship with one another. At the close each day, transactions are cleared in the same way that banks clear checks.

The payee to whom you give your check for, say, $100, deposits that check with his bank. His bank doesn't take the check to your bank to demand $100. Instead, all checks within the city are delivered to the central clearing agency that local banks have setup to determine each day how much, net, each bank owes or is owed on all the checks presented for collection.

Each futures Exchange has a similiar facility called an Exchange Clearing House or some such name. After transactions on the Floor, each Exchange member looks only to Exchange Clearing as the other side of every open position.

After the last trading day during the delivery month, all open positions must be settled. All of the sellers who have open short positions must make delivery of what they've agreed to sell—corn, lumber, crude oil or whatever; all of the buyers who have open long positions must make payment for what they've agreed to buy. Few contracts, however, are settled by delivery and payment.

At any time before the close on the last trading day, both the longs and the shorts are free to liquidate in the open market by entering into identical contracts on the opposite side. Thus in the open market, a person long can sell; a short can buy in. In either case, long or short, liquidation satisfies the contractual obligation to make payment or to deliver.

To sell out, the long need not go back to the original seller; to to buy in, the short need not go back to the original buyer. An open market, offsetting transaction goes to the Clearing House and is matched off against the open position.

Here, however, there's one hitch. The market, likely, has gone either up or down. Somebody is going to lose, somebody is going to win, just as they would if they were betting on a football game. But in the futures market, all of the losers lose a bit more than the winners win. And all the winners win a bit less than the losers lose. There are other participants, the two brokers—one representing the buyer, the other representing the seller.

On every trade, each broker is paid a commission. One commission is paid by the buyer, another by the seller. If buyers and sellers, the customers, just trade actively enough and long enough, all of their money will disappear into the pockets of their brokers.

The money that the winner makes in a futures transaction can be no more than the loser loses. That's also true in options. Neither futures nor options is an investment. It's not like buying property, real estate or common stock that can enhance in value. Futures and options are nothing but bets.

During my years as a broker, I saw maybe two or three commodity speculators make money. Almost all were losers. I'd never risk my money in futures—or in options.

Now you'll think I'm contradicting myself when I tell you that futures markets serve a function that is important, perhaps essential, to our free, competitive economy. Futures trading serves as a pricing mechanism.

As a young broker in Corpus Christi in 1947, I was asked by a group of grain sorghum farmers to explain the futures markets. As to their interest in futures, they told me that when the crop of milo maze, as they called it, was cut in that area, the few buyers who came down from Kansas City seemed to be in collusion. They would pay only the same, low price. The farmers were having to take what they could get—only the same, low price. A futures market, they reasoned, would provide for an accurate, fair, open market price that Kansas City buyers would have to meet. They were right. The trade and speculative interest in milo, however, has never been sufficient to support a futures market.

For many years, the marketing of crude oil was so concentrated and, I suspect, so controlled by the big oil companies that they were able to forestall public trading of crude oil futures. Only in 1983 did trading commence on the New York Mercantile Exchange. Afterward, I read that futures trading in crude and the resultant flow of continuous, up-to-the-minute price quotations introduced honesty in the conduct of the oil business.

Beyond the pricing function, futures markets serve another useful purpose, hedging. Rather than attempting a definition, let me relate a real-life example.

During the late 1960s, I worked in Memphis. As you may know, Memphis is world headquarters for cotton. The cotton growing Mississippi Delta begins, they say, in the lobby of the Peabody Hotel—where each day, six or eight mallard ducks are brought down by elevator from the roof to the lobby, to waddle off to the fountain where they spend a delightful evening jumping in and out. I first saw their procession in the summer of 1933. The progeny of those ducks, I'm told, are those paddling around in the fountain today.

One of the larger Memphis cotton merchants in the '60s was a client of ours. Each year, shortly after cotton was planted in the Delta, he contracted with planters to buy their crops in the fields. They agreed upon a per pound price based on grade and staple—the whitest, cleanest, long-fiber cotton fetching the highest price. To make the most money on his crop, the planter had to get the highest yield per acre and produce the best possible grade and staple.

Although planters wouldn't finish picking cotton until the first hard freeze, the merchant carried the risk of owning that crop from the moment he contracted to buy it. It was a risk, however, that he did not want. He was not a speculator.

As a merchant, our client hoped to make a reasonable profit when he sold to mills or for export. As soon as he bought a crop in the field, he sold futures. (One futures contract, you'll remember, is 100 bales, 500 pounds each.) In the futures market, he sold the same quantity of cotton as he expected to own when the crop came in. So now, he was long, cotton that would be picked in the fall. And against that actual cotton, spots, he was short cotton futures for delivery in maybe October or December. He was hedged.

If the price of cotton went up, the merchant had a profit on the cotton he'd bought in the fields and a loss on his short futures position. If the price went down, he had a loss on the cotton in the fields and a profit on his short futures. The loss on one was offset by the profit on the other. That's the effect of a hedge. For him, it eliminated the price risk.

And who were the buyers of those futures contracts that the merchant hedger was selling? Who was on the other side of the market? Many, surely, were speculators, convinced that the price of cotton was going up. They bought futures with the hope of making a profit.

So the futures market is used to transfer risk from a merchant, a mill or a planter, who can't afford to take price risks, to speculators who are willing to carry the risk for the opportunity of profit. The futures markets provide that useful function, hedging.

One year in the early winter after the price of cotton had been going up, I became concerned about short positions we were carrying for clients who had sold futures at lower prices. Did they have on deposit with us enough money to cover their losses? If the market continued up, would they have the money to meet maintenance calls? Would I have to buy-in client's short positions to protect my firm's capital?

By that time, the cotton crop was in, and presumably our large merchant client had cotton in warehouses. But I had no way of knowing. If he didn't, losses on his enormous short futures position with us could have left him broke and owing me money he didn't have. Yes, he'd signed our hedging letter, a form stating that his futures position would be offset by his spot position. Yet hedging agreements don't mean much. Lots of speculators claim to be hedging and sign the letter to get reduced margin requirements. And because brokers are eager to get the business, and because firms fear offending their brokers, firms sometimes accept their brokers' assurances that speculator clients are legitimate hedgers.

I remembered, however, that our client had told me that he would do his futures business only with us and his banking only with one, local bank. I called a friend who was in charge of that bank's cotton department and offered to exchange information. That was one relieved banker. He hadn't been sure that the merchant's spots were hedged; and if the price of cotton had collapsed, the bank might have been left high and dry. But sure enough, warehouse receipts for the thousands of bales pledged to the bank corresponded almost exactly to the size of the merchant's short futures position with us. And needless to add, this was one relieved broker.

So the risk of owning all of that cotton was being carried by speculators and others who had bought futures from our merchant client. He was hedged and his risks were minimual. Now all he had to do was to sell his spots to mills, or wherever, at prices that would allow him to make his profit. Whereupon, he would buy-in his short future positions to lift his hedges. Until then, whether the price of cotton went up or down, the merchant could not be seriously damaged. And in a rising market, I wouldn't have been left holding the bag on his large short position in futures.

Although speculators in futures can suffer ruinous losses, futures markets serve the useful, economic purposes of establishing fair, continuous pricing and providing a vehicle for transferring risks. You and I, nevertheless, will live happier lives if we stay away from futures trading.

Commodity traders are not rational. A story, or joke, is told of a client who consistently had lost money speculating in pork bellies. With the hope that a change might bring better luck for the client, his broker suggested to him that instead of continuing to trade bellies, he trade soybeans. A few days later, the client told his broker, "I've been thinking about what you said. I've decided to stick with bellies. I don't know anything about soybeans."

No one can forecast successfully the price of anything that trades in futures markets. Yet anyone speculating in futures has deceived himself to believe that he can. Or foolishly, he's listened to some broker who pretends that he can.

A few pages back, I mentioned futures trading in the S&P 500 Stock Index. In 1982, Congress authorized trading in stock index futures—a big mistake, I believe. Although futures contracts were developed for the Major Market Index, which approximates the DJIA, the NYSE Composite Index and the Value Line Composite Average, most of the trading activity went to the S&P 500 Stock Index futures on the Chicago Mercantile Exchange—the Merc.

Futures trading in stock indexes is exactly the same as futures trading in cotton or soybeans. Only settlement is different.

As a stock index is neither bushels nor bales, and as receipt and delivery of shares for the 500 underlying stocks would be impracticable, the S&P futures contract is settled by receipt and delivery of—guess what—money. Loser pays off winner, just as you would settle a bet. The S&P futures contract is worth $500 times the S&P Index. Thus if the S&P Index closes at 250 on the last trading day for S&P futures, the S&P futures contract is worth $500 X 250 or $125,000.

Let's say a trade is made at 250. Whether beans, bales or stocks, the price, remember, is set when the trade is made, maybe months before the contract finally is settled. Assume that the position remains open past maturity, through the last trading day when the S&P Index closes at 260. The futures contract then would settle at 260. As that's 10 points higher than the trade at 250, seller is loser and buyer is winner. In settlement, seller pays buyer $500 times 10 points or $5,000. Of course, either buyer or seller could have come out earlier by selling or buying an offsetting contract before the contract matured and trading ceased. Most positions are closed out like that, by open market liquidation.

Investors buy stocks and own stocks with expectations of making money on advancing prices. To make money, an investor must accept the risk of losing money. His goal is quite different from that of the Memphis cotton merchant. Although both investor and cotton merchant would wish to be protected from losses, the merchant, to get that protection, is willing to forego market gain. The investor is not. He buys stocks to make money. But just like the cotton merchant, the investor can't have it both ways. If he wants to make money in the market, he must accept the risk of losing money in the market.

Hedging a portfolio of stocks by selling S&P futures makes no sense. If S&P futures are sold against a portfolio, any profit on the portfolio will be wiped out by losses on the short S&P futures. An investor in stocks who hedges by selling S&P futures is out of the market; he just doesn't know it. He'd have found it cheaper never to have gotten into stocks to begin with.

And yet among young portfolio managers in 1987, big talk about S&P futures as portfolio "insurance" became fashionable. They seemed to have understood that no profit could be made on a portfolio of stocks while, against it, they maintained short positions in S&P futures. So they devised a scheme that would let them have it both ways—profits from the stocks, protection from the futures. Their idea was that once they knew that the market was about to fall (as though they ever would know), they'd sell futures; on the short side of the futures market, they'd make the money that they would lose on the long side of the stock market. A splendid idea.

The only trouble with their theorizing is that they, along with everyone else in the world, had no way of knowing when the market was about to drop. So in 1987 when the Crash came, they all rushed in on October 19 to sell S&P futures. Not only were they too late, their deluge of sell orders found few buyers on the Merc. Their orders to sell futures were executed 10, 20, even 40% below the S&P Index itself—at prices way below the value of the 500 S&P stocks then trading on the NYSE. They had sold into panic, near the bottom. They took a bath when the stock market rallied. Their short futures moved up with the stock market and then moved up even further to close those 10%-to-40% differentials. Portfolio insurers discovered, to their dismay, that they had lost money, not only in stocks, but in futures as well.

Too bad those young men knew nothing about the cotton market. A cotton merchant who wants protection—"insurance"—knows that he must be hedged from the moment he's bought spots. He knows that he cannot outguess the market, that he cannot have it both ways.

Contributing to the big NYSE "meltdown" of October, '87, were other users of S&P futures. While the portfolio "insurance" boys were recklessly selling futures, "program traders" of large NYSE member firms immediately saw their opportunity for index arbitrage.

Using computers, program traders can fetch up in an instant the present, aggregate value of all the 500 S&P stocks trading on the NYSE and can compare that package of stocks with one of the Merc's S&P futures contracts, one maturing in, say, three months. Their computer programs take into account the dividends that they would expect each of those stocks to pay and the interest cost of whatever amount of money would be tied up to simultaneously buy S&P futures and sell the stocks—or to buy the stocks and sell the futures.

Program traders know that the S&P Index and the S&P futures will come together, at exactly the same figure, when the futures contract settles on the last day of trading. During the months and weeks before that futures contract settles, they watch for any price disparity between the total market value of the 500 stocks that make up the S&P Index and the market price of the S&P futures. During market frenzy when the gap between the two widens, a program trader sells S&P futures and buys the major stocks of the S&P 500 Stock Index or buys the S&P futures and sells the stocks—putting on a riskless arbitrage. That price difference is a locked-in profit that he will receive on the last trading day for the futures contract, or earlier, by liquidation in the market, if that spread closes.

To simultaneously put on both long and short positions, program traders must have access to the NYSE DOT system. DOT is for Designated Order Turnaround.

Before DOT started up in 1976, orders for round lots, 100 shares and multiples of 100 shares, had to be phoned or teletyped to the member firm's booth just off the Floor. From there, a Floor broker had to trot out to the trading post to execute the order—usually with the specialist. With small orders, there's no trading opportunity. During the 1960s, Don L.,an old friend of Training Class 4, then a Floor broker, let me spend a day with him. His job, he said, could have been done just as well or better by a Western Union messenger—because the boy would have had a bicycle.

The DOT system allows orders to be sent electronically out to the Floor, to the 20 or so posts where the specialists stand and trade. Although developed to execute small, troublesome public orders, the DOT system put program traders in business. Their several hundred orders to buy or sell S&P's 500 stocks (actually fewer because some are too small to be significant) can be sent to arrive simultaneously at the trading posts. On October 19, all of their orders, prepared in advance to sell the big stocks of the S&P 500 Stock Index, were ready to go.

At the opening, portfolio managers began selling the S&P futures as "insurance" or hedges. The Merc proved to be a poor market. With little or no support from the locals, futures fell out of bed, falling much faster than the 500 stocks that make up the S&P Index. The spread widened, 10%, 20%, 40%. Thereupon, program traders began hitting the buttons on their computers to spew out surges of orders to sell thousands of shares of the big stocks of the S&P Index. Simultaneously, they bought S&P futures on the Merc, where they were about the only buyers. Many locals had left the Floor. Selling stocks and buying futures, program traders locked in the differences—short stock, long futures.

Portfolio managers who sold futures as "insurance" were not buyers of stocks. Already invested, they just held on to what they had. Sellers of stocks, therefore, found no bids from them. About the only bidders were some of the NYSE specialists.

In the panic, specialists and brokerage firms needed money. New York banks did not step forward. Some banks even began calling outstanding loans to brokerage firms—until they heard from the New York Federal Reserve which saw disaster in the making and told the bankers to get with it. Money, at last, was advanced to specialists and brokerage firms. Major corporations announced that they would buy large quantities of their own stocks. The NYSE shut down the DOT system. That effectively stopped program trading. The ship did not capsize.

So selling S&P futures as portfolio "insurance," money managers had pushed the prices of futures far below the value of the 500 underlying stocks that make up the S&P Index. Program traders had jumped in to capture the profits they could make by selling stocks and buying futures. Buying futures on October 19 was easy; there were no other buyers. Selling stocks, however, program traders were selling along with what looked like everybody else in the U.S.A.; there were almost no buyers.

How much of the day's 508-point decline was attributable to program trading? No one ever can know. Program traders, nevertheless, were sellers of stocks. Selling drives down prices.

Now I can understand how a cycle becomes vicious. The portfolio "insurance" boys sold futures. The spread between futures and stocks widened. The program traders—arbitrageurs, actually—jumped in to buy futures and sell stocks. Their selling pushed the stock market even lower. The falling stock market brought in more selling of futures as "insurance." That widened the gap, attracting more program selling which, in turn, attracted more selling of futures as "insurance." It became a whirlpool, sucking stocks down.

Although a high-priced learning experience, the Fed, the banks, the brokerage firms and the Exchanges now know what must be done to avert a panic. So maybe October 19 wasn't all bad.

How did the October 19 players perform in the panic? The heroes seem to have been the president of the Federal Reserve Bank of New York, Chairman of the NYSE, and perhaps a third of the 50 NYSE specialists.

Who didn't cover themselves with glory? Perhaps two-thirds of of the NYSE specialists, many of whom were net sellers on the day; almost all of the OTC firms, many of which wouldn't answer their phones; most of the locals on the Merc, those who left the pits. Goats? Portfolio managers selling futures as "insurance." Jackals? Program traders.

And what did we learn? Stock Index futures have about the same importance to the economy as a deck of cards or a pair of dice. The stock market requires no futures market for pricing stocks. Index futures cannot be used as "insurance" to hedge a portfolio of stocks.

As to options—puts and calls—their only economic justification is that they generate commissions and provide nice incomes for brokers. Yes, it takes somewhat longer to lose your money in options than in futures. But lose you will. Our lives will be doubly happy if we stay away from both options and futures.

Gratuitously, I might offer the same advice to brokers. It's impossible to build a clientele of futures or options traders. When a client goes broke, the broker must find another innocent and eager person to replace him. Good clients are hard to find.

➤   ➤   ➤

Index arbitrage, which accounts for most of the program trading, can cause sudden market panics and sudden market frenzies, but it has no effect on fundamental values of stocks. Once the storm has passed, earnings expectations determine stock prices.

In the highly-emotional, volatile futures markets, wild speculators carry futures prices, both on the upside and the downside, far beyond rational limits. Index arbitrageurs, like a bunch of vultures, watch the price action of index futures—the S&P 500, the S&P 100, the Major Market Index (which comprises only 17 stocks of the 30 DJIA). Patiently, they wait for mad frenzy or panic to rise from the trading pits.

When index futures prices go crazy, program traders close in on the stock market to buy stocks and sell futures when futures are too high or to sell stocks and buy futures when futures are too low. Their arbitrage buying and selling of stocks brings the insane panic and frenzy of the futures markets to the New York Stock Exchange floor to temporarily distort stock prices.

Index arbitrage forces the prices of stocks and futures back into line with one another. In fact, if there were enough active program traders, their buying and selling would keep stocks and futures from ever getting too far out of line. So program trading doesn't create bull markets and bear markets, it only adds to volatility in the stock market.

You should know, however, that institutional brokerage firms and managers of large stock portfolios do use stock index futures and stock options to facilitate executions of large trades. As an example, to complete a number of sell orders for an institution, a brokerage firm buys some of the stocks for its own account to sell out piecemeal over several days. To protect itself against the possiblity of a sharp drop of the overall market during that time, the firm might sell index futures as a hedge. To hedge an individual stock, the firm might buy put options. Either way, price risks are then assumed by speculators on the other side of the market.

What we don't need, in my view, is stock index futures. With no futures market, there could be no index arbitrage.

PART THREE

THE BOND MARKET

Chapter 25

Invest for Income

"How much investment income do you need?" the broker asks his client or prospect. The answer, almost always, is the same, "Oh, I'll take all the income I can get." Maybe that's what the investor wants, but he hasn't answered the question: how much investment income does he need? not want. The distinction is important.

To get investment income, you must buy fixed-income securities. Maybe some day that will change. Maybe dividend returns on stocks again will be higher than yields on bonds. But presently and for many years, to get income, investors have had to buy bonds, lending their money to a corporation, a state or municipality or to the Federal government. The issuer of a bond promises to repay you, on a specified date, the amount borrowed—that is, the face amount of the bond, usually $1,000. Until maturity, your bond pays interest at a fixed rate. Nothing more.

The amount of investment income that you need should tell you how much of your capital you must invest in bonds, in fixed-income securities. If annually you need $10,000 of investment income, and if bonds are paying 10%, you must invest $100,000 in bonds. That $100,000, committed to producing income, is $100,000 that won't be available to you to produce profit, to invest in stocks.

The more money you put in bonds, the less money you'll have for stocks, the less money with which to make money. Why buy any more bonds than necessary to produce your need of investment income?

Saying to your broker, "I'll take all the income I can get," tells him, "No stocks, please. Show me nothing but bonds. I need more investment income than my investment capital ever can produce." If that's what you mean to say, okay. But don't go back to that broker at the top of the next bull market and ask, "Why don't we own any stocks? Why did we miss the market?"

As investors, almost all of us, at some time, will have to invest for income. Almost all of us, probably, will buy bonds, and you can lose your money in bonds just as easily as you can lose your money in stocks. Every investor, therefore, must understand fixed-income securities and, more specifically, bonds.

Before going any further, however, I want to be sure that you and I have the same understanding of some words that are used and misused in the bond business. Also, I want to explain some of the confusing practices and customs of the business. Anyone who hasn't found bonds sometimes baffling either has bought blindly whatever has been recommended to him—and that's a mistake—or he never has talked with a broker.

Yes, you know what a coupon is. You know what yield is. You know what accrued interest is. So do I.

But fellows in the securities business use those words somewhat differently than their clients. To know what they mean, you've got to know how the words are used.

Coupon

Until sometime in the 1960s, a bond was issued as one, large sheet of heavy paper. On the left side was printed the bond itself: "XYZ Corporation promises to pay the bearer $1,000 on [date] and until maturity will pay interest at 9 1/2% annually." Something like that. Printed on the right side were the coupons, each about twice the size of a postage stamp, one for each interest payment that would become due. Bond interest, then and now, usually is paid twice a year, such as January 15 and July 15 or March 1 and September 1. Printed on each coupon were the interest payment date and the amount due—on a 9 1/2% bond, $47.50.

That's called a bearer bond. The issuer had no record of its bondholders. On each interest payment date, the bondholder would cut off the current coupon and deposit it with his bank. The bank collected the $47.50 and credited the investor's account.

That $47.50 coupon was for six months' interest. But if someone in the securities business were asked about that bond, "What's the coupon?" his answer would be, "Nine-and-a-half percent." That, of course, is the annual rate, not the amount of interest paid on the coupon itself. So when you hear, "It carries a nine-and-a-half percent coupon," you know that's the annual interest rate, $95, not the amount of a single, semiannual coupon, $47.50.

At maturity, the holder of the bond would surrender his certificate, along with the last coupon, and the issuer would repay the $1,000 plus $47.50 interest on the last coupon.

In more recent years, bonds have been issued only in registered form, certificates without coupons. The owner's name is typed-in on the face of the certificate, and the issuer of the bond keeps a record of its bondholders. The Federal government took that a step further: it stopped altogether the issuance of certificates for Government securities and now makes changes of ownership only by "book entry." Except for holders of old coupon bonds issued some years ago, investors no longer clip coupons; they receive checks in the mail. Nevertheless, we continue to ask, "What's the coupon on that bond?" "Nine-and-a-half percent." "When's the next coupon due?" "January 15, it pays January and July." Depending upon the way the word is used, coupon can mean either the annual, 9 1/2% interest rate or the $47.50 paid twice a year.

In every business, I suppose, word usage often is imprecise. "When I use a word," Humpty-Dumpty said, "it means just what I choose it to mean—neither more nor less."

Yield

The word yield also can be confusing. First, there's current yield, simply annual interest divided by present market value. Say the coupon—the annual interest—is 9 1/2% or $95 per $1,000 bond and that you just bought that bond at 87 or $870. The current yield is $95 divided by $870, which is 10.9%. As an investor for income, that's what you want to know: How much money will I get on the money I've invested?

But then there's yield to maturity that takes into account other benefits.

Let's say your bond matures in seven years. Every six months, you will receive an interest payment of $47.50. During the next seven years, you'll get 13 or 14 interest payments. Each of those interest payments can be reinvested, on the day it's received, to earn for you interest on interest. That's a benefit.

Upon maturity in seven years, you will surrender your bond for repayment of the $1,000 principal. That will be $130 more than the $870 you paid for your bond—another benefit. It's as though each year nearer maturity, you're gaining one-seventh of that $130 discount from par. Actually, that $130 now is worth only about $69, the present value of $130 that you won't see for seven years. Each year that passes, the $130 discount is worth a bit more, until at the end of the seventh year, it's worth the full $130.

So semiannual interest payments and interest on interest plus recovery of the $130 discount, all related to the price of the bond, give you yield to maturity. The arithmetic, in fact, is more complex. What you and I need to know, however, we can get from a yield book or a bond calculator. In this example, a bond, trading at 87, with a 9 1/2% coupon and maturing in seven years would have a yield to maturity of 12.325%. That's from my calculator.

Also, you'll see bonds selling at premiums, at prices above par. To produce the same, 12.325% yield to maturity, a bond with a 14% coupon and maturing in seven years would sell at 107.697 or $1,076.97. In that case, the bondholder would be losing, each year, some part of that $76.97 premium he paid, because at maturity he will get back only $1,000.

Almost never does a broker speak of, or even think of, current yield. A broker will offer you a bond only on a yield to maturity basis. He wouldn't say, "You can buy this bond for $870 giving you a current yield of 10.9%." Instead, he'd say, "I can offer you this bond on a twelve-thirty basis." That means a yield to maturity of 12.30%.

If you need investment income—and that is your reason for buying a bond—you'd want to know the current yield, how much money each year you'll be getting on your investment, the 10.9%. But from your broker, you'll hear only yield to maturity. That's the only honest, accurate way that he can offer a bond to you. So you'll have to figure current yield for yourself, which isn't too tough to do.

Accrued Interest

To the individual investor, accrued interest is always both a surprise and a confusing nuisance. In the securities business, interest on bonds is figured on a 360-day year—12 months each of 30 days. Why? In the days before we had calculators, figuring interest on 31-, 30-, 29- and 28-day months was just too tedious.

Let's say that on June 1 you bought that 7-year, 9 1/2% corporate bond, as in the earlier example. Coupon dates, January 15-July 15. On June 8, five business days after purchase, your trade would settle. You must pay for the purchase; the seller must make delivery to your broker. The cost, we'll assume, is still $870. Added to your cost will be the accrued interest, the interest to which the seller is entitled from date of last coupon, January 15, to settlement date, June 8. That's 143 days' interest—four 30-day months plus the last 15 days of May and the eight days in June.

Annual interest of $95 divided by 360 days is 26.39 cents per day. For 143 days, accrued interest would be $37.74. So you'd owe $870 plus $37.74 or $907.74.

On July 15 when you receive the full $47.50 interest payment, you would keep it all. Of that, the $37.74 that you already have paid to the seller is returned to you. The difference, $9.76, is your interest from settlement date, June 8, to interest payment date, July 15.

Now let's move on to investing for income, in fixed-income securities, bonds.

CHAPTER 26

BONDS

An investment is either equity or debt. By equity, I mean ownership—ownership of common stock or real estate. By debt, lending your money—buying bonds or mortgages. Whether equity or debt, you invest with the confidence that you'll get back a flow of money that will be greater than the cost of your investment. Investing, then, is buying with today's dollars what you hope will be a lot more future dollars.

What you're after is money. Whether earnings and dividends from stocks or rents from real estate or interest and return of principal on bonds and mortgages or profit upon resale of any investment, all will be payments to you of money. Only money, nothing else.

So what is any one of those investments worth? The current price, always, is the marketplace guess as to the present value of those future dollars.

You probably want to know, how many dollars in the future can I expect to flow back to me? And when do I get those future dollars? When it comes to buying a bond, those are easy questions, assuming you're buying a good quality bond that won't go into default. The number of dollars you'll get back will be interest payments at six-month intervals and, at maturity, return of principal. Nothing more.

That introduces another question: When I get those future dollars, how much will they be worth? That depends upon rate of inflation during the years ahead—upon the buying power of those future dollars. On a bond, you want a yield high enough to compensate you for any loss of buying power.

If bond investors begin to have serious doubts about the value of those future dollars, if they become convinced that the dollar will lose, say, half its buying power during the coming five years, they won't pay much for the investment. A future flow of badly depreciated dollars is worth, today, not too much. Buyers of bonds will hold out for more future dollars, for higher rates of interest. In the secondary market, they drop their bids on low coupon bonds issued in earlier years at par. Prices of low coupon bonds fall to produce higher yields. New issues of bonds, offered at par, must carry higher coupons to attract buyers. So expectations of inflation and depreciation of the value of the dollar result in lower bond prices and higher bond yields, higher interest rates.

From ownership of a stock, an investor expects a flow of increasing benefits—higher earnings, higher dividends and a higher price on his stock. A bond never will pay more than its stated interest, never return more than the principal. Bondholders can look forward to no pleasant surprises.

From my young brokers, I used to hear many stories of businessmen clients and their investments. Evident in every story was one fact always surprising to me. The businessman didn't know what to do with his money. Trying to impress the young broker, he had put up a big front, but his investments told a different story. What he was doing with his money often made no sense.

A fellow in good health, earning more income than he needs, having 10 or 15 years to work, ought to be buying investments that can give him growth of his capital, to provide for his happy retirement. But in almost every one of those discussions with a young broker, I'd hear the same story. The client or prospect wanted nothing to do with common stocks. He wanted bonds with the highest yields, hang the quality. And he wanted to invest in something, anything, that would give him a break on his income taxes.

In fairness to those investors of the early 1980s, one must recall that they had had some wretched experiences. Many had been burned in the stock market in the 1970s. Then when the market took off in August, 1982, few owned stocks. By early '83, when investor confidence began to grow, the public was buying stocks of companies that had something to do with computers. High tech was the place to be. But by year end, the public once more was bagged and once more disenchanted.

When stocks at last broke out on the upside in 1985, the public was on the sidelines, waiting for the buying opportunity, the big setback. When it came in the autumn of 1987, it wasn't a setback, it was a Crash and, once more, a generation of investors took the pledge never to own stocks.

Young brokers related to me their conversations with investors obsessed with avoiding income taxes. Simply for the satisfaction of paying no tax on the interest, they'd buy municipal bonds—even though they needed no investment income. From what they'd bought, we could see that some of them had given little or no thought to quality, to the safety of their investments. They wanted only tax-free income, the highest return they could get.

Other clients, seeing even higher yields on corporates, bought junk bonds issued by shaky companies. To stay in business for a few more months, to borrow money, those companies were willing to pay any rate of interest. Those bonds were about as secure as a loan to your brother-in-law. Clients bought those bonds without giving any thought to the income tax they'd have to pay on the interest—assuming that interest payments would be made. For some of those folks, greed had overcome their bitter feelings about paying income taxes.

When I'd ask the broker if his client needed investment income, whether tax-free or taxable, the answer often was the same, "No, but he says he likes to get those checks." The money that the client had in bonds, remember, was money not available for investment in stocks, for growth, for profit. To get current income that he didn't need, the client had denied himself the chance of growth of his capital.

Stocks, surely, come with no guarantees, but with inflation continuing to eat away the purchasing power of the dollar, why would anyone, needing no investment income, buy bonds, a fixed-income security?

Few persons active in business have any awareness of the fixed-income investments they already have. How about yourself? You've bought life insurance of some sort, perhaps term life or, through your company, group life insurance. You may have an ordinary or level premium life insurance policy with accumulating cash value—a fixed number of dollars earning a fixed, low rate of interest. If life insurance can be called an investment, it is fixed-income. Its benefits to you and your family are in fixed numbers of dollars—even before you get them, dollars that can only depreciate in value.

Unless you are a Government employee or a member of the Armed Services, the pension you'll receive upon retirement never will be increased to offset the rising cost of living. Your pension is a fixed income investment made in your behalf by the company for which you work. You earned your part of the money with which that pension plan was funded. Social Security, to which both you and your employer have contributed, has been paying retirement benefits with a COLA, Cost of Living Adjustment. Don't be too sure that COLA will last forever—or even Social Security itself. In future years, benefits might be paid only on a basis of need, to those with income below the poverty level.

We all have more fixed-income assets than we realize, and the value of each is vulnerable to inflation. During the 10 years 1975-85, most people had but one major asset that kept up in value with inflation—their homes. But is your home an asset that you can sell to get spendable money? No, you've got to live somewhere. If you sell your home at a good profit, the new home that you might buy will be just as inflated in value as the one you sold. Owning a home, however, you do know that you'll not be subject to rent increases.

Again, why would anyone needing no investment income buy bonds? Well, bonds can be bought—maybe not always rationally—for two other reasons. Speculators sometimes buy bonds for capital gains. Conservative investors buy bonds for safety and stability.

In mid-1983, just before retiring, I bought U.S. Treasury bonds as a price speculation, for capital gain. At that time, the rate of inflation had come down, but long-term interest rates remained high. It appeared to me that interest rates, in relation to inflation, were too high. I felt that long-term interest rates could decline significantly, that long-term bonds could rise sharply.

Was I forecasting the bond market? Yes, in a way, I was. I was betting against inflation, which had dropped from around 13% to below 5%. And although Treasuries had recovered somewhat, long-term yields still were at 12%. To me, that yield looked too high, Treasuries too cheap — unless, of course, inflation heated up again. Anyway, I did buy bonds, U.S. Treasuries.

Treasury bonds? fully taxable? Why not tax-free municipals? For a couple of reasons. But remember, I was buying, not for income, but for capital gain, to sell at a profit.

Why not munis? First, some municipals are callable at any time at small premiums above par. Often you'll see a bond callable at a premium of maybe five points—callable, that is, at 105—in the years immediately after the bond is issued, then at lower prices each year or so until it becomes callable at par, 100. To the investor, that means no matter how low interest rates might fall, his bond never will sell much higher that the current call price, because as interest rates might fall, the issuer will call the bond and pay off the holders with money from the sale of a new issue with a lower coupon.

An occasional municipal issue will have a latent call feature that no one seems to know about. I've seen bonds selling at nice premiums, 111 or 112, called at par to the complete surprise of everyone and at significant loss to the bondholders.

U.S. Treasuries are non-callable. True, some Treasury issues have an alternative maturity date five years earlier than the regular date. If interest rates are low, the Treasury can declare the bond matured on the earlier date, pay off the bondholders and refund at lower coupon rates. But that alternate maturity date always appears in the description of the bond. You know exactly what you're buying.

The other reason is the thin market for municipals. Actually, the market is worse than thin. Trading is sporadic. If you're a seller, you can get a bid, all right. Seldom, however, can a buyer select the bond he wants, find that bond offered and place an order. Buyers' choices are limited to bonds that dealers, at the moment, have in their inventories—bonds that dealers have bought, marked up and are reoffering for sale. A large, reputable dealer, typically, will mark up long-term municipals 3-to-5 points, or $30-to-$50 per $1,000 bond. That means a 3-to-5 point spread, the difference between the bid and asked prices—what you must pay when you buy and what you get when you sell.

For illustration, assume that you bought a bond that cost $950 and that almost immediately, with no change in the market, you had to sell it. Probably you'd get $920 or $900. You'd lose that wide spread. You'd buy on the offer, $950, and sell on the bid, $920 or $900. Buying and selling municipals is expensive.

Treasuries, by contrast, trade continuously. Dealers maintain both bid and asked prices on every issue. And trading is active, billions of dollars worth every day. Competition among Government bond dealers is fierce. And they compete almost entirely on price. Spreads, in consequence, are narrow, in thirty-seconds of a point— a buck or less per $1,000 bond. Treasuries are easy to buy, easy to sell.

So how did my speculation work out?

After I bought those Treasuries in '83, the market was down a bit or up a bit but never as strong as I had anticipated until four years later. I made money on them, but it took a long time. That often happens with a short-term speculation. It can become a long-term investment. A poor way to acquire your investments. Even so, bonds can be bought for capital gain, as a speculation on a drop of interest rates.

The second reason for owning bonds can be for the sense of safety and stability, something to fall back on in bad times such as the Depression of the 1930s. Then, fears were basic: unemployment, eviction from one's home, not having enough money for food, clothing. To have Treasury bonds in such circumstances would be a great comfort. However, another 1930s depression, when no one had money, seems unlikely. If economic cataclysm befalls us, it could be for the very opposite reason: money becoming worthless. In that event, Government bonds—Treasuries—would be just as worthless as the money.

Logically, if I were to buy bonds just for the certainty of protecting a fixed number of dollars, I'd buy Governments maturing in not more than five years. Long-term Governments at times can be every bit as volatile as stocks. Owning bonds, therefore, is not necessarily the best cure for one's anxieties. Bonds can lull you into a false sense of security. Losing money in bonds is no more genteel than losing money in stocks or anything else. When the rate of inflation is rising, T bills would be the best fixed income investment, because you get back all of your money within the year and are exposed to almost no market risks.

So bonds can be bought for capital gain, and bonds can be bought for a sense of safety and stability, but I couldn't advise you to buy bonds for either of those reasons. If you buy for capital gain, for price appreciation, you are deceiving yourself to believe that you—or your advisor—can forecast the bond market. If you buy bonds for safety and stability, you have forgotten how rising interest rates can wreck the bond market.

Bonds are for income.

I want to tell you about a lady who phoned our office in 1981 to inquire about investing for income. But before going into what might have been done for her, let's take a look at the plight of a person who has money to invest but who knows nothing about investing.

To whom could that lady have turned? Probably no one she knew. She had heard of our large brokerage firm and must have assumed that she could talk with some sort of expert. She phones the local office. She asks the receptionist if she might speak to someone about investing.

To a brokerage office, call-ins are a worthwhile source of new clients. Most brokers are eager to get those calls. An office manager, however, will instruct his receptionist to direct call-ins to his newest brokers, to help them build their clienteles. From the roster of new brokers, one will be designated each day to get call-ins. Although the young broker can be well intentioned, he's inexperienced and under pressure to produce business—commissions.

There's nothing wrong with that. Doing business is expected of everyone who works. The opportunity to make money has made the U.S.A. the wonder of the rest of the world. Free enterprise is like sex. It's instinctive, it's selfish, but it's marvelously productive. So instead of faulting someone who's striving to compete, you should contrast that person, who's paid only for results, with an employee, say, of the post office.

The caller-in usually gets a new broker who doesn't know how to identify an investor's needs. Unfortunately, that's true of most

brokers, regardless of the time they've been in the business. Brokerage firms, moreover, do little to help them. Whatever training a firm
offers its brokers emphasizes the sale of a specific security, a
product. Client investment need is not taught. Brokers who learn
something about investing must learn at the expense of their earlier
clients. Some brokers learn nothing in their entire careers, so all of
their clients continue to pay the price of dealing with them. But
that's true, too, of some lawyers and some doctors and some
preachers.

All of that is to tell you, again, that any person you rely on for
investment advice may be either incapable of offering good advice or
more concerned with making money for himself than for you. An
investor, to be successful, must become self-reliant.

Now about the lady who called in.

Obviously, some people need more investment income than
their capital can produce. That was this lady's problem. Her call was
transferred to a rookie broker. She asked him how she could get
maximum income from $20,000. The young man came to me with
the question. Typical of most brokers, he had learned nothing about
the woman. And being a new broker with few clients, he had heard
only "twenty thousand dollars," which he immediately translated
into a nice production credit.

Would one of our packaged bond funds be appropriate? Or an
electric generating utility stock with a high dividend yield? Possibly. But what other assets does the lady have? Her present income?
Her need of additional income? What risks can she take with the
$20,000?

He'd call back.

In a second conversation, the broker learned that the lady was
about 70, living on Social Security plus a pitifully small pension and
interest at a munificent 5 1/4% that a bank was paying on the
$20,000. Nothing else. No family, no property. She couldn't quite
make it on what she was getting.

The lady had to get maximum income. But she could accept no
risk. If she were to have become seriously ill, medical bills could
have been more than her $20,000. And for other emergencies, she
might have required immediate cash.

On the $20,000, the 5 1/4% the bank was paying her brought in
$1,050 annually. It was a great arrangement for the bank, not so
great for the lady. Her money, however, was immediately available
to her. That could have become important. The penalty for withdrawal would have been the possible loss of only a few dollars of
earned interest.

With minimum risk, how could she get more income?

First, how much of the $20,000 had to be available as cash to cover the cost of unforeseen emergency? That, of course, could be only a guess. We assumed that $5,000 would be enough.

She either could leave $5,000 in her bank savings account drawing 5 1/4% or put that money in a money-market fund that invested in T bills, high quality commercial paper (corporations' IOUs for 270 days or less) and bank certificates of deposit—all short-term stuff maturing in less than a year. Rates that money market funds pay change daily, but the fund then was paying 10%. On $5,000, she would get $500 a year compared with only $262.50 at the bank's 5 1/4% rate. Also, from a money market fund, she could withdraw her money at any time without penalty. So that was an easy choice to make.

Why not put all of her money, all of the $20,000 into the money market fund and let her pull down $2,000 a year for the rest of her life? It sure would beat what the bank was paying her.

You couldn't do that. Rates on money market funds change daily and unpredictably. If those rates were to have fallen in a big way, her income could have been reduced, conceivably even below the 5 1/4% that the bank was paying. So all of her money could not have been put in the money market fund. To provide for emergencies, however, $5,000 in the fund gave her, for then anyway, a return of 10% and access to cash with no penalty for withdrawal.

To get that liquidity, that immediate access to cash, she had to give up certainty of income. Ups and downs of short-term interest rates would increase and decrease her income.

With the remaining $15,000, we wanted to lock in, for at least a few years, what looked like a high return on U.S. Government bonds.

The safety of Governments is absolute. The U.S. Treasury will make every interest payment that falls due and, upon maturity of its bonds, will pay off at par, $1,000 per bond. Until the bonds mature, however, open market prices move up and down, sometimes over a wide range. Suppose, as an example, you buy at par a bond that pays interest of 10% or $100 annually, and suppose that afterward interest rates rise to 15%, who's going to pay you $1,000 for your 10% bond when, for the same $1,000, a buyer now can get 15%? Hence, you can sell your 10% bond only at a price that will yield 15%—on a bond maturing in 20 years that would be 67.27 or $672.70, a good bit below $1,000.

Once the lady bought bonds, interest rates might go up, and the price of her bonds would fall. Or rates could go down, and the price of her bonds would go up. Or rates could remain unchanged, and the price of her bonds would remain unchanged. Which would happen, no one could know. But the shorter the maturity of her bonds, the nearer the date, that is, upon which her bonds would be paid off at par, the less widely the price would fluctuate. For example, if a bond were maturing next week, who would take anything but a few cents less than $1,000 for his bond?

Impacted by changes of interest rates, bond prices swing like a barn door. The hinge is today. A bond that's about to mature, about to be paid off at par, is getting close to today, close to the hinge, the side of the door that doesn't swing too far in either direction. The price of a short-term bond doesn't swing far in either direction.

A bond that won't mature for 30 years is at the far side of the door, the side wih the latch. Away from the hinge, 30 years until maturity, the door swings wide in both directions. So does the price of a 30-year bond.

Let's take a look at two Treasury bonds. Both carry a 12% coupon, both pay $120 a year on the $1,000 par value. One matures in five years, the other in 30.

You've bought the five-year, 12% Treasury at par, $1,000. Afterward, the bond market advances and the yield on your five-year bond drops to 10%. To yield 10%, your bond would sell at 107.72 or $1077.20. But suppose the bond market declines and the yield on your five-year bond goes up to 14%. At a yield of 14%, your bond would drop to 92.97 or $929.70.

Contrast that with the 12% 30-year bond also bought at par. If the market rises and the yield drops to 10%, the 30-year bond would sell at 118.92 or $1,189.20. And if a sell-off in the market resulted in a yield of 14% on the 30-year bond, it would be worth only 85.96 or $859.60.

Tabulated, those numbers are easier to compare. Again, both bonds are 12% Treasuries:

Maturity	@ 12% yield	@ 10% yield	@ 14% yield
5-year	$1,000 (par)	$1,077.20	$ 929.70
30-year	$1,000 (par)	$1,189.20	$ 859.60

On a drop in yield of just two percentage points, or 200 basis points, the five-year bond will gain $77.20; the 30-year bond, $189.20—almost two-and-a-half times as much. On a rise of just 200 basis points, the five-year bond will lose $70.30; the 30-year bond, $140.40—almost twice as much. It's just like the barn door. As the door swings through its arc, the price of the short-term bond, close to the hinge, moves only a short distance; the price of the long-term bond, out toward the latch, moves a much greater distance.

We had to protect the lady from wide price swings. If she had bought a long-term bond maturing in 25 or 30 years and interest rates went sky-high, bond prices would collapse. Then should the lady need her $15,000 and have to sell her bonds, she would take a serious loss. If at the other extreme she bought T bills maturing in just a year or sooner, we'd have to be reinvesting the $15,000 every six, nine or 12 months. That's called rolling T bills.

Upon each maturity, she'd have to take whatever yield she could get—the same uncertainty as to income as having her $15,000 in a money market fund. If near-term interest rates fell so low that she could get no more than maybe 3%, she might not have enough money to live on.

To avoid those unhappy extremes, we bought for the lady $15,000 of a five-year Treasury paying 12%. That gave her a good return on her money with limited price risk. If afterward she needed her principal, the $15,000, we wanted to be able to sell her bond at a price close to what she had paid. Even in the worst of circumstances, even if the bond market went down the tubes, the bond would be redeemed in just five years. And every year she owned the bond, it was moving closer to maturity—ever closer to the hinge, resulting in ever smaller price swings until, after five years, the U.S. Treasury would pay her off at par, $15,000. Meanwhile, she could count on getting the 12% or $1,800 every year for those five years.

To get certainty with respect to income, she had to accept some market risk. Only after five years, upon maturity, would the Treasury redeem the bond and return to her the $15,000 principal. If she needed any part of that money before then, she'd have to sell bonds in the open market. To get a certain 12% for five years, she had to accept the small price risk.

So the lady's income on her $20,000 was $500+ from the money market fund and $1,800 on the five-year Treasury, a total of $2,300—better than twice the $1,050 that the bank was paying her in the 5 1/4% savings account.

Now let's go back to the beginning. Do you remember that the young broker asked whether he should recommend to the lady one of our packaged bond funds and an electric generating utility stock with a high dividend return? Well, what about a bond fund and a common stock? Why not?

A packaged corporate bond fund, called a unit trust, consists of something like $100 million worth of corporate bonds bought by the sponsoring brokerage firm. That portfolio, in effect, is broken up into 100,000 identical pieces, or units, each worth $1,000. With the Securities and Exchange Commission, those units are registered as a security and sold publicly.

Most of the bonds in a conventional corporate bond fund are of fairly good quality, rated A or better. On the rating scale used by Standard & Poor, AAA is the highest quality, double-A the next step down, then single-A, which is an investment quality bond safe enough for the private investor. BBB is good quality. Below—BB, B, CCC, CC, and C—are bonds of successively lower quality. (Later, we'll go into safety of bonds.)

Investors won't buy a bond fund unless they can get a high yield. So to make the yield enticing, a few dubious, probably nonrated issues are thrown in.

And brokers won't sell the bond fund unless they can get a big production credit—and brokerage firms must make a profit. So to pay the broker and to leave a profit for the firm, units are marked up a good bit. A 3 1/2% sales charge, $35 per $1,000 unit, comes out of what the investor puts in. His remaining $965 now must yield significantly more than $1,000 invested in a Treasury bond.

So to produce an attractive, above average yield to the investor, to arouse the brokers' interest in selling the units and to make a profit for the brokerage firm, some safety must be sacrificed—thus the inclusion of some bonds of not-so-hot quality.

Also, most maturities of bonds in a fund go out 20 years or more. Yields on long-term bonds usually are higher than yields on medium- and short-term bonds, because risks are greater. Who knows what will happen over the next 20 or 25 years? Some of today's great corporations could be out of business. Or inflation might wipe out another two-thirds of the purchasing power of the dollar.

Although bond funds take on risks to get higher yields, there are some offsets. Funds include bonds of large numbers of corporations. Some funds have no more than 7 1/2% invested in bonds of any single issuer. That diversification is a safety factor. Even if one corporation were to go broke, only 7 1/2% of the principal would be lost.

A second advantage of a unit trust is marketability. A corporate bond, especially in small quantity, can be hard to sell even at a knock down price. If you wish to sell a bond fund, you can get an immediate, fair bid. The brokerage firm sponsor that creates a bond fund and sells the units engages an outside agency such as Standard & Poor to price the bonds in the fund, and the sponsor maintains a bid based on those prices. A unit owner who wishes to sell will be paid that bid price. The brokerage firm buys back the units, tacks on another 3 1/2% sales fee and resells the units. Even so, a corporate bond fund is neither as safe nor as marketable as a U.S. Treasury bond. Also, 20-year bonds drop sharply when interest rates rise. Still, a unit bond fund is not a bad vehicle for income.

And the electric generating utility stock? For a 70-year-old lady living on the brink of poverty, stocks were out, for no one can forecast the stock market. Owing to the perversity of the market, prices always are down if you are forced to sell to raise money. Stocks should be bought only with capital for which one has no foreseeable need. And that lady had more foreseeable needs than money.

You must understand an unfortunate fact. A broker who spends much time with poor folks soon will be out of business. He can't afford as a client the 70-year-old lady we've been talking about. That seems cruel. But what surgeon can afford to treat patients with athlete's foot? What attorney can afford to sue for a bent fender? What preacher can afford to bury paupers?

My rookie broker lost money on his lady client. The profit margin on Treasuries is paper thin. On the entire $15,000, the mark-up would be only $10 or $15. Brokerage firms make money on Treasuries only in million-dollar multiples. And on a $5,000 deposit into a money market fund, a broker makes nothing.

To the broker, $15,000 in a five-year Treasury and $5,000 in a money market fund would be a total credit of $15, of which he would be paid maybe 35% or $5. Buying $15,000 of a corporate bond unit trust and, say, 450 shares of a utility stock at $11 a share, commission credits would be $28 per unit on the fund, or $420, plus a commission of $50 on the stock, a total of $570. At 35%, the broker would get $200 on those trades. Not great, but it beats $5. And it's worth a phone call. Which recommendation would the broker, any broker, make? Probably the purchases that paid him more. Everyone is inclined to act in self-interest. Once more, however, that's not all bad.

In a free economy, everyone is out for himself. And brokers are salesmen. They're paid on the commissions they can generate. Understandably, they're attracted to clients who can do big business, and investors of limited means get, at best, short shrift. The self-interests of brokers, however, are consistent with the needs of the national economy. Huge sums of investment capital must be drawn into the economic system. Brokers and brokerage firms persuade investors to commit the capital that our economy must have. Also, they provide the secondary markets through which capital can be shifted out of declining companies and industries and into growing companies and industries. Investors with large sums of money, obviously, are more important to those needs.

Ironically, all of my concerns for the safety of the lady's $20,000 were for naught. After 1980-81, interest rates trended down and bond prices up. No serious disasters wrecked the corporate bond market, and corporate bond funds were good investments. The stock market, too, was strong. Some electric utility stocks doubled in price. Many increased dividend payments. The lady would have been better off had she gone with the ideas of the rookie broker. But we didn't know that, and she couldn't have afforded the risks of betting on rising markets. Every tomorrow is an abyss. We got for the lady the best investment results with the least risks.

So much for the 70-year-old lady.

Bonds and rising interest rates

One risk of owning bonds is that of rising interest rates. When interest rates go up, bond prices go down. To give you a look in the rearview mirror of just how damaging to bond prices rising interest rates can be, how about this?

In *The Wall Street Journal* or *The New York Times,* turn to quotations of U.S. Treasury bonds, notes and bills. Some bonds are above par (prices above 100), some are below—depending upon the strength or weakness of the bond market at the time you're looking. Does it occur to you that every one of those bonds was offered, initially, at par? That the bond market can be just as wild as the stock market? For an example, I'll use a Treasury bond that I bought just before retiring in 1983, an 8 3/8ths of 2000/1995.

In 1975, the U.S. Treasury sold that issue to mature in 25 years or, alternatively, in 20 years—maturing, that is, in the year 2000 or, at the option of the Treasury, in 1995. On the initial public offering in 1975, that bond, as every new issue of Treasuries, came at par, $1,000. Because investors bought at par on that offering, they must have been convinced that 8 3/8% would be a great yield on their money over the 25-year life of the bond. Yet six years later, in 1981, to bring another new issue, the Treasury had to offer a coupon of 14%. That meant that all long-term Treasuries, in the secondary market, were selling at prices to yield about 14%, and the 1975 buyers of those 8 3/8ths couldn't have gotten more than 65, $650, for their bonds. That was a loss of $350 on a $1,000 bond. And there's nothing wrong, mind you, with any U.S. Treasury bond.

At maturity, every Treasury bond will be paid off at par. When due, every interest payment will be made. So there's no question about U.S. Treasury bonds. Treasuries are safe. The risks are market risks, price risks. If sometime before maturity you need your money and must sell bonds, you may have to take a loss.

Rising interest rates drive bond prices down. Falling interest rates drive bond prices up.

What makes interest rates go up and down? Lots of things, I suppose. Like what? Certainly, changes of expectations as to rate of inflation; also actions by the Federal Reserve Board in its efforts to control credit and money supplies; swings of the economic cycle resulting in change of demand for credit; and spending and taxing by the government. Rate of inflation, however, probably has been the dominant force driving interest rates up and down, yet money supply, demand for credit, interest rates and inflation all appear to be inseparable.

So back to the question, what makes interest rates go up and down? Having no theories to propound, I must retreat to more familiar ground. It's the open market. Buyers and sellers of securities, reflecting everything known, acting upon their hopes and anxieties, arriving at a consensus, set the prices of bonds—and consequently interest rates.

For 40 years from the end of WW II in 1945, bond investors saw an uninterrupted rise of interest rates and fall of bond prices. To finance the cost of the war, the government had imposed controls on the price of almost everything—including wages. Meat, gasoline, auto tires, strategic materials in short supply were rationed. Wage and price controls kept the lid on inflation and allowed the govern-ment to borrow at interest rates of 2 1/2%-3%. Upon removal of controls after the war's end, inflation appeared briefly, but interest rates, curiously, remained low. Maybe it was because individuals and corporations had paid off debt or because there wasn't much to buy, and supplies of money exceeded demand. I don't know.

Interest rates continued so low during the 1940s and early '50s that individual investors who needed income had to go to common stocks. Stocks of even large, high quality companies were selling at prices so low that dividend returns were 6%-to-8%. That tells you that when investment income is a necessity, one can't always insist upon the absolute safety of a Government bond. Safety sometimes must give way to necessity.

From the 1940s and into the 1980s, interest rates rose and bond prices fell. Insurance companies, as I recall, were the only big buyers of corporate bonds. Life insurance was a no-risk business. Companies didn't compete on a basis of premium cost to the buyer. All used the same, antiquated mortality tables prepared from actu-arial experiences of many years earlier when life expectancies were much shorter. Policyholders now were living longer and paying premiums for many more years. Premium charges, therefore, were excessive.

Being able to accurately forecast death benefits they'd have to pay each year for many years out, life companies could invest com-fortably in safe, low-yielding corporate bonds that would cover benefit payments and leave for themselves splendid profits upon which they paid little or no income tax. So bond yields were more than adequate for insurance companies. As they held bonds until maturity, life insurance companies were indifferent to the ups and downs of bond prices in the secondary market.

During the four decades from the beginning of WW II, every bond was a loser. Yes, bonds at maturity were paid off at par. There were, of course, a few brief up-blips, but almost any time a bondholder had to sell, he took a loss. Interest rates kept going up, and bond prices kept going down—for 40 years. In the early 1980s, interest rates peaked-out, and bond prices started up.

During periods of moderate rates of inflation and stable interest rates, bonds can be good investments for income. But one risk of owning bonds is rising interest rates, which seems to be a symptom of disease—inflation.

Bonds and expectations of inflation

Inflation hits bonds in much the same way it hits stocks. Both stocks and bonds are bought to get flows of future incomes—incomes in terms of money, dollars. The big difference is that stocks represent ownership of producing assets, factories that provide goods, transportation facilities that move goods, and distribution and sales organizations that deliver goods to final users. As inflation eats away the buying power of money, prices of goods and services can be raised. As money may become worthless, those same goods and services can be sold for a new money that a government will create. Ownership of equity, common stock, survives.

In contrast, the flow of money from bonds is fixed. Interest rates never will be higher than stated rates; at maturity, bonds are paid off at par, $1,000, nothing more. Therefore, should runaway, ruinous inflation wipe out the value of money, bonds, too, die.

Down here in the South when I was a boy, vestiges of the old Confederacy still were evident. Near the State capitol was a home for old veterans who as boys fought the Yankees. Minie balls from the Battle of Atlanta could be found around Inman Park and along the Peachtree Creek. Occasionally, children would bring to school Confederate money to show off as something of a curiosity. It wouldn't buy for you a nickel Coca-Cola.

Over on Highland Avenue was an old iron foundry that surely must have been here during the Civil War. Ownership quite possibly had been passed down to the prominent, well-to-do family that operated the foundry in the 1920s. Assuming that to have been true, you can imagine that the owners—the stockholders—of that foundry in the 1860s may have been inconvenienced as Confederate money lost all its value, but after the war ended they were selling their products for the new money, U.S. dollars. So long as a company remains in business, the value of the ownership, the stock, survives.

But framed and hanging today on the wall in front of my desk,

I have a $100 bond, Confederate States of America. It's a Cotton Bond payable from a duty of one-eighth of a cent a pound on cotton exported. It was issued in 1861 as a 10-year bond. Interest was payable on March 1 and September 1 of each year. As it was an 8% bond, the coupons are for four Confederate dollars. Coupons up to that of September 1, 1864, were clipped and, I suppose, paid. In September of 1864, four Confederate dollars probably weren't worth the trouble it took to clip the coupon. Confederate money became worthless. The bond, too, became worthless, and bondholders got nothing.

To investors who have put their money out on loan, who have bought bonds, inflation can be ruinous. The longer the term of the loan, the longer the time before the lender is repaid, the more time for inflation to grind down the value of the money. A dollar worth 100 cents when borrowed can be worth only a dime when repaid. Great good fortune for the borrower; great misfortune for the lender. Owning bonds is lending money. Maturity date of a bond, of course, is the term of the loan.

Inflation always is with us. It does not go away. The erosion is insidious. At a rate as low as even 4%, inflation in 10 years will reduce the purchasing power of $10,000 to just $6,756. Money forever is worth less and less, so why keep money? Or why own bonds? A bond pays nothing more than the fixed rate of interest, and although the issuer returns to you the $1,000 you loaned out when you bought that bond, what you get back are 1,000 depreciated dollars.

Investing in bonds, anyone would hope to protect himself from loss to inflation, loss of buying power. During rising inflation and for some time afterward, investors are scared. They won't lend their money unless, and until, they believe the rate of interest offered is high enough to offset future rates of inflation. Expectations of inflation, then, produce high interest rates.

Everything changes, but in my experience, you should own bonds only because you require current investment income and then only because you believe that the interest you will receive will be, not only fair rent for the use of your money, but high enough to offset what you expect to be the annual rate of inflation over the life of the bond.

Perhaps you think that's a dumb statement, ". . . what you expect to be the annual rate of inflation . . ." In a way, it is a dumb statement. Who knows what the rate of inflation will be? No one. Nevertheless, you can anticipate that inflation at some rate will continue over the life of the bond, that your money will be at risk and that you should be paid incremental interest for accepting that risk.

And maybe you should buy only short-term bonds.

Assuming that the certainty of repayment of a loan is absolute, "rent" on money seems to have been, historically, around 3 1/2%. To that 3 1/2%, add an expected rate of inflation—if 7% annually, interest becomes, just to break even, 10 1/2%. That would be the rate on risk-free Governments. Invested in anything other than a U.S. Government obligation, however, money is exposed to another risk, the possibility of default. As an investor, you must be paid for the level of risk you choose to assume. To the 10 1/2%, you now must add percentage points to compensate you for whatever you believe to be the degree of risk of default—about which, more further on. Owning Treasuries, Government bonds, however, you are concerned with only one risk, rising interest rates resulting, probably, from inflation.

In 1985, Treasuries were yielding 12%. Although two or three years earlier inflation had been 10%-to-13%, it had receded to about 4%. Adding that 4% rate of inflation to the 3 1/2%-4% no-risk rent on money, one might have expected Treasuries to have been yielding no more than 8%. But bond buyers obviously had no confidence that inflation could be contained at 4%. They feared, anticipated, a return of higher rates of inflation. Bond buyers and sellers—the market—appeared to expect rate of inflation to rise to around 8% (12% on Treasury bonds less 3 1/2%-4% rent equals 8% or 8 1/2% for inflation).

Bond buyers did not aggressively bid up bond prices to bring down those yields, and the sellers did not hold back their bonds for those higher prices. Fearful that the tide might go out, neither buyers of bonds nor bondholders wanted to be left stranded, holding low yield, high cost bonds. It must have been, too, that bond investors had been burned so badly by inflation of the few years earlier that they were saying to themselves, "Never again." As always, trying to see into the future, the marketplace was reflecting inflation fears and telling us to beware, that inflation at a high rate could return. Although not always right, the market seldom is wrong.

The precarious value of money depends entirely upon public confidence, yet business and industry will survive even catastrophe. The marketplace seems to recognize an almost indestructible value in ownership of corporations that are producers and providers for the nation and, indeed, the world.

Although U.S. investors got a whiff of inflation during the 1970s, I can't remember having heard expressions of serious concern that our moderate inflation could become runaway inflation. Because the U.S., geographically, is at such a distance from most of the rest of the world, perhaps it's easy to tell ourselves, It can't happen here.

In 1985, the annual rate of inflation in Israel was 100%, prices doubling every year; in Argentina, 1,000%, prices up 10 times in a year. Sometimes it gets so bad that a government will declare its money worthless. That's to cancel all debts and all bonds, to start all over again. If that ever does happen here, I don't want to be holding bonds—any kind of bonds.

Bonds and the risk of default

So far, we've been concerned with what happens to bonds when interest rates rise and when inflation heats up. Another risk, an even more frightening specter, lurks about the bond market: default or repudiation by the issuer. Large corporations can collapse. Municipalities that issue bonds can refuse to meet payments of interest and repayments of principal. It does happen. So how does the investor protect himself? Buying a bond or lending your money, what would you be on the lookout for?

Suppose you work for a bank. Suppose you are a loan officer responsible for committing the bank's money. Suppose further that no one can tell you how to do your job. Even though you know just a bit more than nothing about banks, and something less about lending practices, what comes immediately to mind?

This bank, you say, is in trouble?

Maybe so, but that's not what I'm getting at.

How would you go about your new job of lending money? A customer comes in and asks to borrow money. What do you need to know about him so that you can make a good decision?

I shall guess that, first, you would ask yourself, can this man —will this man—pay us back? Has he ever failed to repay a loan? How much already does he owe? Is his business profitable and growing? What, belonging to him, can he let us hold as collateral to make sure he repays us? And if he defaults, could we readily sell his collateral to get back all of our money? Or maybe the loan is such a small fraction of his net worth and he is so reputable, that we need no collateral.

Satisified with all that, how long do you want to tie up the bank's money? The longer time you give the borrower to repay the loan, the greater likelihood of loss to the bank, the greater possibility that the borrower could suffer business reversals or even go broke.

Finally, what interest rate should we charge? You want to make enough money on the loan to cover expenses—including your salary— to provide for unforeseen risks and to make a profit for the bank.

Splendid. You've made a logical analysis of the loan applica-
tion. Too bad that some bankers, and some bond buyers, don't do
as well. Fewer banks would fail, and fewer investors would buy
junk bonds—bonds of financially shaky corporations that must pay
dangerously high interest rates to get investors to buy their . . . well,
their junk.

In rating bonds, Standard & Poor and Moody's probably go
through that sort of exercise in measuring risks. The ratings of both
services are reasonably reliable; otherwise, subscribers would drop
one in favor of the other—competition begets quality. We've got to
depend upon the rating services, for neither you nor I aspires to
become a credit analyst.

When you buy a bond, you lend your money. Certainly that's
evident if you buy your bond on the original offering, in the primary
market. Through the underwriter, an investment banking firm, the
money that you pay for the bond goes to the borrower, the issuer of
the bond. That can be the U.S. Government, a corporation such as
IBM or GE, a state, city or county or an "agency" of some layer of
government. In the secondary market, you buy bonds from other
investors who want their money back, now, before the maturity date
when the issuer is obliged to redeem the bond by repayment of the
full, $1,000 principal.

In lending his money, or buying a bond, one must reckon the
risks of higher interest rates, inflation and the borrower's inablity
to pay interest and repay the principal. All of those risks determine
the minimum rate of interest that a lending bank or bond investor
would be willing to settle for. Those are the forces that push interest rates up.

Holding interest rates down is competition. Another bank may
be willing to make the loan at a lower rate of interest, to take greater
chances. As a banker, you'd learn that if you quote too high a rate
of interest, you may be sending a good customer across the street. As
a bond investor, you'd find that if your yield ideas are unrealistically
high, the bonds you'd like to own have been sold to other buyers at
higher prices. Competition among bond buyers is the force that
pushes interest rates down.

In the open market, bond buyers want to buy at the lowest
prices and highest yields, bond sellers want to sell at the highest
prices and lowest yields. It's a standoff until either an eager buyer
steps up to take the best offering or an eager seller hits the best bid,
and the bond trades. The price of that transaction determines the
yield on that bond—and also the yield on any other bond of the same
quality, coupon and maturity. Interest rates are established in the
free marketplace.

Except for U.S. Governments, any bond you buy can go into default.

Between Government bonds and corporates—between absolute safety and some lesser degree of safety—the difference in yields can be viewed in two ways. Needing investment income, one might say, I can take some risk, buy higher yielding corporates and get more income for the same amount of money that I'd have invested in Governments. The other view: I can take the risk of buying higher yielding corporates, and get the investment income I need without having to invest as much money as I would in Governments.

To illustrate, let's say you need investment income of $7,500 a year and that Governments yield 9 1/2% while A-rated corporates yield 12 1/4%. As always, you work backward.

To see what you'd have to invest in Governments to get $7,500, divide $7,500 by 9 1/2%, or 0.095, the yield on Governments. That comes out to $78,947, so you'd buy $79,000 of Governments. (That assumes that a Government with a 9 1/2% coupon sells at par.) Then you might say to yourself, let me see what income the same $79,000 will produce in corporates at 12 1/4%. Multiplying $79,000 by 12 1/4%, the yield on corporates, you get $9,677.

Buying corporates instead of Governments, you'll have $2,177 more income from your money—$9,677 on corporates minus $7,500 on the Governments = $2,177.

Well, that's one way of looking at it. But don't forget that corporates carry some risk, however slight. With Governments, safety is absolute. Are you willing to accept that slight risk of owning A-rated corporates? Are you willing to expose your $79,000 to that risk to get an additional $2,177 a year? How badly do you need investment income?

The difference in yields can be seen in the other way.

You must invest $79,000 in Governments to get the $7,500 annual income. But if you buy corporates at the higher yield, you won't have to invest that much to get $7,500. With corporates at 12 1/4%, divide your $7,500 income requirement by 12 1/4% or 0.1225. That comes out to $61,224. You'd could buy only $62,000 of corporates, or $17,000 less, and still get the same income. And maybe you need a larger cash cushion, so the $17,000 could be kept in a money market fund. Or for growth, you could buy $17,000 more in stocks.

Once more, don't be distracted by visions of sugar plums. Ask yourself, do I want to assume risk? Another concern is marketability. Governments are easily, quickly, cheaply bought and sold. The spread, the difference between bid and ask, is minimal, scarcely a dollar per $1,000 bond. To buy, you must pay up only that small amount; to sell, you've got to go down only that amount. And commissions are nominal.

Corporates don't trade in such close, active markets. Spreads can be a point or two, $10 to $20 a bond. Even so, they're sometimes tough to buy, tough to sell. And commissions are higher.

At times when corporates yield little more than Governments, you must ask yourself, is the small difference in yields worth my taking even minimal risk? For myself, I can't see it. If, as an example, Governments yield 9% and corporates 10%, why take any risk with my capital to get one percentage point more of income? It's mindless. If I am to accept risk, I want the opportunity to make real money. You must balance the two: risk versus reward. Why take big risk, or any risk, for small reward?

Some investors, however, may have to take risks to get income. A person with limited investment capital might find that the yield on Governments won't produce the investment income he needs. He may have to sacrifice quality, take the risk and buy an A- or BBB-rated corporate to get the income that he must have.

All that relates to the quality of your bond, to the credit-worthiness of the issuer. The risk is default—failure to pay interest when due, failure to repay principal upon maturity. The issuer of a bond, remember, is a borrower, and as an investor you are a lender. In a person-to-person transaction, if you were about to lend your money to someone, what's the first question that would come to mind? Right. Is this guy going to pay me back? When it comes to a corporate borrower, the issuer of a bond, you must take the same skeptical view.

Owning some quantity of bonds can be necessary to produce your need of investment income. Owning a few Governments can meet the emotional need of allaying an old man's unreasoned fear of another 1932-style Depression. But owning bonds in any larger amounts is, to me, frightening.

In the early 1970s here in Atlanta, both borrowing and lending of money was becoming more and more reckless. Real estate developers would undertake construction of buildings just as large as some lending institution was dumb enough to finance. Go-go developers and lenders were unconcerned that reasonable projections of rents couldn't cover interest costs. Loan officers seemed to be rewarded, not for making good loans, but for making big loans. By 1975, a Wall Street bank analyst was telling me that Federal regulatory authorities had three Atlanta banks on their "trouble list"—owing to bad real estate loans.

In the years that followed, many banks, nationally, approached the precipice—bad loans to oil and gas operators, to overextended farmers and, of course, to real estate developers. We saw major banks fail. The Federal Farm Loan Bank was broke. Latin American governments were in default on loans from U.S. banks, and large chunks of those loans were being written off. In 1989, Congress had to appropriate $166 billion to bail out, buy out or close hundreds of Savings & Loans, S&Ls, that were under water because of incompetence and fraud.

The U.S. Government debt doubled in just six years. Consumer installment debt had risen to 20% of after-tax, personal incomes. And brokerage firms and banks were aggressively marketing home equity loans by which the owner, using his home as collateral, applied for a line of credit, paid a big fee to get it, then simply wrote checks against the equity in his home. (When one of those brokerage firms begins foreclosing on home loans, I'd hate to be one of their local office managers.)

As we got to the end of the 1980s, debts were being discharged, more and more, not by repayment but by refinancing or even repudiation. Once a disgrace, personal bankruptcy became commonplace, granted by courts with seeming indifference. Maybe it was because of their heavy caseloads or maybe because judges saw banks and other lenders as having accepted some responsibility when knowingly they made credit freely available to persons clearly not creditworthy— for encouraging profligacy.

Ridiculous borrowing and ridiculous lending led to what, surely, was ultimate absurdity in corporate finance.

So you'd like to own, all for yourself, a large, national corporation. How was it done? Simple. Select your company. Team up with some Wall Street firm. Arrange with them a temporary loan, a bridge loan, to buy up, at a price far above the market, all the stock of the company. For permanent financing, file with the SEC a huge issue of junk bonds that will have to carry some astronomical coupon.

To witless buyers of the bonds, tell them of your plan to sell off parts of the company to reduce the debt. Give them a glowing projection of enhanced profitability that will result from your skillful repositioning of assets and restructuring. Explain that yields on high coupon bonds, historically, have more than offset the few defaults. Show them how safe their bonds will be.

When you get the bonds sold, pay off the bridge loan. And, presto, you own a large, national corporation.

But how did it really work? Actually, just as I've described it, but to make the transaction seem believable, I'll substitute the vocabulary of Wall Street's merger and acquisition, M&A, experts who sometimes call themselves merchant bankers—although neither merchants nor bankers. And allow me to play the part of the corporate raider, the buyer-outer.

To take over the large, national corporation, I'll make a leveraged buy-out, an LBO. Leverage, as always, is using money that belongs to someone else. Buy-out is paying off the stockholders at a price double that at which their stock has been trading. Such a deal. Why wouldn't they be happy?

I team up with a Wall Street investment banking firm eager to make its mark in creative financing. They've earned a reputation for being able to distribute high coupon bonds of egregiously poor quality —junk bonds.

First, my investment banker goes to commercial banks to arrange a stand-by bridge loan. As an interest rate, the big number he uses arrests attention. Then he tells them about the handsome fees we're willing to pay. He's got the bankers licking their chops.

Now, my investment banker goes to institutional clients such as pension funds, insurance companies, S&Ls and high yield bond mutual funds and unit trusts—all of which invest other people's money. To arouse interest, he tells some of them that the stock of an unnamed corporation soon will be in play. (In the 1920s, it was called manipulation.)

With, let's say, the CEO of an S&L, my investment banker makes this arrangement: "We'll tell you the name of the corporation, then, before this gets out, you can buy for your S&L—and for yourself— all the stock you want. In return, you must commit your S&L to buy some minimum quantity of the junk bonds we'll bring to market to pay off the bridge loan that we'll use to buy up the stock. You can sell your stock into our buy-out bid and make a bundle. The stock will be in play any day now, because we've tipped off some risk arbitrageur friends who quietly are buying stock for themselves. They've agreed to gang up with us to fight off any other raiders— or some white knight merger partner that will let present management keep their jobs. The arbs know which side their bread is buttered on."

(Risk arbitrageurs neither arbitraged nor took risk. They bought and sold on inside information. One had the brass to write his autobiography in which he explained to the gullible public that his success was based on his genius that had been recognized when he was a child.) Selling the bonds, the investment banker tells his S&L client, "Our firm will make a market in the bonds, so if you ever you need your money, we can work off your bonds in the secondary market. You can depend on us. Your S&L will get its money back okay. You'll make it big in the stock, and our client [that's me] will take over the company."

Here, you ask me, "What if you can't pull it off and the deal falls through?"

I say, "That's not a problem. Present management of the company will buy our stock from us at a premium above the market to get rid of us and keep their jobs. We'll make a killing."

You ask, slightly aghast, "But isn't that some kind of blackmail? What they call green mail?"

"Well," I say, "some people get upset about these things, but it's just free enterprise forcing efficiency and improving productivity."

You ask, "Is that why you're doing all this?"

"Well," I say, "not exactly, but let me tell you how we're structuring this deal. First, the corporation's employee pension plan is overfunded—more money than's neccessary [so long as the stock market keeps going up] to pay out future retirement benefits. So we'll return that money to the corporate treasury where it belongs. With that money, we can buy in some of those junk bonds— which probably will be selling at a nice discount in the open market—to bail out some of our underwriter's institutional investors. We can't let them get burned too badly, because we'll need them when we do our next deal. Also, we'll sell off some of the corporation's divisions and subsidiaries to get the money to buy in more of our bonds. [The corporation's capital still will be 95% debt.] And I'll end up owning the large, national corporation."

"Congratulations," you say, "but what happens when the economy goes into a recession? If you're not operating at full steam, how can you pay the interest on such a staggering debt load?"

I say, "The worst that can happen is that we go into Chapter Eleven [bankruptcy] and restructure our debt."

You ask, "But what about the bondholders? are they left holding the bag?"

"Uh," I say, "we probably can work out something with them, but that's the risk they take, that's why we pay them such a high interest rate on those bonds."

You ask, "What about the suppliers, customers, creditors, the employees and their families?"

"Well," I say, "I'm taking my chances, too. By the way, have you seen my picture on the cover of *Business Today*? They call me an engaging, entrepreneurial buccaneer. How about that?"

You say, "How much of your own money have you got in this deal?"

"Well," I say, "none. You can't ask me to take all the risks."

Managements of many corporations, to avoid buy-outs and perpetuate themselves in their jobs, borrowed huge amounts of money with which to buy-in vast quantities of their own common stock and to load the boat so heavily with debt that corporate raiders could see no opportunity of using the target corporation's own credit to finance their buy-out schemes. In the next economic downturn, survival of those companies, too, would be questionable.

Many junk bonds ended up in high yield mutual funds and unit trust bond funds that were unloaded on the public. Many junk bonds remained with S&Ls that anyway were going broke. To keep their jobs a while longer, managements of those S&Ls were happy to have the high income that those debt-ridden corporations might be able to pay for two or three years, until bankruptcy. Also insurance companies selling high yielding, single premium deferred annuities, invested those premiums in high risk bonds to get the investment income they had to have to make good on their promises. When the junk bonds defaulted on interest payments, investors who had bought those annunites were bagged.

Federal income tax laws have encouraged corporate management to finance growth and expansion with borrowed money. From taxable incomes, corporations can deduct interest paid on borrowed money. That reduces the tax bill and increases earnings. With a tax rate of, let's say, 40%, interest expense of $1 cancels out $1 of profit on which the corporation, otherwise, would pay income tax of 40 cents. It's easy, therefore, for management to rationalize paying interest on borrowed money by saying, Interest doesn't cost us $1, Uncle Sam is paying 40 cents; our cost of borrowing is only 60 cents.

The Federal government, then, subsidizes corporate borrowing by reimbursing 40 cents of every interest dollar paid. The Federal government also subsidizes the lending banks. The cost of what banks sell, money, is reduced by 40%. It's a Christmas sale. Pay only 60 cents, and save a tax dollar. In contrast to the favored tax treatment of interest costs, dividends paid to stockholders come from after-tax profits. That seems upside down.

One would suppose that tax laws ought to penalize borrowing and reward common stock investors who accept the risks of ownership and whose capital strengthens corporate underpinnings. Instead of allowing corporations to deduct interest expense, why not exempt corporations of taxes on profits paid out to stockholders as dividends? Although bankers and investment bankers would scream, wouldn't that be more consistent with American virtues of thrift and enterprise? More consistent, too, with national interests?

I see lending money as a crummy business. Pocketing the money he so desperately needs, the relieved borrower, for the moment, is grateful to the lender. Borrowed money, however, spends more quickly than earned money. Soon, the borrower sees owing the money as a blight on his future. Festering in the borrower's mind is some vague sense of inequity that the money—which may not have been used wisely—must be repaid. Having to carry the burden of debt begins to seem something of an injustice. When his loan falls due, the borrower has no kindly feeling for the lender.

Buying a bond is lending money. Borrowing corporations and governments, just like people who borrow, have no love for lenders, their bondholders.

I see lending money as a risky business. National governments that print their own money can let internal debt pile up. To balance the budget, to reduce the debt, what politician would risk favor with his constituents by requiring harsh economic sacrifices? Certainly no one in the U.S. Congress or White House. Politically, it's safer to continually borrow and refinance, issuing new bonds to pay off maturing bonds and let inflation erode the value of the dollar owed. Knowingly, recklessly, advancing money that won't be repaid, managements of some banks make bad loans to produce, temporarily, higher interest income, higher current earnings and a higher price on the bank's stock—and hope to have been retired when the loans go into default. And just as ruthlessly, managements of some corporations borrow money, take on debt that will sink the ship in the next economic squall—expecting then to have moved on to other opportunities.

I see owning bonds as risky business. If you need investment income, you probably will have to buy bonds. If you're smart, you'll forego the lure of high yield and stick with high quality. High yield, anything much higher than the yield on Governments, puts you on notice: This bond is unsafe as to both interest and principal. The higher the yield, the greater the risk.

Bonds, nevertheless, can be bought for profit when prices are low, when yields are high and when, according to expert opinion, prices surely will go lower and yields higher. Any consensus among experts always is a reliable signal to travel in the opposite direction. For the nimble speculator, therefore, bonds can be bought profitably during a panic, but it's a game played on a slippery, downhill slope.

I just never saw investors get rich off bonds. I know that's a one-sided view, because bonds went down and interest rates went up from the 1940s to the mid-1980s, during almost my entire career as a broker.

CHAPTER 27

THE MUNICIPAL BOND MARKET

Municipal bonds are bonds issued by states, counties, cities and their many agencies—by layers of government below that of the Federal government. In the business, we speak of them as munis, pronounced MEW-nees. But when a broker phones you to offer a muni, he'll call it a tax-free bond. That's to grab your attention at the beginning of the conversation. He knows that almost anybody wants to hear about a tax dodge.

Interest on munis is exempt of Federal income tax. That's based on the idea or fiction that under the U.S. Constitution the states retain sovereignty and cannot be taxed by the Federal government—that the power to tax is the power to destroy, and the states don't want to be destroyed. Actually, I suspect, our senators and representatives in Washington don't want to incur the wrath of back-home politicians by cutting off their great source of low cost borrowing—which would happen if interest from municipal bonds were taxed. For whatever reason, the Federal government does not tax interest that investors receive on municipals.

Investors are taxed, as you know, on interest from Governments and corporates. So when you hear tax-free bond, you know it's a muni. But don't forget that the profit one might get on the sale of a muni, bought at a lower price, is taxable as a capital gain. Only the interest is exempt.

How attractive, to you, is tax-free income? It depends upon the rate at which you pay Federal income tax. The higher your income tax rate, or bracket, the more attractive tax-free income becomes and the more you'd be willing to pay for munis.

Let's say that you are paying Federal income tax at 25%. You need investment income and ask your broker what he can suggest. He says that he can offer, at par, a corporate bond or a corporate bond fund or even a Government—anyway, a taxable bond—with a 10% coupon. The yield, of course, is 10%. You ask about a tax-free bond. He pokes his quote machine and tells you that he can offer, at par, a muni with a 7% coupon. Assuming that the bonds are of the same maturity and comparable quality, which for you is the better buy?

Well, the annual interest of $100 that you'll get on the 10% corporate will be taxed at 25%, leaving you with $75. That beats the $70 you'd get on the 7%, tax-free muni. So you'd buy the corporate.

But suppose you're in a 35% tax bracket. On interest of $100 from the corporate, you pay tax of $35, leaving you $65—not as much as the $70, tax-free, you'd get from the 7% muni. Now in a higher tax bracket, you'd buy the muni.

So how attractive to you is tax-free income? It depends upon your income tax bracket. But for tax-free munis to produce for you more income than you can get from taxable corporates or Governments, you've got to be in a fairly high tax bracket.

Investors in the highest tax bracket get the greatest tax advantage of tax-free income from munis. Consequently, they are the most aggressive buyers of munis. Their buying advances prices. Munis become more expensive. That tax-free, 7% coupon costs more money. Muni yields drop. To buy that bond, you may have to pay a premium, a price above par. Meanwhile, corporate prices and yields are unaffected and stay about the same. More investors in lower brackets find that they can get more income buying corporates, or even Governments, and paying income tax on the interest. Only investors in the highest brackets come out better in munis.

Any tax-law change that raises or lowers the top income tax bracket has an immediate impact upon the municipal bond market. The impact, in fact, is more than immediate, because the market follows shifting political winds and anticipates changes of the tax law.

Let's suppose that Congress raises the top bracket from 35% to 70%. (For a while after WW II, the top rate was 90%.) Now, instead of being able to keep, after taxes, 65% of your interest income from a taxable corporate or Government, you'd end up with only 30%. Headlong, investors in that top 70% bracket would rush into the municipal bond market. Their buying would drive muni bond prices up and drive tax-free yields down—down almost to 3%, where a tax-free $30 would be the same as getting $100 on which they'd have to pay income tax of 70% or $70. Yielding 3%, a 15-year muni with a 7% coupon would sell at 149. High income taxes result in high prices—and low yields—in the municipal bond market.

Now suppose that Congress decides to cut that top-bracket tax rate. Investors with all their money tied up in municipals wouldn't be too pleased. How about that? Rich folks who wouldn't want taxes reduced. Why? Because market values of their muni investments would drop. A lower tax rate would diminish the advantage of owning munis for tax-free income. Investors would begin to see that even after paying the tax on interest from corporates and Governments, they'd end up with more income. Muni buyers would drop their bids, and some muni investors would sell their munis to buy corporates and Governments. In the muni bond market, lower income taxes result in lower prices and higher yields.

If we had no income tax at all, the tax-exempt feature of munis would be meaningless, and munis would sell at the same prices and produce the same yields as corporates. If corporates were yielding 10%, that muni with a 7% coupon would drop from par down to around 77 or $770 on a 15-year bond—low enough so that it also would yield 10%.

The same thing, of course, would happen if municipal bond interest were to become fully taxable. That would eliminate the advantage of owning munis. Muni prices would drop, yields would rise.

States, too, can have income taxes. Here in Georgia, the top rate is 6%. As states can tax one another, a Georgia resident must pay Georgia income tax, as high as 6%, on interest on out-of-state municipals. States can tax interest on corporates, too. But Government bond interest is exempt from state taxes, because states cannot tax the Federal government. As you might guess, interest on municipals of the state of Georgia, its cities, counties and agencies are exempt from Georgia state income tax. So given a choice between two comparable munis, one a Georgia bond and the other out-of-state, a resident of Georgia would buy the Georgia issue.

Bond Daddies

Public financing through the sale of municipals is nice business. Lots of money passes around. Local politicians are the key players. Big fees are paid to an engineering firm for a feasibility study, to a law firm for its legal opinion, to consultants for recommendations as to site and availability of Federal matching funds, maybe to a financial advisor, certainly to a bank as trustee, interest disbursing agent, transfer agent and registrar. And of course an investment banking firm is engaged to underwrite the bond issue—buying, marking up and selling the bonds. Many worthy folks have their hands out. And then, sometimes, in some places, politicians get kickbacks. Why give up those opportunities? Fight for states rights. Keep out the Federal regulators, the Securities and Exchange Commission. And municipal bond investors, many of whom are influential locally and some of whom are campaign contributors, have a parallel concern. They own munis and want to protect their tax-free incomes, so keep out the Internal Revenue Service.

To members of Congress, the political costs of intrusion are too great. Legislate, regulate anything, but why kick a hornets' nest?

Only in the early 1980s did the Municipal Securities Rulemaking Board come into existence as a not-too-harsh, self-regulating trade organization. The only effective restraint on municipal dealers, however, remained the threat of civil suit for fraud. Even that was not much deterrent, because victims of the many scams of the unregulated market have been banks and savings institutions, the officers of which are disinclined to call foul for fear of exposing their own foolishness or stupidity.

How about regulation by the states? In some states, regulation has been effective. Most states, I must guess, do a poor job of it.

And so the municipal bond business runs with the throttle wide open, laissez faire, caveat emptor.

I'd never heard of a bond daddy until we moved to Memphis in 1967. We'd been living in Macon. There, the biggest industry appeared to be loan sharking. Almost every third storefront was another small-loan office.

In Memphis, the many hospital buildings led me to believe that the major industry was sick folks. It didn't take long, however, to learn that healthcare was small potatoes. The big action was in municipal bonds. Successful muni salesmen were called bond daddies.

Around the time we got to Memphis, a man named George Lenox was murdered. Lenox, I was told, had begun his career with the municipal bond department of one of the major banks. The bank itself was a muni dealer selling bonds to surrounding country banks and, I assume, to high income individuals. Seeing how profitable the business was, Lenox had split off to start his own firm, as others did afterward. The bank became the spawning ground of independent muni bond firms.

By 1970 when we moved away from Memphis, the number of municipal bond firms was estimated to have been 150 and the number of full-time muni salesmen located in Memphis, 1,500.

One of the earlier abuses was the so-called adjusted trade. To overcome sales resistance of the muni buyer at the country bank, the bond salesman guarantees to buy back the bond, at any time, at the price the bank pays. That sounded okay, coming from the big city bank. The country banker goes along, saying to himself, How can I lose?

Afterward, however, when the price of his bond has collapsed and the country banker asks the salesman to make good on his buy-back guarantee, the salesman explains that he can pay the higher, original price only if the banker buys another bond at the same price. The second bond is worth no more, of course, than the first—probably a lot less. It's a swap, therefore, of a $10,000 cat for a $10,000 dog, both priced by the bond salesman. Between salesman and banker, it is understood that the dealer firm's printed confirmations of the two transactions, a sale and a buy, will show the same, artifically high price. That arrangement obviated question by the country bank's directors as to why the officer was losing money when he traded munis for the bank's investment portfolio.

Another sales technique was tail-gating. Working in collusion, three or more bond salesmen, call the same country banker, at intervals of about 30 minutes, to offer the same bond. Each offering is at a higher price and lower yield. Correctly assuming that the banker now is becoming frantic for fear of missing out on a good deal, the first caller phones again to say that he is about to raise his original, low offering price, would the banker want to reconsider? Yes, he would. And he buys.

Obituaries were useful. The muni salesman reads in the paper that a well-to-do man in a small Mississippi town has died. For the account of the dead man, a package containing a bundle of bonds, with a draft attached, arrives promptly at the local bank. When the banker inquires of the dealer firm, he's told that the dead man had bought the bonds a few days earlier and, for payment, had instructed the firm to draw a draft against his account at the bank. Lugubrious banker advises grieving widow. Now, what widow would go against the wishes of her late husband? (That, really, wasn't too imaginative. Custom-made shirts, too, are sold that way.)

But what of George Lenox? the dealer who was murdered?

Beyond the reaches of Tennessee, where he'd had legal problems, Lenox lived and worked across the state line into Mississippi. He had, I believe, three offices from which sales staffs sold municipals. A fancier of Tennessee walking horses and an early riser, Lenox was on the way to his farm one morning at dawn, driving inconspicuously in a gold Cadillac. He never made it to the farm. He was found shot to death. Afterward, a doctor told me that his left thigh had been punctured to the bone, maybe with an ice pick, maybe to get his attention. A Memphis judge told me that a reliable, firsthand source had told him that two torpedoes from out-of-state had come to Memphis with instructions, "Get our money or kill him." No one ever was arrested.

If a Memphis dealer wanted to buy bonds out of my firm's inventory, he could call our New York trading desk. I didn't want the business. I saw enough combat in WW II.

Memphis became second only to New York in volume of municipal bond trading. Ranked on innovative sales practices and effront-ery, Memphis was the undisputed first.

Dealer firms hired anybody—milkmen, used car salesmen, preachers, undertakers. In two days, the new salesman had mas-tered the yield book. (Back then, we had no calculators and comput-ers.) He could turn the pages to coupon rate, find the column for number of years and months to maturity and, knowing the dollar price, could get yield to maturity—or knowing the yield to maturity, get the price.

Now the salesman was assigned a geographic area for solicita-tion. In a large firm, he might have a state or part of a state; in a small firm, maybe a third of the U.S.A. He was ready to go. All he needed was a bank directory that gives the capitalization of each bank, names of officers and directors and, most important, the phone number. Leased WATS lines, used all day long, cut dealer firms' long distance costs.

Selling bonds requires no special talent, just brass. It goes like this:

Calling cold, the salesman gets the bank's receptionist on the phone, "Who's y'all's muni buyer?" She connects him. The salesman goes into his prepared pitch.

"Mr. Banker, this here is Herbert O'Connell of First Honesty Securities. [Never mention Memphis; the banker might hang up.] We've just picked up a tax-free, Tennessee muni for, I mean, cheap. It's a City of Jackson, Tennessee G.O. [General Obligation] six per-cent of January two thousand that I can let you have on a six-forty basis. Since we've never done business with y'all's bank, our man-aging partner's letting me offer you fifty of these bonds with no profit to our firm. Pretty attractive buy, don't you think?"

(The G.O. of a town the size of Jackson is a good credit. The city's taxing authority stands behind the bond. The bond carries a 6% coupon and matures in 2000. The 6.40% yield, higher than the 6% coupon, tells the banker that he'd be buying at a discount, below par, at a better yield than he would have expected from a G.O. And you can be sure that the salesman and his firm will make a nice profit on the sale.)

That's just about all the salesman knows about the bond and the bond market. From here on, the only way he can make the sale is to bully the buyer: "You gotta own this bond" or "You won't see a deal like this again."

Click. The banker hangs up. The salesman calls right back: "We musta been disconnected." And persistence pays off. After several calls the banker buys the bond.

A few years later when the next coupon on that bond is due and the bank clips it and mails it to the paying agent, the coupon is returned unpaid. The issue is in default. Only then the bank learns that the bond it owns is not a General Obligation of the City of Jackson, Tenn., it's a Jackson, Tenn., Gas Revenue bond—and income from the sale of gas in Jackson, Tenn., is not sufficient to cover interest payments on the bond. Try to find that salesman. Try to find that firm.

Dishonest firms, moreover, make unconscionable profits simply by overpricing their bond offerings. A 10-point markup, I've been told, is not unusual. That's a profit to the firm of $100 on a $1,000 bond.

Principals of Memphis bond firms heaped gifts upon their stars, the bond daddies. Cadillacs for Christmas presents were fairly common; in good years, one for every salesman. Some dressed in pastel suits and alligator shoes. Lots of girls, booze and weekend trips to the Caribbean.

At length, the state decided that bond daddies were doing little to enhance the good names of Shelby County and Tennessee and began to enforce its securities regulations. Bond dealers scampered. Some moved across the Mississippi River to West Memphis, Arkansas, some to Atlanta and some to Ft. Lauderdale where, predictably, the same cast of characters became dealers in another unregulated security, Government bonds. How about that? No regulation of the Government securities market.

In the mid-1980s, S&Ls trading in Governments got hit; some went broke. What did them in were repurchase agreements—in the business, called repos (pronounced RE-pose).

Nothing wrong with a repo. A large, reputable firm such as Goldman, Salomon or Merrill Lynch needs to borrow money to carry its huge Government bond inventory. Big employee benefit funds, like the state of Georgia, maintain enormous cash balances invested short-term to meet liquidity requirements—but they can't make loans. So the two, let's say Merrill Lynch and Georgia's employee health and welfare fund, enter into a repo agreement by which the state fund buys from Merrill Lynch maybe $20 million Governments, and Merrill Lynch promises to repurchase the bonds from them, after some agreed-upon number of days, at a price that will give the fund an attractive return on its money. The firm delivers the Governments; the state fund pays over the $20 million. The state fund holds those bonds. Thirty days or whatever later, the transaction is reversed.

Thus the state fund nets, risk free, $100,000 or $150,000—a slightly higher return than they could get on T Bills. And Merrill, in effect, was able to borrow at a slightly lower rate than a bank would charge. State employee benefit funds, as you know, are closely audited.

The S&Ls, few of which ever got high marks for shrewdness, also entered into repos—with small, unknown Government bond firms. But instead of getting delivery of the bonds, some of the S&Ls paid out their money on oral assurances of crooked dealer firms that the bonds were being held for them by some depository. They trusted the dealer firms.

What do you suppose those dealer firms did? Right. Under repo agreements, they sold the same bonds to other S&Ls and, on every repurchase date, made new repo agreements, pushing forward the day of reckoning. After a few of those S&Ls asked for their money, the music stopped. No money. No bonds. The biggest scandal involved a big S&L in Ohio that was trading with a Ft. Lauderdale firm. Several folks spent time in the slammer.

As an investor in muni bonds, you must depend almost entirely upon oral representations of the bond salesman. You'd better deal only with large, well known, national securities firms. You'd better be talking with a broker who is both knowledgeable and honest. Buying a muni for myself, I'd talk with the firm's regional muni bond manager, as well as the broker, to make sure I knew all the features of the bond I'm about to buy. I'd find out what option the issuer has to call the bond for redemption prior to maturity. Every bond issue is different.

A few other things you should know

Munis don't trade in a continuous market. Continuous market means that market makers or dealers stand ready, at all times and with their own money, both to buy securities at the prices they publicly bid and to sell those securities at the prices they publicly ask—either way, buy or sell. Government bonds, some corporates and almost all publicly held common stocks trade in continuous markets. Municipal dealers would love the sort of high volume that would allow continuous markets in munis. So let's not blame the dealer firms for that.

Transactions in munis are more like transactions in real estate. Each parcel of land is unique. That isn't to say that each muni is only one of a kind, but quantities of identical bonds are limited. However large an entire municipal issue may seem, it's broken up into relatively few bonds maturing in each of 15 or 20 years. Each maturity is a different bond; one maturity cannot be substituted for another. In such relatively small fragments, a continuous market is impossible.

To do business, to have merchandise for their salesmen to sell, municipal departments of larger firms must carry inventories. Firms are eager, most of the time, to buy bonds that investors, for whatever reasons, wish to sell. Yet a firm's trader can't bid too aggressively for a bond offered to him. He must bid low enough to mark it up 3-to-4 points, $30-to-$40 a bond, to compensate the salesmen, leave a profit for his firm and still reoffer that bond at a price and yield competitive with comparable bonds being shown in the market. A trader can bid too high and have to sell out at a loss to his firm. Do that too many times and a trader must consider the possibility of another loss—his job.

The result is a wide spread between the price at which a trader will buy-in a bond and the price at which he will reoffer it. That spread, necessarily, is a cost passed along to you as the buyer. Unless you view your purchases as permanent or, at least, semipermanent investments, don't buy municipals. And, of course, buying and selling munis is too costly to allow for trading.

That brings us to bond swapping for tax purposes, best explained by an example.

Two years ago, you bought at par $25,000 of munis. Interest rates since have gone up. Now the best bid you can get for those bonds is 80, $20,000 for the lot. If you sell, you will have a loss of $5,000. Maybe some of the loss can be used to reduce taxable earned income or investment income, or maybe the loss can be applied against $5,000 of a capital gain on which you otherwise would have to pay tax.

Your broker tells you that if you don't sell the bond to take the loss, that if you sit with it until it returns to par, you've passed up the opportunity to save money on this year's income tax. But you want to continue your investment in munis. And you don't want to sell out at 80 only to watch the bond go back to 100.

The tax law doesn't allow you to sell and immediately buy back the same security. That's a riskless transaction, a wash sale, the loss from which would be disallowed as a deduction. To use a capital loss to reduce taxable income, the security sold may not be bought back within 30 days. And if instead you buy first to double up before you sell to take the tax-loss, you must stay doubled up for more than 30 days before selling. Internal Revenue thinks of everything.

(Let's stop here for a moment. You must remember that tax laws change. I'm not giving tax advice. Talk with your accountant.)

Here, your broker will explain to you that you can simply swap your bond for a different but comparable bond and thereby stay invested in munis and avoid the wash sale rule. To make the swap attractive to you, the trader usually will cut his markup, but he probably won't trade for less than 1 1/2 points, $15 per bond, which still comes out of your pocket, one way or another. You must give up something. The bond offered to you may cost more than the one you're selling. If you insist upon an even-dollar swap, you may have to accept fewer bonds, a lower quality bond, a longer maturity, a lower coupon and lower current yield or lower yield to maturity.

And the tax savings may not be of much value to you.

Instead of swapping, if you keep the first bond until the market recovers and sell it at par, you'll have no tax to pay. You would have bought at par, sold at par. But if you swap, if you sell to take the tax-loss on your first bond to switch into the second bond at 80 and then ride it up to par and sell, you'll have to pay tax on that $5,000 capital gain.

So to me it looks like a bond swap only postpones payment of taxes. And only if you're in the top income tax bracket will a swap work. Also, finding a comparable bond into which to swap isn't easy. For their clients, brokers do a lot of tax swaps. In blocks of 50 and 100 bonds, it's great business, for them. For the clients, I'm not too sure.

Every transaction ought to stand on its own economic merits. Those who enter into clever schemes just to beat the income tax usually blunder into booby traps. Many seemingly normal people, however, react strangely to paying income taxes. To them, avoiding tax, even illegally evading tax, is some kind of righteousness. What some folks will do to beat the income tax, you wouldn't believe.

How about those wide spreads on munis? Are dealers taking you to the cleaners?

Munis are not bought by one investor direct from another with brokers in between. The only sellers are dealers, willing to sell to you the bonds they own. If you're the seller, the only buyers are dealers who buy your bonds to put on the shelf, into their own inventories. To stay in business, municipal dealers must make a profit, and their profit is a part of that spread. Profit must be enough to cover big losses they sometimes must take on their own inventories. Over-night, unexpected news can wreck the bond market. Next morning, a dealer firm can have losses of two, three, five points on its entire bond inventory of $50 or $100 million.

If the business were a risk-free gold mine, muni dealers would outnumber fast food joints. Yes, spreads are wide. No, reputable firms are not gouging their clients. Competition, moreover, keeps most of them honest.

But don't forget the vermin who crawled out of Memphis to set up shop in cities not identified with bond daddies. They're still out there, marking up bonds eight and 10 points and lying about the quality. Every business has its crooks, offering something for nothing, waiting for suckers like you and me. The person who gets taken succumbs, not to the guile of the swindler, but to his own greed. He's entitled to little sympathy.

Municipal bond funds, unit trusts, are similar to corporate bond funds. Sales charges, around $35 per $1,000 unit, are about the same. Underlying bonds, probably, are okay, A-rated or better. Yes, a few poor quality issues have been thrown in to make the yield more attractive. Nevertheless, good features probably outweigh the bad. Like corporate bond funds, muni bond funds are widely diversified. That protects your capital. One of the best features of any bond fund is the willingness of the sponsoring brokerage firm to buy back units at a fair price. An investor with less than $100,000 available for municipal purchases may be better off in a muni bond fund. I think he is.

Whether taxable or tax-free, bonds bought for income ought to be safe. The only reason for buying a less-than-A-rated muni is to get a slightly higher yield. I don't risk my money to get one or two percentage points. For myself, I'd insist upon a rating of no less than double-A, preferably triple-A.

I'd buy no industrial revenue bond. What's an industrial revenue? Well, it's tax-free . . . but let me give you an example of how one might have been issued.

A manufacturer, looking for a factory site in a rural area, goes to the county commissioners to tell them that their county is being considered for a new industry that could mean jobs and a boost to the economy of the area. Then he asks, "What can you gentlemen do for me? Tax and zoning concessions? water and sewer lines? access road?" Maybe, but all that costs money. At no cost, the county can create an industrial agency to issue, in the name of the county, tax-free bonds with which to raise money for building the factory. Those bonds, industrial revenues, do not become debt of the county. The county is only a conduit between the manufacturing company and the bondholders. Through the county's industrial agency, the manufacturer pays interest on the bonds and, upon maturity, repays principal. Because the interest is paid in the name of the county, that interest is tax-exempt to the investor. That enables the manufacturer to borrow at a rate of interest lower than he could get at a bank.

Hospital revenue bonds and bonds for nonpublic enterprises are issued in the same way. One town issued industrial revenues to finance a hamburger stand. The county has no liability for the debt. When the business goes broke, the bondholders are stuck.

Most of the excesses have been corrected, but why industrial revenues were ever tax-free beats me. I suppose it's politicians again. Congressmen in Washington want no part of shutting off a source of cheap financing that brings business to their districts. So offensive is the abuse of tax exemption that one wonders why courts have not declared the practice a sham and the interest subject to Federal income tax.

Although you should look askance upon any revenue bond, a municipal water and sewer revenue can be an excellent credit. The user, threatened with having his water cut off, will pay his water bill. Even so, don't buy the bond unless the rating is A or better.

A general obligation bond of a city, county or state, in most instances, is a more reliable credit than a revenue bond. Again, insist upon a rating of A or better.

No Federal regulatory agency exercises control over municipal financing. Prospectuses or other descriptive material rarely are available. Investing in munis, you sometimes are buying a pig in a poke. Your dependence upon representations of the salesman is total. For myself, I'd buy munis only if I needed tax-free income and only if I knew exactly what I was getting into.

CHAPTER 28

LIONS, TIGRS, CATS—ZERO COUPONS

In 1982, we began selling what are called TIGRs, another of those acronyms, for Treasury Investment Growth Receipts, or something like that. We were doing a brisk business in TIGRs when an impertinent rookie broker asked, "What's a TIGR?" We all knew that TIGRs had to do with Government bonds, but what we were selling had an odd par value, $4,500, which none of us understood. When someone at last got up the courage to inquire of our fixed income specialist in New York, his first response was, "I thought no one ever would ask." That seemed to suggest that no broker in the firm knew what he was selling. We surely didn't.

You'll remember, at the beginning of this part of the book on fixed income securities, the description of a bearer or coupon bond: a large sheet of paper with the bond itself printed on the left side and the coupons printed on the right side—one coupon for each semiannual interest payment.

Now suppose you have a U.S. Treasury 9% bond that matures in 20 years and that you cut off, separately, each coupon and spread out all the pieces on a table top. The 40 small pieces would be the coupons—one for each of the 40 interest payments of $45 that will be made, at six-month intervals, until maturity. The large piece, of course, would be the $1,000 stripped bond.

Further suppose that in the same way you strip 99 more bonds so that now you have 40 stacks of coupons, 100 coupons in each stack, and a pile of 100 stripped bonds.

A TIGR is either one of those stacks of coupons or a pile of stripped bonds.

The specialist explained that the firm had bought $50 or $100 million U.S. Treasury 9% bonds maturing in 20 years. What we were selling were stacks of 100 semiannual coupons, each stack worth $4,500 on interest payment dates, and, without any coupons, piles of 10 stripped bonds, each pile worth $10,000 when redeemed in 20 years. As the Treasury no longer was issuing coupon bonds, we had no clipped pieces of paper to sell. Instead, the buyers got a confirmation of ownership.

The firm had appointed a bank as trustee, and at the Federal Reserve that bank was the nominal owner of the $50-to-$100 million worth of bonds. Every six months, upon the interest payment date, the bank would receive from the Treasury the semiannual interest payment on those bonds. As trustee, the bank then would pay off all the investors who had bought that current coupon. That explained the odd $4,500 principal amount—100 coupons, each for $45.

Let's say the investor bought a $4,500 TIGR due November 15, 1995. He then owned 100 coupons for the November 15, 1995, interest payment on 100 bonds, $100,000 principal amount. Shortly after November 15, 1995, he would receive a check for the interest on those 100 bonds: $45 X 100 = $4,500, the par value of his TIGR. Only then would the TIGR be paid off.

The stripped bond itself also was a TIGR. The only differences were par values and pay-off dates—the owner of a TIGR for 10 stripped bonds would be paid $10,000 when the bond matured 20 years later. So that's what we were selling, clipped coupons and stripped bonds.

TIGRs produce no interest, no return. To cash in, the investor must wait until the interest payment date of his coupons or until maturity of his stripped bonds. We did make an active secondary market in TIGRs, however, so he could sell whenever he wished.

Suppose today is November 15, 1990. Suppose you buy a $4,500 face value TIGR of November 15, 1995—that's the coupon payable 11/15/95 on $100,000 U.S. Treasury 9% bonds. What's the present value of that $4,500 that you won't get until five years from now when the trustee bank receives that interest payment and mails its check to you? You know what you're going to end up with, but you don't know what $4,500 in the future is worth today.

First, you'd have to know what five-year U.S. Treasuries are yielding in today's market. So let's say that five-year Treasuries are yielding 10 1/4%.

With the same arithmetic we used to determine present discounted value of a T Bill, we'd work backward. Also, we'd have to subtract out coupon interest we could have gotten every six months on a U.S. Treasury bond or note—interest payments we won't get from a TIGR.

According to my bond calculator, the TIGR, bought to yield 10 1/4% and paying off in five years, would be worth $60.655% of par. Par of $4,500 multiplied by 0.60655 is $2,729. So on a 10 1/4% yield basis, you'd pay $2,729 for a TIGR that would return to you a face value of $4,500 when the November 15, 1995, interest payment is made. Each year that pases, that TIGR would appreciate in value until the final pay off.

What about the bonds without the coupons? The stripped bond is sold in the same way, at a discount. The holder of a TIGR for 10 stripped bonds gets $10,000 from the U.S. Treasury only upon maturity of the bond. He's entitled to no semiannual payments of interest. Those interest payments on the stripped bonds have been sold to someone else.

Don't think that owning TIGRs you'll get off scot-free of income tax. The Internal Revenue Service makes you pay tax on "imputed" interest. IRS assumes that, each year, the value of a TIGR "accretes" in an amount equivalent to the interest you could get on an interest paying bond. That assumed gain is taxed as though it were interest income to you during the year. The TIGR owner, therefore, pays tax each year on money that he won't get until the payment date of the coupon or the maturity date of the stripped bond. For some persons, that could be troublesome. Nothing coming in, taxes going out. That cost of ownership actually reduces the value of the investment but is not taken into account in its pricing.

How 'bout them CATs? and LIONs?* Same as TIGRs, just sold by different firms. In each day's *Wall Street Journal,* you can find them quoted under Treasury Bonds, Notes & Bills. They're called Stripped Treasuries.

Zero Coupon Bonds

About the time TIGRs were introduced, we began seeing zero coupon bonds. Perhaps the concept of TIGRs gave issuers and investment bankers the idea. Just like TIGRs, zero coupons, both corporate and municipal, are sold at deep discounts, pay no interest and, upon maturity, are redeemed at par.

Talk about mortgaging our children's futures, how about a city that might issue a 20-year zero coupon muni at, say, 8% to pay for maybe street repairs. What will the city get today from the sale of that bond maturing in 20 years? $156. That's right. Today, the city sells a $1,000 bond for $156, uses that money to repave streets and 20 years from now lets the next generation come up with $1,000 for the bondholder. Unless the U.S. dollar depreciates badly, that coming generation isn't going to be too happy about paying $1,000 for $156 worth of paving done 20 years earlier. Does that suggest to you that the second generation might refuse to pay off those bonds? It's an issue that a politician could use to get himself elected.

---

*Not to be confused with LYONs, for Liquid Yield Option Notes, zero coupon bonds convertible into common stock. And you can count on Wall Street to breed many other strange animals.

Describing TIGRs and zero coupon bonds as fixed income securities is a contradiction. Neither pays income. Instead, each accumulates incremental value as it approaches maturity. If you need investment income, you wouldn't want either. If you want growth, you'd be guaranteed price appreciation of the difference between the discounted purchase price and, at maturity, the par value—but no more. Yet a high rate of inflation could wipe you out.

Comfortable with that, you may wish to inquire a bit further. What about volatility? price fluctuation? What about the cost of buying?

As a LION, TIGR, CAT or any zero coupon bond, by definition, pays no interest, market prices exaggerate the impact of change of interst rates. For example, let's compare a 15-year, 9% interest-paying bond bought at par, with a 15-year, zero coupon bond bought to yield to maturity the same 9%.

	15-year 9% Coupon Bond	15-year, 9% Zero Coupon Bond
Bought at 9% yield basis	$1,000	$267
Price at 7% yield basis	1,184 +18%	356 +33%
Price at 11% yield basis	855 -15%	201 -25%

Assume that you know that long-term interest rates are about to drop. You really don't know, of course, but say you're convinced that rates will drop. You call your friendly broker to buy some bonds. "Why buy bonds?" he says. "Why not some of our TIGRs [or CATs or LIONs]? You can make almost twice as much on your money." You buy the TIGRs. And sure enough, long-term rates do drop, from 9% to 7%. On bonds, you'd have made only 18%. But on your TIGRs, you've made 33%. Not bad.

Supposing, however, that rates don't drop. Contrary to all logic, long-term rates rise, from 9% to 11%. On the bonds, you'd have lost 15%. On your TIGRs, you've lost 25%. Not good.

If you wish to speculate, if it's leverage you're after, buy the zero coupons.

And what about the cost of buying?

On zero coupons, TIGRs, CATs, etc., the brokerage firm figures its markup as a percent of par value, $1,000. Relate the dollar amount of that markup, maybe $20, to the deeply discounted price of the zero, $267 in the table above. That's 7 1/2%. Pretty steep. An extraordinarily large part of the cost of a zero is markup. Brokers, as you might guess, prefer to sell you the zero coupons.

Within a few years of retirement, one might consider zero coupon corporates or TIGRs in his Individual Retirement Account

(IRA) which is tax deferred. With a child four or five years away from entering college, one could buy a zero coupon corporate or TIGR in an account for the minor. Income tax on the imputed interest would be little or nothing.

However, if I needed income, I'd buy an interest paying bond. If I wanted long-term growth, I'd buy a common stock.

CHAPTER 29

GINNIE MAES

For income, should you buy a Ginnie Mae?

To answer that, I must tell you something about Ginnie Maes. As you know, GNMA is Government National Mortgage Association. Created by Congress in 1968, GNMA applies a Government guarantee to $1 million packages of home mortgages. Those packages then become marketable securities in pieces as small as $25,000. That, of course, has brought billions of investment dollars to the home mortgage market. To better understand what GNMA does, recall your own homeowner experience.

When you bought a home, you put down 15 or 20% and borrowed the rest. Your mortgage was for maybe 20 years. Your fixed monthly payments were for both interest and repayment of principal—mostly interest in the earlier years, mostly principal in the final years. Now put yourself in the shoes of the mortgage lender.

When you buy a Ginnie Mae, you become a mortgage lender. Those fixed, monthly payments come to you. Actually, what you're getting is your share of payments from a $1 millon package of mortgages that a mortgage banker has put together, turned over to a trustee and has had guaranteed by GNMA—U.S. Government guaranteed. But all is not peaches and cream.

Just like Government bonds, Ginnie Maes go up and down with swings in long term interest rates. They go down, of course, as interest rates go up. But do they go up when interest rates go down? Well, maybe not.

When interest rates drop, homeowners pay off their mortgages and refinance with new mortgages at lower rates. As a Ginnie Mae investor, a mortgage lender, you get paid off at par. The part of your investment that's paid off never gets a chance to trade at a premium above par. So you're fully exposed to the risks of the downside, but your opportunities on the upside are severely limited.

Government bonds, remember, are non-callable and can trade at big premiums as interest rates might fall.

If you buy Ginnie Maes for income—and that's the only reason to own them—you'll have a monthly bookkeeping problem of keeping separate the payments of interest and principal. You wouldn't want to spend the principal, because you'd end up with nothing. And to reinvest that principal, you probably would have to let those payments accumulate in a money market fund.

I believe you'll be happier with a Government bond even though the yield may be slightly lower.

PART FOUR

AVOIDABLES AND UNAVOIDABLES

CHAPTER 30

PAY YOUR TAXES CHEERFULLY

In Macon back in the mid-1960s, a woman client on her way out of our office stopped by to talk with me. She said that she'd just bought some municipal bonds. She was pleased with her purchase and seemed eager to tell someone about it.

"The reason I bought municipals," she explained, "is because I want to leave my daughter as much as I can without her having to pay inheritance tax. Since the bonds won't have my name on them, I'll put them in the safe deposit box that we have in both our names. Then after I'm gone, she can take them out and just say nothing."*

Beating taxes is seen by some people, not as dishonest, but as a sport that demands ingenuity of which to be proud.

The lady client made no mention of needing investment income. If she'd wanted income, she might have done better to have bought higher yielding corporate or Government bonds and paid income tax on the interest. But I doubt that she cared whether the interest payments were taxable or tax-free. Anyway, she didn't mention it. Obviously, she had bought munis only because she could get nonregistered, bearer bonds that probably wouldn't be identified as part of her estate.

I don't remember having seen that lady client ever again. I'm sure we delivered the bonds to her and that she put them in the safe deposit box she had jointly with her daughter. And maybe after the lady died, the daughter did evade estate tax on that part of her inheritance. Whether or not, how smart was it of the lady to have invested only to gain what she saw as a tax advantage?

Let's suppose that the munis she bought were 15-year bonds, maturing, that is, around 1980; further that the daughter kept the

---

*Many otherwise law-abiding citizens must have used the same scheme to beat estate taxes. In later years, the IRS required banks to report the Social Security number of any person who presented clipped coupons for collection of interest. Thus the IRS knew that the bank's customer owned the bonds. Since 1983, all bonds have been issued in registered form, and checks for interest payments automatically are sent to the registered owners.

bonds until maturity. Redeeming the bonds, the daughter would have been paid off with 1980 dollars that would have bought for her about one-third of what the same dollar would have bought in 1965. That's to say, two-thirds of her buying power had been lost to inflation.

For the moment let's forget about estate tax and income tax. What purposes could the mother have had for investing? To begin with, I'll say that she must have had no need of investment income. She wanted only to leave her daughter as much as possible. Clearly, that would have required investing her money to make money, to profit. For that purpose, she should have bought stocks, not bonds. Had she invested in a high quality, common stock mutual fund, she probably would have protected herself against the loss of buying power of the dollar. However, she must have been so obsessed with ways of not paying taxes that she never considered the risk of inflation nor the possibility of investing her money to make money— more money than the estate tax ever could have been.

What the mother's net worth was, I don't know. Yet I suspect that her estate was not large enough to have been taxed much at all. Whether or not, her scheme for beating the tax likely was a disaster. She'd have done much better had she never heard about estate taxes.

Tax evasion, running the risk of a jail term, is a stupid way of reducing one's tax bill. Smarter persons do it legally. They get the tax law changed.

Most of us, I'm sure, would like to believe that congressmen represent the public interest. Too often we see that most of them represent private interests—very privately. Most congressmen represent the interests of those from whom they receive money, what they describe as campaign contributions. The big bucks come from business and industry associations that expect, in return, changes of the tax law to exempt them from having to pay taxes. They seem to get their money's worth.

In 1986, however, something different happened.

Over the years, responding to the demands of their contributors, congressmen had amended the old tax law so many times that not only were all the "special interests" relieved of the burden of paying taxes, even specific companies and persons were favored. Congressmen scarcely could find another place in the law to cut out another loophole. The tax law, instead of being a ladle for collecting revenues, had become a sieve.

Although I hope not, a cynical thought may occur to you. If all the big contributors already had been accommodated, from whom could a congressman expect further contributions? Cynical, indeed, it's a thought that may have occurred even to some of our congressmen, What do we do? And some nimble mind had the answer. Join the tax reformers, wipe out the whole damned thing and start all over again—new demands for tax relief, more campaign contributions, more special exemptions. Thus, likely, was born the Tax Reform Act of 1986.

The 1986 law was supposed to have eliminated the more egregious abuses and made the tax on incomes both fair and simple. It all began with the idea that a flat tax ought to be levied against all gross incomes above some minimum level. It would end the many deductions that can be taken to reduce the amount of one's taxable income. Everyone's income, regardless of source, would be taxed at the same rate, at an across-the-board percentage. Maybe no more than just 15% on everyone's income would balance the budget.

What a splendid idea. The entire tax code could be printed on a single sheet of paper. Your tax return could be a postcard. Put to a national referendum, such a proposal would receive the enthusiastic, affirmative vote of nine out of 10 Americans.

But that's not what we got from the Tax Reform Act. Not exactly every deduction was wiped out. The oil and life insurance industries continued to enjoy preferential tax advantages. Other industries, companies and even individuals were favored.* The politically emasculated tax-paying public continued to carry the burden. And the enormous annual deficit added to the staggering national debt. Those problems, however, are not our concern in this exercise.

Reflecting back, I must say that most investors worry too much about taxes. So often, a person would seem less concerned with the investments he was about to make, less concerned with making money than with the taxes he might have to pay. Although he had no capital gain, although he hadn't made the investment, already he was bristling with resentment of maybe having to pay taxes. With such a mind set, how could he have made a rational investment judgment? even a rational tax judgment?—if there is such a thing.

Time and again over the years, I heard the lament of an investor with almost all of his wealth represented by a single stock— stock of the company with which he worked or stock of the company to which he had sold out his business or stock he had received as an inheritance.

"Almost everthing I've got is tied up in this one stock. When I got it years ago, it was a nice nest egg. Since then, it's grown beyond anything I could have imagined. Now the annual dividends are more

---

*The "Gallo amendment," promoted by the wealthy California wine family and sponsored by Georgia Representative Ed Jenkins, allowed the transfer of as much as $2 million to a grandchild without paying any special tax.

than the stock was worth when I got it. I don't even know how many times it's split. My cost is 10% of today's market value. If I sold it, almost all of what I'd get would be profit. The income tax I'd have to pay would be more money than I want to think about. I know that the company doesn't look so great anymore. I know the stock's high and the market's high. But I just can't afford to sell."

In those circumstances, anyone who concludes that he just can't afford to sell, that he just couldn't pay such a huge amount of income tax, probably is approaching a time when he'll no longer have to worry about making the decision. The market just may decide his problem for him. Let the price of that stock fall far enough and he'll have no profit on which to pay tax.

In the summer of 1983, most of what I had was in the stock of the firm with which I worked. The stock had had a prolonged, powerful advance. It had outrun the market but now had begun to falter. The stock lost its steam. It dropped off a bit and then began to fall on heavy volume. I sold out.

As I'd bought the stock many years earlier, most of the market value was profit and taxable at the capital gains rate of 20%, which I had to pay in the following year. Certainly I couldn't afford the risk of reinvesting money that I owed the IRS. Nor did I want to become emotionally attached to money that I couldn't keep.

I knew how much I'd owe in the following April, nine months later. In a separate account, I deposited 20% of the proceeds of my sale and bought U.S. Treasury bills maturing in April. I never looked on that money as mine. In fact, I never looked at the account until the bills matured. I paid my income tax and forgot it. That's one way to obviate the shock of having to come up with a lot of money when you see your tax bill.

Whether such a sale as that later proves to have been a good decision depends, first, upon how the remaining, after-tax proceeds were reinvested and, second, what afterward happened to the price of the stock sold.

After tax, you have only a part of the proceeds to reinvest. If it's 80%, as in my case, each 80 cents reinvested in other stocks must outperform the 100 cents that you would have had in the stock you sold. You're asking a lot of your 80 cents. But if the stock you sold falls badly enough, you may find yourself better off to have made the sale and paid the tax. Investment judgment, therefore, is far more important than tax decisions.

As a broker, I always was happy to see year-end tax loss selling begin. In years when the market was trending down in November and December, tax selling was especially good business for us. As an investor, however, I seldom have seen worthwhile benefits from selling stocks to take losses for tax purposes. In that respect, I'm an atypical investor—or taxpayer. Most investors seem more concerned with income taxes than I.

Why sell a good stock to save a few bucks on income tax? The risk/reward ratio isn't attractive. So that the IRS won't disallow your loss as a wash sale, you must either double up a month before you sell or stay out of the security a month afterward. Either way, you run the risk of the market's turning against you during the month that you're either doubled up or out altogether. Too, commission costs are expensive.

Most states have a Gift to Minors law that allows a custodian, who usually is a parent, to hold money and property in behalf of the minor, to invest and reinvest, and to use the money to pay for the child's maintenance and education. Brokerage firms will carry accounts for custodians for minors—but not for minors, because minors cannot enter into contracts.

For whatever reasons, social, economic or even political, Congress has encouraged gifts to minors by providing small tax breaks to custodians.

Most custodian accounts for minors that I saw were used as a way of investing money to pay for children's college educations. For that purpose, almost any parent could consider a custodian account for a minor child. The education fund can grow and accumulate without being fully taxed as income to the parents.

Giving money to children can be a way of avoiding estate tax on the amount of the gift. Doting grandparents sometimes do that perhaps out of genuine affection or, as I sometimes suspected, just to feel good about themselves.

I've observed that a gift of money can be damaging to a child. As custodian, the parent might say, Oh, this money will never become a problem, because I'll always have the say-so as to how it's spent. Well, possibly so. A child, however, doesn't forget that the money's out there for him. And state law doesn't allow you to be an Indian giver. When that boy is 21 (18 in some states), the money is his to spend as he wishes, whether the custodian likes it or not. If the young man is headstrong, he may decide that he knows better than his parents how to spend that money, and they can do nothing about it.

Money given to a young person can deny him opportunity to succeed on his own, to gain self confidence. A father who indulges his son does so, possibly, to exhibit his own wealth. If so, the father's ego may be more important to him than his son's success and happiness.

My children were responsive to my directions only so long as they needed me to pay their bills. Money gives a parent remarkable control over children. Once your children can provide for themselves, however, your authority is gone. But that's the way it ought to be.

After age of about 40, most persons have developed habits of work and conduct that allow them to handle a windfall satisfactorily.

If I were looking for a way to reduce my income taxes, I'd find something better than a custodial account for my minor child. Nor do I see the wisdom of trying to get around estate taxes. Most of those tax dodges require that your money, after your death, go into trusts with limits upon what your wife and children can do. Why tie them up? I can't know the future. I can't foresee the needs they may have.

I can see, however, what's ahead for me—lock step, as an associate once told me, to the garbage heap. So I can see the need of a standby trust arrangement by which my children can take over my affairs if I become senile. And after I'm dead, I'd rather they make their own mistakes.

Getting older, I don't need complications and vexations. It's easier to pay the taxes and free my mind for more pleasant things. Furthermore, I've had it both ways: no income and no taxes to pay; good income and lots of taxes to pay. I'll take the good income and the taxes that go along with it.

CHAPTER 31

TAX INVESTMENTS WON'T DO MUCH FOR YOU

Annuities and Life Insurance

For some years, we tried to get our brokers to sell life insurance. Few were interested enough to study for the exam that the state of Georgia requires of life insurance salesmen, so few of our brokers were licensed. But after passage of the 1986 tax law, life insurance and annuities were about the only surviving tax-advantaged investments. The life insurance lobby had done its job with Congress.

Years ago, annuities were sold to people who needed retirement income. Annually, they paid in some fixed amount and after age 65 got some small monthly income for a limited number of years—or some smaller monthly income for life. In more recent years, inflation had left those hard working, thrifty people with incomes that would buy only a fraction of what they had expected. People wised up. They stopped buying annuities.

The insurance industry stepped forward to offer variable annuities. Instead of the insurance company investing the money and raking off everything above the guaranteed, low rate of interest, the buyer of the annuity is given the choice of having his money invested in one or more of the insurance company's funds—a stock fund, a bond fund and a money-market fund. But the insurance company is taking care of itself, too. Its commissions, fees and penalties for early withdrawal produce nice profits.

Only life insurance companies can offer annuities, because some death benefit feature must be included to qualify an annuity for the special tax advantages. On the money paid into an annuity, interest, dividends and capital gains are allowed to accumulate, tax-free, until money is withdrawn. But if money is taken out before ages 59 1/2, the Government hits you with its penalty—10%. That's in addition to income tax. Investing in an annutiy, you tie up your money possibly for many years.

Unless you could get the tax advantage, you wouldn't buy an annuity. You'd buy a common stock mutual fund of your own selection and, if you needed life insurance, buy separately a term policy. So your only reason for buying an insurance company's annuity is to get the tax advantage.

The insurance company, however, isn't giving you that tax advantage for nothing. You're paying for it. And the insurance company is charging you as much as it can without completely eliminating the tax advantage to you. That makes it a better deal for the insurance company than for you. The insurance industry didn't spend all that money lobbying Congress to make money for you.

So it's the tax-deferral that sells annuities. However, with the insurance company's commissions, fees and probable penalties taken out of the money that you pay in, you'd have to stay with an annuity for many years to finally come out better than if you had just bought a mutual fund direct and paid the taxes.

The same can be said of variable life insurance.

Single premium variable annuities or single permium variable life insurance may sound impressive, but when you go into partnership with an insurance company, you put up all the money; they take a split of the profits. Their take may be more than those tax advantages are worth to you.

Tax Shelters

Although the tax law of 1986 wiped out many of the tax loopholes and, along with them, most of the tax shelter business, you can be sure that every session of Congress will respond to demands of campaign contributors for new tax exemptions and exceptions. Each new loophole will bring forth a new tax shelter investment. The demand is out there. Some people are so preoccupied with taxes, especially income taxes, that they seem happier to save a tax dime than to make ten dollars.

I can recall no investor whose tax avoidance skills made him rich. Quickly, however, I must qualify that observation.

Through the 1970s and mid '80s, Federal income tax laws were so skewed to favor real estate that investments in office buildings, shopping centers, warehouses, apartments and so on, were made largely to obtain the extraordinary tax advantages. But of those who got rich, few were public investors.

The big killings were made by the developers and by promoters who sold partnership interests in those properties. Public investors, as the limited partners, paid prices based on the most optimistic assumptions of tax deductions for rapid depreciation and forecasts of high rates of inflation. Inflation was expected to translate into escalating rents, ever increasing resale values and, within five or ten years, handsome capital gains, taxed at a maximum rate of—at that time, only 20%.

Other tax shelters sold publicly were oil and gas drilling programs and equipment leasing deals. Buyers were eager investors with aversions to paying income taxes. But most tax shelter investors that I knew did no better than the lady who stashed away the muni bonds for her daughter.

Promoters of tax shelters were the big winners—not because of money they saved on their own taxes. They made it from their fees and mark ups. Nor did those of us in the brokerage business do badly. Commissions were large enough to arrest the attention of every deserving broker. One of our offerings that I recall of was partnerships in barges, an equipment leasing deal.

At Memphis, the Mississippi River is a sight of greatness and grandeur. From the Summit Club on top of the First National Bank building, one could see across the river into Arkansas, down the river into Mississippi and up the river for many miles. A tow of barges moving up or down the river is a thrilling spectacle. A single barge is big. Close up, it's real big. A tow is a lot of barges lashed together. Unless age has badly affected my memory, tows that I've seen from the bluffs were of as many as six barges across and eight deep, 48 barges in a single tow. It looked like acres of barges. If you've never seen a tow, you should know that it's pushed and not pulled or towed. But it's still a tow. The towboat must be little more than a tub to float the huge diesel engines that turn the propellers.

In increments of $20,000, we sold limited partnerships interests in barges. You could borrow some of that $20,000 and deduct the interest cost from your taxable income. The depreciation, too, was a deduction, and you could get an investment tax credit (ITC) of 10% that could come right off the income tax that you otherwise would have to pay. Lots of tax goodies. All the while, someone was paying you rent on your barge which was being pushed up the Mississippi with a load of oil or gasoline and then back down with grain or coal or something.

It was a great investment idea. A barge has no moving parts. It just floats. If a careless towboat captain pokes a hole in it, a piece of iron plate can be welded over in a trice. What a sweet deal. Nothing can happen to a barge.

During the first year that our barges were in service, however, something happened to the river. A drought in the Great Plains states and up the Ohio river valley cut off the water. The Mississippi almost dried up. Our barges, empty, I suppose, sat it out, high and dry on mud banks. No rent coming in, interest and insurance being paid out. Scarcely a great year for barges as a tax investment.

Other equipment leasing partnerships were owners of IBM computers, railroad box cars and hopper cars and almost anything else you might think of.

When oil prices were advancing by leaps and bounds, oil and gas drilling partnerships were especially easy to sell. With the collapse of oil prices, many partnerships went broke. That created severe problems for the investors. The IRS takes the view that partnership debt wiped out by bankruptcy is the same as income and that each partner, therefore, must pay income tax on what had been his share of that debt. What an unpleasant surprise, to find yourself paying income tax on money you never got. Too, there is recapture. IRS required partners, in some instances, to pay back-taxes on incomes that had been reduced by deductions taken in prior years.

Long before tax shelters had become a part of the investment business, anyone could appreciate the adage, "No good oil deal ever gets out of Texas." Being romanced by some promoter, you'd have to ask yourself, as the prospective buyer, Why me? How was I selected to be offered this unique opportunity? Such a cinch—and they want to cut me in? Too often, investors become so intent upon beating taxes that they ignore the investment merits of what they're buying.

If ever you're being sold something that has an appealing tax avoidance feature—a tax shelter, that is—stop. Ask yourself, "Without the tax breaks, would I buy this investment? What am I looking for? profit or income? Apart from the tax advantage, would this investment meet my need?" Your answers to those questions probably will tell you, "Don't buy a tax shelter."

It's almost impossible, legally, to completely avoid paying taxes. Tax shelters, more likely, allow you only to postpone payment. To achieve that, you always must meet certain requirements imposed by the law and IRS regulations. For one, you always must put your money at risk. For another, you always must put your money beyond your reach for some period of time; you must relinquish control, which may be something more than an inconvenience. And if ever you want to sell out, you'll find that there's no market for your partnership interest.

To assuage whatever qualms you may express about not paying your taxes, a tax shelter salesman will have a plausible, even patriotic explanation for you. The tax advantage, he will tell you, was created by Congress to direct investment capital toward areas that the Government has identified as requiring development to meet some noneconomic purpose, some social or national security need, or to stimulate the economy. That's a way of saying that whatever the Government's purpose, the tax-favored area, viewed on its own merits, can't attract capital and, therefore, may not be a great place in which to sink your money. Examples might be public housing or synthetic fuels. Proceed, therefore, only with caution.

Publicly offered tax shelters, those available to you and me and the investing public, seldom are bargains. Before one ever is offered to you, a lot of folks have lined up to get a cut of your investment dollar. Someone who owned the real estate or the mineral rights for an oil deal or the equipment to be leased, has sold it, at a nice profit, to the promoter of the tax shelter. An agent probably was involved; he made a commission. For his own time and talent, the promoter expects something more than minimum wage.

Attorneys must prepare the offering prospectus, and their fees seem to be in direct relation to tonnage of printed material they produce. Accountants must project incomes and expenses and vouch for the accuracy of all the numbers; that doesn't come cheap. Printing, promotional expense, advertising all cost money. Finally, you pay the salesman's commission. For a commission of less than 6%, a broker won't pick up the phone to talk about a tax shelter. You might be shocked to know how little of your money actually gets invested for you.

And to buy a tax shelter, you all but sign your life away. A fellow office manager once confided in me his apprehensions about any of our investment "products" that required the client's signature on a sales agreement. Too many had blown up. Requiring a signed agreement, we were telling the investor that the risks were too high for us to accept any responsibility for his losses. The signature isn't to protect the client, it's to protect the broker. To open a cash account with a brokerage firm, to buy and sell stocks and bonds, no signatures are required. My advice to you is to sign no sales agreements.

I'll guess that publicly offered real estate partnerships were the most numerous of tax shelters. Many of the good ones probably worked out okay. No great shakes, but fewer losses.

Many of the tax breaks that over the years had been slipped into the law to reward special groups for their political support were eliminated by the tax law of 1986—but that won't be forever. Our political system remains the same. Among candidates for political office, we elect those who have raised the most money to spend for television appearances to tell all of us what we want to hear.

Politicians who get the big campaign contributions are those, I suspect, whose principles are the most compromised. You may be sure, in consequence, that special interests, in return for their contributions, will continue to receive special advantages with every amendment of the tax law. Each new loophole becomes another opportunity for creative promoters to develop investments contrived to appeal to investors' eagerness to dodge taxes.

The tax shelter business is something of a flimflam. Something for nothing is the come-on. To get hit by a confidence man, the pigeon must be both a bit stupid and untroubled of conscience. How, otherwise, would he fall for the story of a trunk of stolen money in Mexico and fork over $2,000 so that the con man can go down there to bribe the police to release it?

Maybe tax shelters aren't quite that bad, but I've observed that those who create tax shelters and those who sell them come out a lot better than the buyers. Buyers probably have lost more money than they ever saved on their taxes.

A long time ago, I concluded, that for myself, life is too short to worry about taxes. My time was better spent trying to do my job, trying to make money. Why agonize about taxes? Just pay 'em. Anyhow, I don't want to take the chance of going to hell for a few thousand, lousy tax dollars. Whether religious or just superstitious, I see that as an unattractive risk/reward ratio.

CHAPTER 32

OTHER PROFESSIONALS
HOPING TO SHARE YOUR WEALTH

Seeing some self-styled investment professionals in action, I often thought of a cartoon picturing two old tramps. One is saying to the other, "If you're so smart, why ain't you rich?"

To you and me as investors, hundreds of investment professionals offer their services. Some are honest and competent. Some, however, are not. So the odds are not in our favor. I've written enough already about brokers, securities analysts, technicians, traders, investment counselors. What about some of the other professionals who make a living selling investments and their investment advice?

Market letter writers who forecast the stock market for their subscribers must be endowed with undiminished faith that, next time, they'll call the turn. Some market letters are forever bearish. Stocks soon will be wiped out. Sell out, buy gold, move to an underground home in the mountains and stock up on canned goods. Consistently developing that theme—supported by stories in every day's newspaper—the market letter writer can count on a brand-new crop of subscribers with every break in the market, every recession. A stopped clock is right twice every 24 hours.

A doomsday letter writer who called himself Major Angus kept the faith for 20 years—from the 1940s into the 1960s, while the DJIA went from 160 to 1,000.

The first market letter writer that I ever actually saw was an elderly sitter in the boardroom of our firm's Pine Street office in New York. It was 1946. The little old gentleman had divined that the one common denominator in all the U.S.A. was the funny paper. The most popular strip at that time was "Bringing Up Father," which ran each Sunday in color on the front of the comic section. The leading characters were Maggie and Jiggs. Jiggs smoked a cigar. The old market letter writer had established, in his mind, a correlation between the stock market and the direction that smoke took from Jiggs' cigar. When the line representing the smoke had been drawn straight up, the market was about to go up. As I can't recall having seen the smoke from Jiggs' cigar going down, I guess that the old market letter man was a constant bull. Someone told me that the S.E.C. had made an inquiry of his forecasting methods and had concluded that the funny paper was as good a market indicator as anything else.

Several advisory services are useful, but I'd not waste my money on a market forecaster.

Preparing wills and trusts, some attorneys get into offering investment advice. Because a law practice often involves local real estate and business transactions, some attorneys may discover local investment opportunities. But most attorneys can give you no better stock and bond advice than you might get from most doctors or preachers.

I shall say the same thing about accountants. Often before making a securities transaction, I phone my accountant to ask her a tax question, but I don't know that I've ever let taxes influence my investment decision. It's just that I don't like surprises when in April she tells me how much income tax I owe.

Among the more egregious fakirs of the investment community, I believe, are some financial planners. It all started with life insurance salesmen and estate planning. Only after many years did insurance companies discover that people don't want to talk about dying, so they began to call it financial planning which, one must admit, sounds more cheerful. Estate planners became financial planners. That let just about anybody into the business.

Some financial planners charge a flat fee for their services. Others, notably brokerage firms, offer financial planning services as a way of generating transactions for which they charge commissions—quite all right if you know that at the outset. A third group charges clients fees for their advice and then turns around and charges commissions on the products that they have pushed their clients into buying. And sometimes those are commission splits received under-the-table from other salesmen.

Anybody can be a financial planner. It's an unregulated business. No qualifications necessary. The wide open opportunities attract lots of folks. Look in the Yellow Pages under Financial Planners and Financial Planning Consultants—almost as many listings as you'll find under Escort Service.

Either by interview or having you fill out a form, a financial planner gets the information he needs from you. Most of them enter the numbers into a computer programmed to figure your income tax liability and to show you what you have left after taxes—not much. Not much, multiplied by the 15 or 20 years left of your working life, equals not much. That's the discouraging picture of what you can expect to have when you retire. Now, your unique situation is carefully analyzed. Only then are you told what the financial planner knew that you wanted to hear: you are paying out too much in taxes. But for you there is hope.

The computer program now assumes that you apply several sophisticated tax avoidance opportunities. Since tax shelters have been limited by the 1986 tax law, the most widely suggested tax dodge is to turn your money over to some life insurance company. The computer recalculates your tax bill, cut dramatically, and revises the projection of your accumulation of capital: tax-free and growing like yeast. Magically, that is shown on a computer-generated graph. Who can argue with a computer? You're impressed. In 15 years, you'll be the richest man in town, just from tax savings. You give your financial planner the okay to implement the program.

You are about to be loaded down with life insurance and annuities and maybe a few limited partnership deals in real estate and oil drilling. After a year or two, you'll discover that the tax avoidance schemes have been poor investments.

As one of three arbitrators of a dispute between a financial planning firm, which was also a registered broker-dealer in securities, and one of its former Wealth Consultants (how about that for a title?) I gained a rare insight into their business.

The Wealth Consultant was the claimant. He had taken legal action to require his former employers to pay him the commissions that he said he'd earned.

An arbitration proceeding is informal. No rules of evidence, no courtroom stuff that you see on TV. An arbitrator can interrupt at any time to ask anything he wishes to know.

The commissions in dispute were on tax shelters that the W.C. had sold to an out-of-state doctor client. We listened to the W.C.'s long story of how he had worked assiduously with the doctor to prepare a comprehensive plan for his complete financial security and how tax shelters had been sold to him. At length, one of the arbitrators asked the W.C. about the doctor's investments, his stocks, bonds, real estate. He had none. No investments. Just tax shelters. That was the firm's entire business, professionally recommending tax avoidance and then charging big commissions on the sale of tax shelters. Financial planners call that financial planning. You'd better do your own financial planning—and your own investing.

The investment practitioners for whom I have the least respect are those who pretend to manage their clients' investments by switching money back and forth among the several funds of a no-load mutual fund group—among its "family" of funds. The fund group will have a common stock fund for growth, a bond fund for income and a money-market fund for cash reserves. Nothing wrong with the fund group, nothing wrong with its funds. For only a service fee of maybe $5, the fund group allows its investors to switch between its funds once or twice a year. The adviser, however, for his skills, charges an annual fee of 2-to-3% of the client's capital. He calls himself a market timer and speaks of "asset allocation." This is what he tells you.

When the stock market is about to start down, I take you out of the stock fund to preserve your capital and go into the money market fund to wait until things calm down. Then we [it's always we, even though it's your money]—*Then we move into the the bond fund to pick up a nice return while the stock market is consolidating. When I see that the stock market is about to start back up, we switch out of the bond fund and back into the stock fund for the big move.*

My job is to protect your money in the down markets and let you make money in the rising markets. I get you in and out at the right time.

Sounds great, doesn't it? And great it would be if anyone could do that, if anyone could know today what the market will do tomorrow or next week or next year. Implying that he has such a skill, the market timer is dishonest.

With any devious investment scheme, you'd be surprised how often religion is part of the selling job. A businessmen's prayer breakfast. A salesman who piously explains that he's had a "religious experience" and has been born again. Hearing that, you can know that the Christians are about to suffer.

Investing other folks' money is big business. The dollar volume of money moving in and out of investments must be second only to the volume moving in and out of the nation's banks. It's as though every day is another California gold rush. Some people went out to work the mines, others went out to work the miners. Of those flocking to the marketplace, some hope to make their fortunes in investments, others hope to make their fortunes from their dealings with investors.

Most investors are overwhelmed, I believe, by what they imagine to be the bewildering complexities of securities and the markets. That's exactly the reaction some investment professionals wish to encourage. Baffled or worse, some investors tend to be vastly relieved when they can turn over their money to professionals—who quite possibly will take advantage of them. What you may see as complexities are mainly unimportant details deliberately thrown out to confuse you.

For you and me, investing our own money, all that we need to decide is our purpose. Do we require income? if so, how much? and how much must be invested to get that needed income? Now, what's available to invest for profit?

To accomplish our purposes, two types of securities can be bought, bonds for income and stocks for profit. Whether investing in stocks, bonds or both, I buy nothing but highest quality. It took me most of my working life to figure out that simple logic. I need no complicated investment products, no advice from any market forecaster or investment genius.

As an investor, I can't expect to make it on my own. For reliable information, interpretations and opinions, I must depend upon the support of brokers, analysts, technicians, traders and other investment professionals. Whatever I accept and use, however, must be understandable and logical, must pass the test of good common sense. It's my money. I'm taking the risk.

If I lose money, I have no one to blame except myself, my own greed that got me into a something-for-nothing scheme. Accepting total responsibility for my investment decisions and my investment results, knowing that I'm entirely on my own, I'm less likely to become careless about investing or casual about my securities.

As investors, our best protection is our own common sense and skepticism.

Appendix

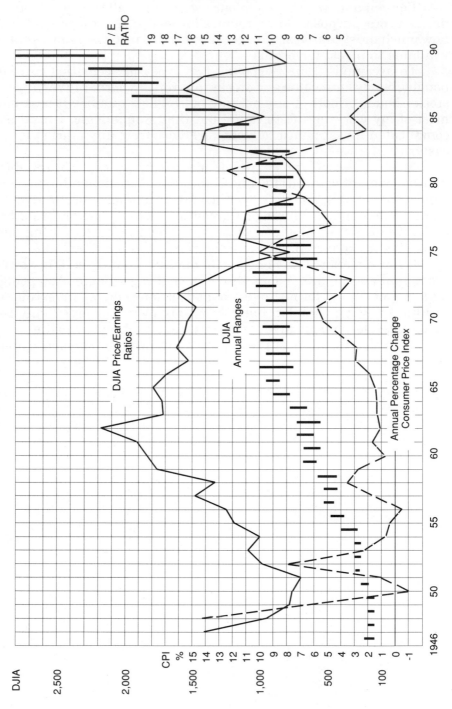

(Enlarged version of chart 1 on page 59)

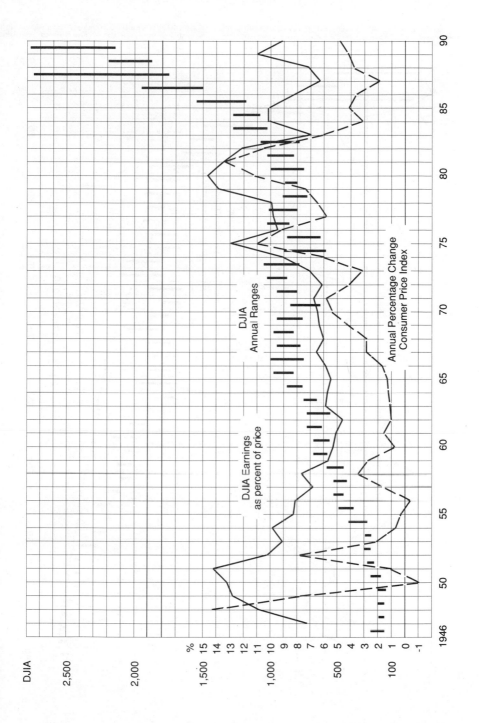

(Enlarged version of chart 2 on page 59)

280

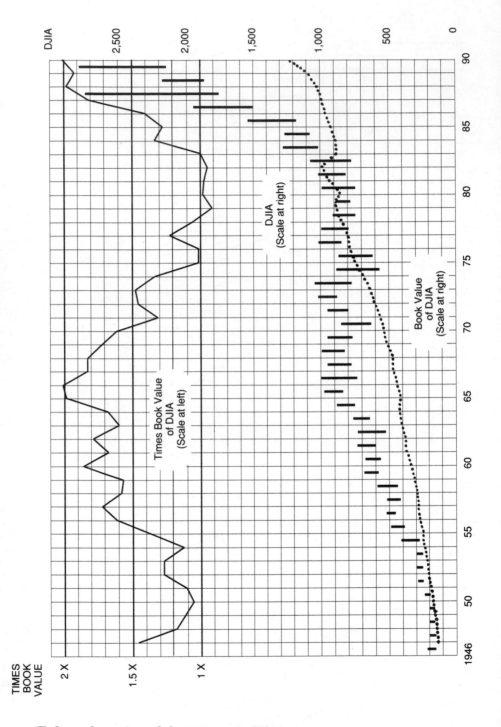

(Enlarged version of chart on page 65)

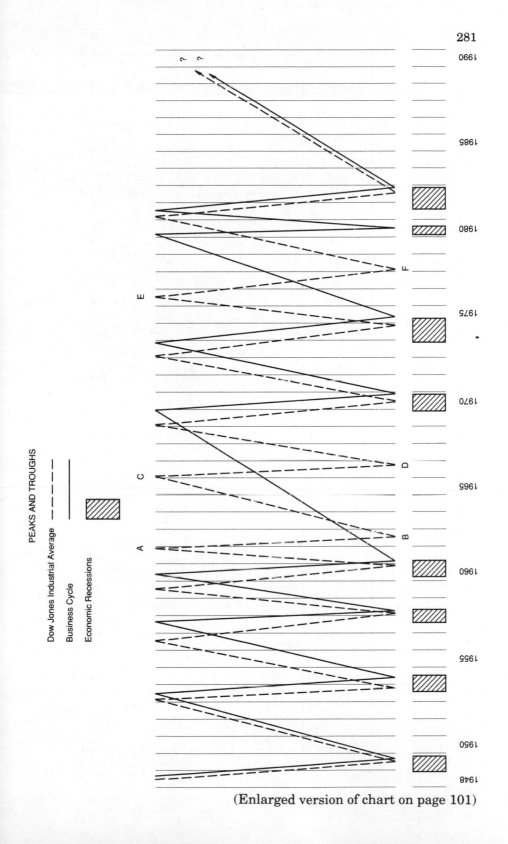

PEAKS AND TROUGHS

Dow Jones Industrial Average - - - - -

Business Cycle ———

Economic Recessions

(Enlarged version of chart on page 101)

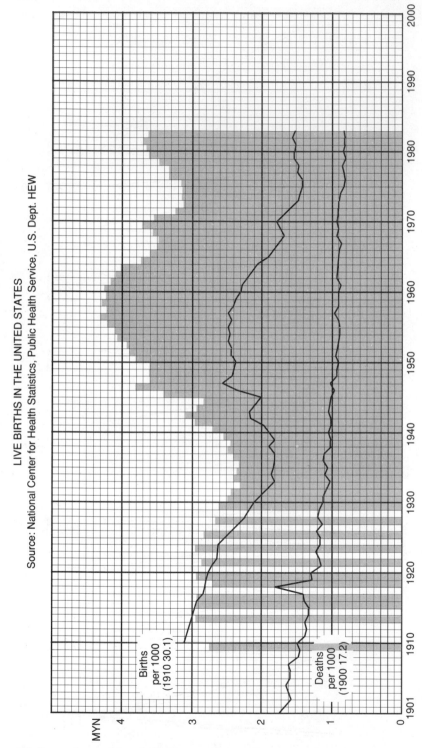

LIVE BIRTHS IN THE UNITED STATES

Source: National Center for Health Statistics, Public Health Service, U.S. Dept. HEW

Births per 1000 (1910 30.1)

Deaths per 1000 (1900 17.2)

(Enlarged version of chart on page 106)

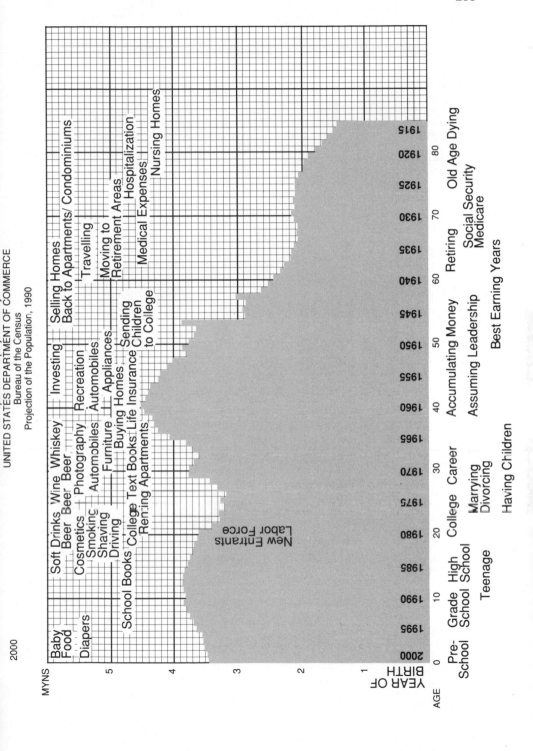

UNITED STATES DEPARTMENT OF COMMERCE
Bureau of the Census
Projection of the Population, 1990

2000

MYNS

5

4

3

2

1

YEAR OF BIRTH

AGE

0

| 2000 | 1995 | 1990 | 1985 | 1980 | 1975 | 1970 | 1965 | 1960 | 1955 | 1950 | 1945 | 1940 | 1935 | 1930 | 1925 | 1920 | 1915 |

0   10   20   30   40   50   60   70   80

Baby Food
Diapers

Soft Drinks Wine Whiskey
Beer   Beer   Beer
Cosmetics Photography
Smoking Automobiles
Shaving
Driving

Investing
Recreation
Automobiles
Furniture Appliances
Buying Homes
Life Insurance

Selling Homes
Back to Apartments/ Condominiums
Travelling
Moving to
Retirement Areas
Hospitalization
Medical Expenses
Nursing Homes

School Books
College Text Books
Renting Apartments

Sending
Children
to College

New Entrants
Labor Force

Pre-School

Grade High
School School

Teenage

College Career

Marrying
Divorcing

Having Children

Accumulating Money

Assuming Leadership

Best Earning Years

Retiring

Social Security
Medicare

Old Age Dying

(Enlarged version of chart 1 on page 108)

284

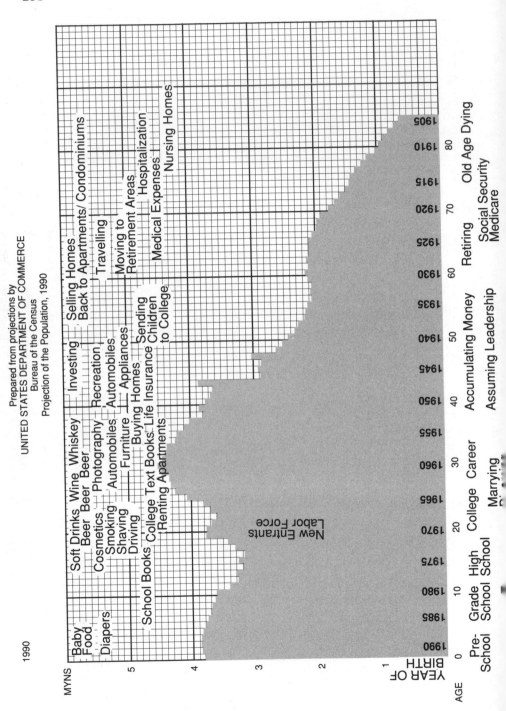

(Enlarged version of chart 2 on page 108)

INDEX